Additional praise for *Sweet and Natural*

"McCarty contends that 'you don't need to desert dessert just because you want to eat healthy' and offers more than tempting delights to prove her point. . . . For the dedicated health food fan, her carefully constructed recipes will be welcome—especially the opportunity to trade in a plain apple for some guilt-free Chocolate Pecan Bourbon Bundt Cake."

—*Publishers Weekly*

"Meredith McCarty has done her homework. This book is as valuable for the extensive research on ingredients as for the luscious recipes that will surely please anyone who tries them."

—Annemarie Colbin, CHES, author of *Food and Our Bones* and *Food and Healing,* founder of The Natural Gourmet Cookery School, NYC

"Meredith McCarty is a genius in the kitchen. Her recipes are wonderful and, from a health standpoint, they're just what the doctor ordered. I highly recommend this outstanding collection of healthy desserts."

—Neal Barnard, M.D., President, Physicians Committee for Responsible Medicine

"Meredith McCarty's fantastic desserts have introduced thousands of people to a balanced, natural way of eating. Thanks to pioneers like Meredith, the whole world is beginning to change in a healthier, more peaceful direction."

—Aveline Kushi, world-renowned macrobiotic cooking teacher and author

"*Sweet and Natural* is great! For those of us who love sweets, yet also love the joys of health, this beautiful book is a godsend."

—John Robbins, founder of EarthSave International and author of *Diet for a New America*

"Meredith McCarty's healthy and satisfying recipes are an essential ingredient in the Kellogg Wellness Cuisine. We serve to hundreds of executives every day."

—Ron Griffin, Director of Dining Services, Northwestern University, Kellogg School of Management

"*Sweet and Natural* will convince the most discerning palate that the use of healthful ingredients does not mean giving up the pleasures of eating sweets—rather, it means giving up the consequential poor health and weight gain expected from typical desserts."

—John McDougall, M.D. Medical Director of the McDougall Program, St. Helena Hospital, Napa Valley, California, and Mary McDougall, author of lowfat, pure vegetarian cookbooks

Also by Meredith McCarty

Fresh From a Vegetarian Kitchen

MEREDITH McCARTY

Sweet & Natural

More Than 120 Sugar-Free
and Dairy-Free Desserts

St. Martin's Griffin
New York

Photographs copyright © 1999 by Jeanne Stack
Illustrations copyright © 1999 by Magué Calanché
Food Stylist: Amy Whelan
Props courtesy of Crate & Barrel, Pottery Barn, Cornelia Park,
Christina Eckland, and Victoria Yee

ISBN 0-312-20029-3 (hc)
ISBN 0-312-26782-7 (pbk)

Designed by Pei Loi Koay

www.stmartins.com

10 9 8 7 6 5 4 3 2

This book is dedicated to the readers

for bringing Sweetness into their own lives

and into the lives of so many others.

Contents

Acknowledgments

Infinite thanks to my mother, Betty James, for her sweet and very natural love and support.

And to my former husband and real friend, Patrick McCarty, and to our former secretary and friend, Karen Bandy, for their support over the twenty years of designing and serving these desserts to the people who came to our natural health center in Eureka, California, for classes, dinners, and counseling.

To my teachers in macrobiotics, Michio and Aveline Kushi, Shizuko Yamamoto, Herman and Cornelia Aihara, and Jacques and Yvette de Langre.

To fellow natural health consultant and chef Linda Redfield for her valuable feedback on both the ingredients sections and the recipes and for her research in formulating the charts and doing the nutritional analyses.

To my editors at St. Martin's Press, Marian Lizzi and (formerly) Barbara Tomchin.

To the recipe testers Arlene Luft, Laverne Whitehead, Linda Redfield, Sierra Laidman, and Barbara Rutner, and to recipe tasters extraordinaire, Alex McIntyre and Cindy and Dennis Thompkins.

To experts in their fields, Lorenz Schaller, Russ Bianchi, and Selina de Langre for clarification in the Whole Grain Flours, Natural Sweeteners and Sea Salt sections respectively. To Caroline Flagiello for photographic advice.

To the San Francisco Chronicle food writers for all they have shared in the excellent food section over the years, especially Marion

Cunningham, Tom Seitsema, Joyce Goldstein, Michael Bauer, Flo Braker, and Sharon Cadwallader.

To Martha Stewart and Mollie Katzen for the color and beauty in their approaches to food.

To the organizations and persons who provide well-documented information about the effects of our diet and lifestyle on personal and planetary health, especially Physicians Committee for Responsible Medicine, EarthSave, One Peaceful World, Preventive Medicine Research Institute (Dr. Dean Ornish's organization), and to the late Dr. Benjamin Spock and his wife, Mary Morgan, and Dr. John and Mary McDougall.

I continue to learn much from the good work of my peers, especially Jan Bellame, Rebecca Wood, Annemarie Colbin, Mary Estella, Lorna Sass, Harriet McNear, Susan O'Toole, Lenore Baum, Laura Stec, Jennifer Raymond, Joyce Guthrie, Gary Alinder, Chuck Collison, Susanne Jensen, Anka Bagic-Sayre, Patricia Becker, Natalie Jung, Rachel Matesz, Christina Pirello, Jane Quincannon, and Jan Snyder.

And lastly, heartfelt thanks for their loving support go to personal friends Steve Miller and Yvonne Schell, Irith Shalmony, Alice McGovern, Meryl Kolevzon, Anne Bruce, Marjorie McClain, Betsey Lekan, Chuck Lowery, Anne Wilbur, Colette Penne, Tia Rich, Karl Schmidt, Steven Wrobel, Patti Kilpatrick, Barbara McFarland, Christina del Gallo, Thea Chalmers, Randy Wood, and to my sister, Leone Webster.

Preface

My fascination with healthy desserts was ignited by the first good old-fashioned apple pie I learned to make in a beginning macrobiotic cooking class back in 1974. I was working as associate editor of the East West Journal *(now* Natural Health *magazine)*, and having had a diagnosis of mononucleosis a couple of years before, I wanted to learn to satisfy my sweet tooth in a conscious and loving way.

In cooking class and at lunchtime at work, we were gifted with a magnificent natural foods feast. I liked even the simplest of meals—the split pea soup with miso, the brown rice with sesame salt, and the sautéed vegetables seasoned with toasted sesame oil, soy sauce, and ginger. But the pie was what won me over and kept me going. Knowing how to prepare little else in the dessert realm until many cooking classes later, I made it once a week and ate a big slice every night. While I regained both my vibrant energy and my always-inquisitive taste buds, that pie kept me from craving the alcohol, cigarettes, fast food (hamburgers, fries, and Cokes), doughnuts, and other sugary foods that had helped create such a poor health condition.

It was after I left Boston and co-directed a natural health center in northern California that I learned how satisfying it is to present gourmet vegetarian (I call it Healing Cuisine) meals to people at public dinner parties and in cooking classes, especially when the finale is a dessert that is light, bright, and full of flavor. A sense of contributing to the well-being of oneself and others is both comforting and empowering.

I wanted to create familiar desserts redolent with the flavors of the season, some with un-usual culinary twists, and always using the best ingredients. I wanted to provide practical infor-mation on natural foods and how to use flours other than wheat for wheat- or gluten-free desserts. During those twenty years I produced two cookbooks and a video. This third book is an outcome of those good times and of the new ones here in the San Francisco Bay Area where I now have the ecstatic pleasure to reside.

In another role as consultant and personal food coach, I meet with men and women with a wide variety of reasons for wanting to improve their lifestyles, especially their diets. Some are exhausted (as I was), some have allergies and cravings, and some have breast or prostate cancer or heart disease. Sharing with them the benefits and the specifics of a plant-based cuisine is my joy, and learning to use whole foods in creating luscious desserts is part of the delightful and delicious process.

Meredith McCarty
Tiburon, California
January 1, 1998

Introduction

Thinking about desserts evokes sensations of sweetness and richness and a feeling of time-out to enjoy the pleasurable endings to an afternoon or evening meal. In order to eat smart, savvy twenty-first century home chefs seek out whole foods that are in season, locally grown, and organic when possible. How do desserts fit into such a healthy and healing cuisine? And what are the choices for varying levels of wellness?

From a natural health perspective, dessert is an indulgence, neither essential daily fare nor food as medicine. But desserts that are both delightfully satisfying and sweet without being overpowering, can enhance a relaxing sense of balance between the demands of a healthy lifestyle and the sensual pleasure of eating.

The average American eats 42 percent of their calories from fats and 20 percent from sugar, consuming more than a hundred pounds of sugar per year. The heartening news is that although this lifestyle of extremes has led to an epidemic of disease seen nowhere else on the planet—50 percent of our population is dying from heart disease and 30 percent from cancer—most of it is completely preventable and can be reversed.

ALLERGIES, CRAVINGS, AND DISEASE

Both scientists and lay people are discovering that a good diet not only prevents disease, but also greatly improves our vitality, enhances brain chemistry, and creates a deeper sense of well-being. Specifically, refined foods such as white flour and sugar are responsible for a host of bothersome conditions that can easily be avoided.

A food allergy is a response in which the body's immune system overreacts to certain proteins in food. Symptoms of an allergic reaction include skin breakout in hives, swelling of the lips, eyelids, face or hands, nausea and stomach cramps, rhinitis (runny nose), tightening and closing of the throat, asthma, blood pressure drop, and in extreme cases, loss of consciousness, multiple organ failure, and death in as little as ten minutes. The foods that most often cause allergic reactions are dairy products, eggs, wheat, corn, and nuts. The suggested treatment is a diet that avoids these foods.

Termed OAS, Oral Allergy Syndrome includes symptoms such as itching or swelling of the lips, tongue, throat, or roof of the mouth. According to John Yunginger, M.D., in an article entitled "Do Fruits and Vegetables Cause Allergic Reactions?" *(Food Allergy News)*, the dessert ingredients most commonly associated with OAS are nuts and seeds (hazelnuts, sesame, sunflower, poppy, and fennel seeds) and fruits (apple, apricot, banana, cantaloupe, cherry, honeydew, orange, peach, pear, and watermelon). Yunginger points out that because the allergens responsible for these reactions are usually destroyed by heating or digestion, affected individuals can usually eat fruits that have been cooked, as in an apple pie.

Anaphylaxis is the more severe form of food allergy. Milk and eggs as well as nuts and seeds are the dessert foods that may induce anaphylactic reactions.

Another food sensitivity, lactose intolerance, is associated with an inability to metabolize lactose, the sugar in milk and other dairy products. Lactose is concentrated in low-fat dairy products in particular. The disease worsens with advancing age and ultimately affects 60 percent to 90 percent of people in some ethnic groups. Symptoms include abdominal pain, flatulence, and diarrhea.

Gluten intolerance, called celiac disease, is associated with consumption of the gluten part of wheat, rye, triticale, barley, and sometimes oats. It is prevalent in at least 1 per 3,000 in the United States. By abstaining from gluten, the symptoms that are associated with malabsorption—body wasting, anemia, bloating, gas, diarrhea, bone pain, and sugar/starch craving—disappear.

Cookies, one of the most common snack and binge foods, are made from gluten-containing grains. The grains are also refined. That is, the bran layers and the germ have been removed to make white flour. These grains can damage the intestinal lining in gluten-intolerant people. The condition prevents nutrients from being effectively absorbed into the body, causing gut permeability and subsequently immune-mediated allergic reaction, thereby setting off cravings for more simple carbohydrates.

More like drugs or, even more so, alcohol than food, refined (white) flour and highly refined sweeteners, such as corn syrup, white and brown sugar, and blond, turbinado, and raw sugars, contain high levels of simple sugars called monosaccharides and disaccharides. These simple sugars metabolize very quickly, raising the blood glucose level and creating acidity. Requiring little digestion and providing no nutritional benefit (no vitamins, no minerals, and no fiber), they produce fatigue, heart palpitations, and shortness of breath, and weaken the nervous system. In order to be metabolized, refined sugar causes minerals to be taken first from the tissues, then from the organs, and lastly from the teeth and bones. Sugar also kills the appetite for other foods that can't be tasted immediately, or for anything that has to be chewed. All in all, refined sugars depress the immune system and can be highly addictive.

According to Julia Ross, director of Recovery Systems—a New Approach to Alcohol, Drugs and Food Problems, when these substances are withdrawn and replaced with real food (along with supplements, exercise, and counseling), the blood sugar balance is restored and the overpowering cravings caused by blood sugar drops are silenced. Whole grains, vegetables, beans, soy foods, and other protein sources soon become appealing.

Alexander Schauss, Ph.D., with the American Institute of Biosocial Research, has come to the same conclusions, as explained in his books *Nutrition and Behavior* and *Diet, Crime, and Deliquency.* He demonstrates how junk food diets, sugar starvation, vitamin deficiencies, and food allergies can convert a normal brain into a criminal mind. Among many studies, he cites one on alcoholics showing that 97 percent had low blood sugar or hypoglycemia, compared with 18 percent in the control population. The alcoholics' hypoglycemia disappeared once their diet was corrected and as they continued to abstain from drinking.

Another disease, candidiasis, is a condition of overgrowth of intestinal yeast caused by longterm antibiotic or hormone use. The yeast feeds on simple carbohydrates such as sugar and starch (e.g. white flour). As the yeast grows, carbohydrate cravings, a feeling of anxiety or irritability, fatigue, bloating, depression, and mental fog may increase dramatically. These are the same symptoms used by William Duffy in *Sugar Blues* to describe the condition leading to hypoglycemia, diabetes, heart disease, obesity, tooth decay, hyperactivity, and schizophrenia.

Chronic bloating, due to poor diet, makes many anorectics feel fat. When the bloating disappears, they feel much more comfortable eating normally. As they eat, their starvation-caused mental obsessions dissipate. Even the cravings associated with PMS are eliminated as an improved diet restores hormonal balance.

HYPOGLYCEMIA AND DIABETES

A position paper called "Hypoglycemia, Diabetes and Diet," from Physicians Committee for Responsible Medicine (PCRM) states: ". . . diabetes is a disease that is largely preventable and controllable. In most cases, diabetics can manage their disease much better with a food plan that gets most of its calories from high complex carbohydrates while minimizing fats . . ." It turns out that while glucose, a simple sugar, is the body's main fuel, the best sources of it are complex sugars, which the body breaks down over time.

The most common form of the disease is non-insulin-dependent diabetes, which has also been called Type II or adult-onset diabetes. Eight million Americans have been given a diagnosis of diabetes and another eight million are thought to have the disease without knowing it. This kind of diabetes is not due to an inadequate supply of insulin. There is usually plenty of insulin in the blood stream, but the cells do not respond readily to it. Sugar cannot easily get into the cells and it backs up in the bloodstream. In the short run, diabetics may experience episodes of labored breathing, vomiting, and dehydration. In the long run, diabetics are at risk for heart disease, blindness, kidney failure, and circulation problems that lead to amputation of feet and legs.

PCRM goes on to say: "The more fat there is in the diet, the harder time insulin has in getting sugar into the cell . . . Modern diabetic treatment programs drastically reduce meats, high-fat dairy products, and oils. At the same time, they increase grains, legumes, and vegetables . . . The dietary changes are simple, but profound, and they work. Low-fat vegetarian diets are ideal for diabetics."

In research from Harvard University conduced by Dr. Walter Willett ("Diet-Diabetes Link Reported", the *New York Times,* Feb. 12, 1997), it was found that "ounce for ounce, white flour products [white bread and pasta, as well as potatoes and white rice] increase blood glucose levels more than eating sugar itself." Dr. Willett recommended eating foods rich in fiber rather than taking supplements because micronutrients in fiber may be important in preventing diabetes.

Foods that are high in soluble dietary fiber slow carbohydrate absorption and help to prevent swings in blood sugar levels. For some, fruits (not fruit juice, which contains no fiber) may also be a good addition as fructose, the natural sugar in most fruits, does not require insulin to be absorbed into the body cells.

The causes of insulin-dependent diabetes remain elusive. Several recent studies have implicated cow's milk consumption as a possible contributor. A wise conclusion is that good diet and regular exercise can minimize the amount of insulin these diabetics require.

SUGAR AND FAT CRAVINGS

If you look for sweetness
Your search will be endless
You will never be satisfied
But if you seek the true taste
You will find what you are looking for.

—BUDDHIST AXIOM

The emotional issues associated with sugar cravings involve finding ways of rewarding ourselves that truly raise us to higher levels of health, inner peace, and happiness, whether through the broad spectrum of physical activity, intellectual, social, and cultural enjoyment, or spiritual pursuits, and through developing more nourishing relationships. For example, Dr. Dean Ornish's cutting-edge program for reversing heart disease emphasizes meditation and yoga (a combination called stress management) and group support (group therapy and family support) as much as it recommends a plant-based diet and exercise.

Food-wise, as William Duffy says in his classic work *Sugar Blues,* "Changing the quality of your carbohydrates can change the quality of your health and life." The first step in cutting down on cravings for sweets is to eat your sugars with the fiber attached so they are digested very slowly. Eating plant foods—such as whole grains, land and sea vegetables, beans, and fruits—is the most balanced way to consume sugars. (Grains such as brown rice are made sweeter by thorough chewing. An enzyme in the saliva begins to turn the starch into sugar, the first step in its digestion.) The rewards for practicing such a diet are stabilized energy patterns and a heightened awareness of the effects of food on overall well-being.

Complex carbohydrates, which are complex sugars, also called polysaccharides, are found in plant foods. They reduce to glucose during digestion. This slow-burning fuel releases energy steadily for physical stamina, mental clarity, and emotional stability. On the other hand, simple sugar consumption leads to physical, mental, and emotional exhaustion. Even the USDA relegates sweets, fats, and oils to the tiny tip at the top of the Food Guide Pyramid, with the admonition to "use sparingly."

Dessert cravings—the intense desire for both sugar and fat—are an expression of a need to make balance in the rest of the diet. An excessive consumption of animal products (meat, poultry, dairy, and eggs) goes together with sugar cravings because when we eat too many animal foods, which are a concentrated source of protein and fat, our body craves an excess of carbohydrates for balance.

Most Americans satisfy this craving with the simple carbohydrates found in sugar and white flour products. But eating these foods on a regular basis becomes an addicting cycle of meat and sweets that leads to the diseases of our civilization—heart disease, cancer, diabetes, etc.

In the 1990s, margarine contributed more fat calories to the American diet than any other source. The polyunsaturated fats used in margarine are linked to cancer and are "much worse than saturated," according to more research from Harvard by Walter Willett and Alberto Ascherio, published in the *American Journal of Public Health.*

Re-educating the palate to prefer foods with both less fat and less intense sweetness is ultimately the best approach. According to Jean Weininger, Ph.D. in nutrition and a writer for the *San Francisco Chronicle,* research shows that the preference for lower-fat foods can take hold in a matter of weeks, but only if the sensory exposure to the mouth-feel of fat is reduced.

For people already on a plant-based or fully vegetarian diet, sugar and fat cravings derive from other habits such as:

- A failure to serve grains, beans, and vegetables at the same meal at least once a day for a feeling of satisfaction and completion. Some vegetarians leave out protein on a regular basis, which leads to carbohydrate cravings.

Minerals from plant foods are also important in preventing sugar cravings. Plant foods typically contain 25 percent to 200 percent more minerals than animal foods. Moreover, 60 percent of the enzymes in the human body require minerals to function properly.

A quick-and-easy meal plan recommended by PCRM would be: For breakfast, hot cereal (oatmeal or cream of wheat) with whole grain bread and a piece of fruit. For lunch, a salad with raw vegetables, beans, sunflower seeds, and a dressing, as well as bread and fruit. For dinner, brown rice or whole grain pasta or bulgur, beans or tofu, and cooked vegetables. And for snacks, have whole grain bread, crackers, or popcorn with carrot or celery sticks or a piece of fruit.

- Too simple a diet with not enough variety or flavorful seasonings such as fresh and dry herbs and the moderate use of spices.
- Too much salt in the diet from snack foods such as corn chips, or from overdoing salty seasonings such as sea salt, soy sauce, and miso.
- Too little oil used in food preparation (especially the highly flavorful extra virgin olive or toasted sesame oils in dressings), or including too few seeds and nuts or nut butters for a feeling of satiety in an otherwise basically low-fat or fat-free diet.
- Or their lack of fulfillment may stem from not cooking at all, relying on raw foods, or not knowing how to make at least a few good desserts.

The recipes in this book are designed to inspire you to cook luscious whole foods desserts for your great pleasure and increased well-being. Based on organic whole grain flours (including wheat-free alternatives), natural sweeteners, vegetable oils, fresh and dried fruits, nuts and seeds, and sweet spice seasonings, these innovative treats will help you rise to the occasion of healthy eating to produce new dessert classics of your own.

soy milk

About the Recipes and Nutritional Analyses

Ingredients are listed in order of use as described in the recipe. Ingredients within a class, e.g. sweeteners or liquids, are listed in order of preference in terms of taste, texture, and visual appeal, the favorite item being listed first, e.g. brown rice malt syrup, barley malt syrup, or pure maple syrup.

The analyses following each of the recipes are calculated for the original recipe (not the variations) without the optional ingredients, and are figured for the larger number of servings. The analyses were performed on the computer program Food Processor II from ESHA Research in Salem, OR, 1996. Additional data derives from The Nutritive Value of American Foods, USDA Handbook No. 456, The Complete Book of Food Counts by Corinne T. Netzer, and manufacturers' analyses (see Resources section).

CONVERSION CHARTS

All the recipes in this book were tested using customary American measuring cups and spoons. Following are approximate conversions for weight and metric measurements to enable you to make these desserts wherever you may be.

VOLUME CONVERSIONS		OVEN TEMPERATURE CONVERSIONS	
U.S. Customary	**Approximate Metric Conversion (ml)**	**U.S. Customary Fahrenheit**	**Celsius Centigrade**
⅛ teaspoon	0.5 ml	300°F	150°C
¼ teaspoon	1.0 ml	350°F	175°C
½ teaspoon	2.5 ml	400°F	200°C
1 teaspoon	5.0 ml	450°F	230°C
1 tablespoon (3 teaspoons)	15.0 ml		
¼ cup (4 tablespoons)	60.0 ml	**LENGTH CONVERSIONS**	
⅓ cup (5 ⅓ tablespoons)	79.0 ml		
½ cup (8 tablespoons)	118.0 ml	**U.S. Inches**	**Metric (cm)**
¾ cup	177.0 ml	½ inch	1.0 cm
1 cup	237.0 ml	1 inch	2.5 cm

A NOTE ABOUT TECHNIQUE

You don't have to be an experienced baker, cook, or food chemist to make great tasting desserts. Cooking is an art, not a science, imitative as well as creative, and more play than work. A recipe is a series of guidelines to inspire and support you in trying something new, not a rigid formula.

To begin with, read the recipe once or twice, or until you can easily picture both the process and the final result. Inexperienced bakers are served well to follow recipes to the letter until certain techniques are mastered and you develop a feel for the ingredients. Do remember to test new recipes once or twice before you make them for guests. Then, when starting to design your own recipes, keep flavors clean and uncluttered by featuring only one or two dominant flavors.

Prepare mentally and physically for cooking with your whole body, mind, and spirit. The ancient French cooking principle of *mis en place* refers to having all ingredients at the ready to help you work quickly. Before you start shopping and cooking, go through the recipe to be sure you will have all the ingredients and equipment on hand. Gather them together before beginning, then measure or chop ingredients to the recipe specifications.

People get different results from the same recipe because of the way they measure ingredients and the real temperature of their ovens. Measure ingredients accurately. Use nested measuring cups for dry ingredients, liquid measuring cups with pouring spouts for liquid ingredients, and standard measuring spoons for small amounts of both liquid and dry ingredients. In this book, all measurements are meant to be level, ie. 1 teaspoon, 1 tablespoon, or 1 cup. Gently scoop the flour out of the bag. Try not to tap the cup or scoop or the flour gets packed down.

Temperature is very important to the success of baking. Home ovens are often not well calibrated and may be many degrees off, which can spell disaster. Buy an oven thermometer and keep it on the middle or lower shelf. Preheat the oven for 20 minutes before baking. Be sure the oven maintains the desired temperature by referring to it occasionally before and during baking until you can rely on the accuracy of your equipment.

Prepare your baking pans before you begin mixing ingredients. I prefer to line the bottom of the pans with baking parchment rather than brush them with a light vegetable oil.

Taste, taste, taste. In the beginning, follow recipe quantities as stated, but also notice the flavor of the fruit that goes into a pie. It changes with the season and between varieties. Later, once you know the recipe, you may want to include a little more or less sweetener. Observe the moisture content of fruit as well. If apples are quite dry, add a little juice to a pie filling. If ingredients are wetter than normal, for instance if the pears are super-ripe, add more arrowroot powder.

Taste nondairy milks (soy, almond, or rice milk) to be sure they are impeccably fresh. Once opened, oils and nuts and seed butters should be refrigerated to preserve their flavor. If using tofu, ensure freshness by pouring off the liquid in the container as soon as you return from the store, adding fresh water to refrigerate. Use tofu as soon as possible.

To make baking quicker, assemble the dry and wet ingredients in separate bowls in advance, then combine them just before baking. Oils are listed before liquid sweeteners in the recipes because these sweeteners (brown rice syrup, FruitSource, barley malt, sorghum syrup, or honey) slide out easily from a measuring cup when oil has been used in it first.

Avoid overmixing, which removes air from a cake or cookie batter and creates a tough texture. Handle cookie and pie doughs gingerly. Don't knead unless the recipe calls for it, and even then knead just a few times.

One of the most important things to know is that a moist dough is always easier to work with—and lighter in the end—than a dry dough. If a pie dough comes out dry and/or crumbly because either too much flour or oil were added, discard the dough rather than struggling to incorporate more water after the dough is formed. It's only flour, oil, and water and therefore not too wasteful to start again. Avoiding frustration, you'll be a happier cook.

Prepare garnishes such as mint sprigs, rose geranium leaves, or flowers ahead of time and store them in the refrigerator. Other topping choices are fresh fruits or berries, nuts, or chocolate or carob chips. Add the garnish as close as possible to serving time to ensure freshness, crispness, and vivid color.

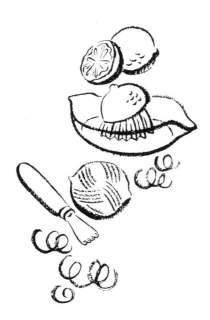

Ingredients

WHOLE GRAIN FLOURS

The vast majority of mankind may be described as grain-eaters and has always relied on a cereal as the basic staple of diet, with wheat and rice—and in America, maize—as the most important examples. According to the Oxford Book of Food Plants, *some of our oldest crops, such as wheat and barley, seem to have come into cultivation in the Middle East between 8000 B.C. and 5000 B.C. In China, rice is recorded as a staple crop as far back as 2800 B.C.*

maple syrup

Wheat products are the staple food of a very large part of the human race, especially those of European descent, although they are also very important in the temperate parts of India and China. Rice, often constituting a very high proportion of the diet, is the typical staple food of enormous human populations in Asia. Maize (the global term for corn, the idiom used in the United States) either is or was a staple food for large populations in South America, parts of eastern Europe, and in eastern and southern Africa.

Health Concerns

Whole grains are good sources of complex carbohydrates, fiber, B-complex vitamins, vitamin E, the minerals calcium, iron, magnesium, phosphorus, and potassium, and essential fatty acids. Organically grown grains and freshly ground flours are best in terms of flavor and nutrition from the bran and the germ, both of which satisfy the need for large amounts of oil or butter.

In terms of baking to create vibrant health, whole grain flours are the key. In a six-year study of 65,000 women done by the Harvard School of Public Health, those whose diets were high in carbohydrates from white bread, white pasta, and white rice (all refined grain products) and potatoes, had two and a half times the risk for Type 2 diabetes as those who ate a diet rich in high-fiber foods like whole wheat bread, whole grain pasta, and brown rice.

Walter Willet, a Harvard professor of epidemiology and nutrition and a coauthor of the study, finds the results of this and other research so convincing that he'd like to see the government amend the Food Guide Pyramid, which recommends six to eleven daily servings of any kind of carbohydrate. "What's important in the diet is not just the total amount of carbohydrates but the type of carbohydrate, and the Food Pyramid is remiss in not pointing that out. They should move white bread and potatoes up to the sweets category because metabolically they're basically the same . . ."

Diabetes is no minor concern. A chronic illness without a cure, diabetes is the fourth leading cause of death by disease in the United States. And it's a growing problem. Scientists predict that by 2007 more than 21 million Americans—about one in every ten adults—will have Type 2 diabetes, the kind that people in their forties and older may develop.

Flours in Baking

Flour forms the framework for whole grain pastries. High-protein flour is great for forming the strong elastic bonds of gluten that give bread its structure, but it makes for a tough cake or cookie. Choose low-protein soft wheat flour called pastry flour, with its higher percentage of carbohydrates, to produce a delicate crumb. Pastry wheat is not a finer grind of bread wheat flour. It is a completely different grain. Whole wheat pastry flour contains 100 percent of the whole wheat berry.

By marrying whole grain flours with white flours, you can create baked desserts with body as well as beauty. I have used unbleached (white) pastry flour in many of the recipes in a proportion of no more than 50 percent of the volume of flour, but if you prefer, all whole wheat pastry flour may be substituted. There are some benefits to flours ground from just the endosperm that don't contain the germ or bran. Doughs made from even some white flour will enjoy greater expansion creating lighter desserts. The bran, no matter how finely ground, has sharp edges that tend to shred the strands of gluten that have been developed in a dough or batter. When the gluten matrix is torn, some of the carbon dioxide bubbles created by the leavening agent escape, resulting in a slightly denser baked dessert.

Whole grains that are ground into flour, thereby rupturing the oily germ of the berry and exposing it to air and oxidation, slowly become rancid over a three-month period in a cool, dry place or six months in the refrigerator when stored in an airtight container, longer in the freezer. The best bet is to buy small amounts often and use them up right away. White flour, on the other hand, can be stored in a cool, dry place for an indefinite period of time.

The other reason to include at least half whole wheat pastry flour is that when it is refined, white flour loses about 70 percent of its nutrients.

Chemicals and Enrichment

Choosing organic flours both supports sustainable agriculture and eliminates concern over the chemicals used in growing and processing white flour. All-purpose flour from the supermarket contains bleached, presifted wheat flour with malted barley flour and is enriched with niacin (a B vitamin), iron, thiamine mononitrate (vitamin B1), and riboflavin (vitamin B2). Self-rising flour or cake flour is the same as all-purpose flour with leavening (baking soda, sodium aluminum phosphate, monocalcium phosphate), salt, and calcium sulphate added.

Bleach alters the protein in the flour and destroys the all-important carotene pigments that are essential to making a nice-looking baked good. It is the pigments that carry the delicate, nutty flavor and aroma of wheat-based pastries.

Chemicals such as chlorine dioxide, benzoyl peroxide, and chlorine gas, all of which whiten and oxidize flour, are currently permissible additives. Cake flours are by definition heavily bleached, since an effect of bleaching is to "strengthen" or toughen the gluten so that a batter made with a bleached cake flour will be able to support the large amounts of sugar and fat that are usually part of cake formulations. High-quality pastry flour, on the other hand, is never bleached as untreated gluten is more tender and, handled gently, will produce a more tender and flaky result.

And according to "The Baking Sheet" from King Arthur Flour, "Although some 'experts' rationalize that these chemicals are virtually dissipated by the time the flour is used, we have it on the authority of one of our labs that both benzoyl peroxide and chlorine gas leave chemically detectable residues in the flours that are treated with them . . . that can be detected as bitter aftertastes . . . Chemical additives are designed to mask and artificially compensate for desired characteristics that are lacking in lower-grade flours."

Other additives include potassium bromate, an oxidizer and conditioner, and enrichment. Potassium bromate has come under increasing scrutiny as tests with it have indicated that it is potentially carcinogenic. As for enrichment, more nutrients are returned to the flour than would naturally exist. And there is controversy as to whether synthetic vitamins and minerals are beneficial or toxic. Dr. John McDougall says in *The McDougall Plan:* "Processing and refining results in new and often undesirable properties for individual components because they are more concentrated and are no longer associated with the minerals, vitamins, fiber, fats, carbohydrates and proteins that surrounded them when present in the natural food."

Wheat Alternatives

Nowadays many people are looking for recipes that feature grains or starches other than wheat (such as brown rice, millet, quinoa, or chestnut flours, or arrowroot powder). Spelt is an original strain of bread wheat to which many wheat-sensitive people are not reactive.

Wheat (and its relatives spelt, kamut, and triticale), rye, barley, oats, and buckwheat contain gluten to which some people with a yeast-related health problem are allergic or sensitive.

The last three—barley, oats, and buckwheat—contain a gluten analogue to which some sensitives are not reactive.

Making muffins and crisp and cobbler toppings is a good way to see how the flours react in combination with the other ingredients used in baking. While doing so, it became clear that all flours make leavened baked goods on their own, but most have textures—either somewhat crumbly and dry or dense and gooey—that are best combined with wheat, a wheatlike flour (ie. spelt, kamut, or triticale), or with other gluten grains.

On the other hand, any flour may be used in a crisp topping since the ingredients, containing no leavening agent, are simply mixed for a sandy streusel consistency.

For gluten-free toppings, substitute the gluten analogues or gluten-free grains such as chestnut or quinoa flour as a base. Include the other gluten-free grains—rice, millet, corn, amaranth, and teff—in smaller amounts because they make very crumbly baked goods that do not hold together well when used alone. See the Wheat-Free Basic Vanilla Cake recipe on page 166.

If a particular flour cannot be found in your natural foods store, make some fresh flour from whole grains by grinding them in a grain mill (most effective), coffee mill or spice grinder, a mini-prep food processor or a small blender container. Or grind flakes such as wheat, barley, or kamut flakes into flour. I have used commercially milled flours in this book because that is what is available to most people. Should you decide to grind your flours fresh, they may require up to 25 percent less liquid than commercially milled flours.

All flour should be refrigerated directly after grinding because it may lose 40 percent of its nutritional value within one to three days after it's ground. That is the major advantage of being able to grind grains fresh, either at the store or at home. So keep your flour refrigerated and suggest that your natural foods store does the same. If any flour doesn't taste good to you, consider the possibility that it has gone rancid.

Whole Wheat Pastry Flour

This flour is the one used most often in this cookbook. Also called soft wheat or soft white wheat, both whole grain and white pastry wheat flour are lower in gluten content than whole wheat bread flour. Pastry wheat flour makes for light, delicate pastries.

Spelt

Spelt, which today is officially classified as a subspecies of common wheat, was one of the first grains to be domesticated. Archaeologists believe it was cultivated in parts of Europe during the Stone Age and in England by about 1000 B.C.

In baking, both whole spelt and white spelt flours are slightly heavier than pastry flour and are very suitable for use in desserts.

Nutritionally, spelt grain surpasses wheat in protein content, amino acids, minerals, and B vitamins. Its genetic makeup is different from today's wheats and it is not hybridized, so some wheat-sensitive people tolerate spelt well. Experiment with care and caution.

Barley

Barley was the most important bread-making grain of the ancient Greeks, Romans, and Hebrews. Today's barley flour is white and fluffy to the touch and tastes bland because the flour is made from "pearled" barley, "pearling" being a process that removes most of the bran layers. If barley flour is hard to find, you may decide to grind your own in a coffee grinder from barley flakes.

The best choice as a base for wheat-free toppings, barley flour is closest to white pastry wheat flour or white spelt flour in both appearance (light buff color) and texture (fine-grained on the inside with a delicate crunch on the outside in cobblers). It is great in cookies combined with oat flour. Baked alone in muffins, the texture is thick and gummy.

Quinoa

Pronounced KEEN-wa, this was the staple grain of the Inca civilization more than 5,000 years ago and, until the Spanish conquest, was one of their principal foods along with maize (corn) and potatoes. Imported quinoa is grown in Ecuador, Bolivia, and Peru. Domestic quinoa is grown in the Colorado Rockies.

Quinoa is a complete protein. In fact, quinoa was named one of the world's most promising foods by the National Academy of Sciences because of its high ratings for protein, calcium, iron, and fiber.

As a gluten-free alternative to wheat, quinoa flour works well in baking as the base. It makes a lovely cake, but the flavor is somewhat strong when used in large proportion. The Quinoa Corporation spokesperson says that this is the natural flavor, that the grain has been desaponized—"water-washed, sun-dried, and cloth-brushed"—before it is ground into flour. To make your own quinoa flour, rinse, drain, dry roast in the oven, and then grind the grain.

Oat

Tan in color with great flavor and a delicate, fine-grained texture, oat flour adds a moist sweetness to baked goods when combined with other flours, especially wheat or barley, brown rice, and millet flours. Its texture is a bit viscous when used alone.

Brown Rice

This flour is surprisingly nice used by itself in baking—spongy texture, light color, pleasant taste. It makes for a slightly wet batter, calling for less liquid (see the Brown Rice Cake recipe on page 167). Its crystalline texture adds a crisp quality to pie crusts, crisp toppings, and cookies when used in combination with other flours such as wheat or barley, quinoa or chestnut.

Millet

Millet is considered one of the least allergenic and most easily digested of all the grains. It has a high protein content, a good mineral content, and is rich in lecithin. The slightly dry and crunchy texture of this pretty yellow flour makes it best combined with other flours like wheat or barley or quinoa.

Kamut

Wheats of this type originated in the fertile crescent area that runs from Egypt to the Tigris-Euphrates valley. The American growers coined the trade name, kamut, an ancient Egyptian word for wheat.

Kamut is higher in vitamin, mineral (especially magnesium and zinc), and protein content than common wheat. It doesn't yield as well as wheat, but it is drought-resistant and performs well without chemical inputs.

Kamut has a very nice texture and taste in baked goods. Muffin batters made from kamut call for more liquid because it is somewhat denser and drier than spelt flour. The resulting texture is spongy like bread.

Chestnut

For historic information on the American chestnut, see the Chestnut Cake recipe on page 192. More like a grain than a nut, chestnut flour is high in starch/carbohydrates, protein, B-complex vitamins, and minerals, and is low in fat.

Chestnut flour's light tan color turns a milk chocolate-brown with baking. Chestnut flour adds sweetness with a hint of chocolate flavor as well as lightness and creaminess to baked goods. Too soft to stand alone, it's great combined with wheat, spelt, barley, oat, buckwheat, quinoa, or millet flours.

Available in Italian markets or gourmet/specialty markets during the holiday season, see Resources on page 247 for an organic source.

Buckwheat

Not technically a grain, but a member of the rhubarb family, buckwheat is considered a grain due to the large number of edible seeds produced.

Buckwheat contains a starchy substance known as a gluten analogue, which means it behaves like grain gluten in cooking, but for many people who can't tolerate gluten grains, buckwheat is not seen as poison to the body.

The gray-blue flour darkens to a tweedy color with baking. Buckwheat has a pleasing flavor and stands up well on its own as the base for a wheat- and gluten-free cake.

Cornmeal and Corn Flour

Bright yellow or gray-blue in color; yellow cornmeal has a very gritty texture, making it best used in small amounts. Blue cornmeal and yellow corn flour are more desirable.

Rye

A darker grain than wheat, along with triticale (a manmade cross between wheat and rye), rye is the only other whole grain containing gluten. Baked alone it reminds one so much of rye bread with its distinct hearty flavor and dense texture, it seems best featured in main dish pastries or in very small amounts in desserts for people with wheat sensitivities who can tolerate gluten.

Teff

This ancient grain comes from Ethiopia where it is made into the national crepelike flatbread called *injera*. The word teff means "lost," since these grains are miniscule. Indeed, the smallest grain in the world's germ and bran ratio to starchy endosperm is higher than other grains, and so teff's calcium content is as much as nineteen times that of wheat or barley.

Teff has a light brown color, less dark than chestnut or buckwheat. It is best used in combination with pastry wheat, spelt, and other whole grain flours and in small amounts due to its distinctive, but pleasant flavor. Baked alone, it has a nice texture at first, which changes to a dry, gummy mouth-feel with chewing.

Amaranth

This whole grain was the staple food of the Aztecs, who used it to make flatbread. It is not a true grain because it is the seed of a broad-leaved plant and not of a grass. But due to its high yield of edible seed, like buckwheat, it is considered a grain.

Amaranth is high in complete protein, is rich in minerals such as iron, calcium, and phosphorus, and contains little fat. Like quinoa, it contains more calcium and calcium-supportive magnesium and silicon than milk. It has a tan color like wheat and a very distinct, hearty and nutty flavor that is nice in small amounts combined with other grains such as pastry wheat, spelt, and barley. Used alone, amaranth makes for a slightly dry dough, but the texture changes to glutinous and sticky when cooked.

NATURAL SWEETENERS

America is on a sugar binge. The average American eats between 120 and 143 pounds of sugar each year, 70 percent of which is consumed in manufactured foods such as breakfast cereals, snacks, specialty foods, and soft drinks. At two cups of sugar per pound, that's between ⅓ and ½ cup per day. According to *Sugar Blues*, the classic book on the history of refined white sugar consumption and its relationship to physical and mental health, ". . . in the 13th century a pound of sugar cost a week's wage. A hundred years ago, the U.S. and Britain ate 300 pounds of wheat and 25 pounds of sugar. Now [1975] the amounts are 120 pounds each of refined wheat, sugar and beef." Sugar has grown from use as an occasional condiment to the leading food additive. In fact, it's very difficult to find a processed food that does not contain sugar.

Health-conscious consumers should read the ingredients labels. Starting with the most prominent ingredient by weight, anything ending in "-ose" is a sugar. Also look for the number of times different sugars appear in the ingredients list. Often a product will contain sugars under three or four different names.

Monosaccharides—Simple Sugars

Glucose (blood sugar), also known as dextrose

Fructose (fruit sugar), also known as levulose

Galactose

Disaccharides—Double Sugars

Sucrose (table sugar) made of glucose and fructose

Lactose (milk sugar) made of glucose and galactose

Maltose (malt sugar) made of two glucose units

Polysaccharides—Complex Sugars

Plant foods

Natural sweeteners are the ideal alternatives to sugar refined from either cane or beets (and its relatives—brown, turbinado, and confectioners' sugars), as well as sugar substitutes such as corn syrup and fructose.

Natural sweeteners have four things in common:

1. They are derived from a natural source that may be organically grown.
2. They use relatively simple, chemical-free processing techniques.
3. They may contain maltose and complex carbohydrates that break down more slowly in the body than the simple sugars sucrose, glucose, and fructose.
4. They may contain vitamins and minerals necessary for their metabolism.

Natural foods consumers are enjoying the rise of more whole-foods-based, low-impact alternatives—brown rice, barley, and wheat malt syrups, sometimes combined with fruit juice concentrates—along with the standards, like maple syrup and honey. Even so, intelligent choices among the alternative sweeteners must be made with regard to origin, processing, nutrition, and versatility.

And it's wise to assess how much sweetener—natural, unnatural, or supernatural—we are consuming every day because even the finest, most impeccably wholesome, minimally processed sweetener can still upset dietary balance when overly consumed. We might be better off eating a luscious piece of fruit than using even the most complex carbohydrate-based grain syrup with its concentrated sugar structure.

I prefer liquid sweeteners in dessert making because their humectancy, the ability to contribute and hold moisture, is greater than with dry sweeteners. This means that you don't need as much fat in the recipe and baked goods stay moist and fresh-tasting longer. With regular baking, the moisture content is provided by hard fats (butter, lard, or margarine) and eggs, ingredients that are high in cholesterol and the hormones, antibiotics, and the questionable feed that factory farm animals are given these days.

Rice syrup and barley malt, two malted grain sweeteners, are closer to whole foods than any other sweeteners. This section covers sweeteners in order of preference, starting with these malted grain syrups and ending with refined white sugar and synthetic sweeteners for a complete understanding by comparison.

Preservatives are seldom used in natural sweeteners because sugar is a good preservative itself. All natural sweeteners keep very well in a cool dry place, unrefrigerated, except maple syrup, which needs refrigeration.

All the sweeteners used in this book are available in natural foods stores; you may need to ask the buyer to order particular brands from their distributors.

Malted Grain Syrups—Brown Rice Syrup and Barley Malt Syrup

As grain is the food that grows in the greatest abundance on the planet, it seems appropriate to derive a sweetener from it. Of the most popular grain syrup sweeteners, (white) rice syrup is lightest in color and has a subtle flavor. Brown rice syrup is slightly darker and sweeter and is the best quality of all in terms of taste, versatility, and wholesomeness; 100 percent barley malt (or wheat malt) has the richest flavor and is darkest in color, yet is mildly sweet. Corn and barley malt syrup is somewhat lighter and much sweeter due to the sugars derived from the corn.

Malted grain syrup sweeteners are the most healthful of all, while still providing a satisfying sweet flavor. They are made by a simple process called malting, which is natural and safe. When we chew grain, the amylase enzyme in saliva breaks down the starch into simple sugars. The malting process does the same thing, as malt enzymes convert the starch in grains into sweet syrup. The difference is that some manufacturers of brown rice syrup prefer to use only the live *Aspergillus oryzae* mold grown on brown rice or barley (referred to as *koji*), while others use enzymes that have been extracted from the mold via mechanical methods.

Malted grain syrups provide a slow but prolonged source of energy that is calming and soothing in comparison to other sweeteners. The sugars they contain are about half as sweet as white sugar. They metabolize slowly and evenly in the body, creating none of the severe stress reactions such as the rapid fluctuations in blood-sugar levels caused by ingestion of the simple sugars (fructose, glucose, and sucrose) found in all the other sweeteners, natural or otherwise. These sweeteners are better tolerated by diabetics because their complex carbohydrate content enables the syrup to be metabolized more slowly and stimulates less insulin production. Grain syrups also contain much of the original mineral content of the grain.

Brown Rice Syrup

Rice malt has been used as a sweetener in the Orient for centuries. Rice malt contains about 30 percent soluble complex carbohydrates, 45 percent maltose (grain-malt sugar), 3 to 4 percent glucose and 20 percent water. While the glucose is absorbed into the blood almost immediately like other simple sugars, maltose takes up to 1½ hours to digest, and the complex carbohydrates are gradually digested and released for up to 4 hours.

Furthermore, 1 tablespoon of brown rice syrup contains 42 calories (about the same as conventional table sugar and less than honey at 64 calories), but it packs potassium and small amounts of protein, calcium, and B vitamins, which are naturally present in whole grain rice. And rice syrup is hypoallergenic.

Nowadays, to produce domestic brands of brown rice syrup, only certain enzymes extracted from sprouted barley are substituted for the actual barley. Barley is sprouted, placed in a centrifuge, and spun until the enzyme-containing layers are removed. These enzymes are then placed in a growth medium to multiply. To make rice syrup, enzymes are added to cooked ground rice to culture the mixture.

> *IMPORTANT NOTE:* To distinguish between the two types in the recipes in this book, the traditional version is called "brown rice malt syrup," while the version containing laboratory-extracted enzymes is termed "brown rice syrup." When only the traditional version works in a recipe, it is called for. When either type works, the term "brown rice syrup" is used.

I agree with traditional makers of rice malt who contend that there is a distinct qualitative difference between their product and enzyme-treated rice syrups. In the traditional process, many enzymes in the sprouted barley are at work holistically digesting proteins and fats as well as carbohydrates, and the full range of flavors is more evident in the well-rounded sweet flavor. The color is like an amber-hued honey. At this time, this kind of brown rice syrup is produced domestically by Suzanne's Specialties, or is imported from Belgium (Sweet Cloud brand) or Japan (Mitoku brand). Ingredients are partially polished organic brown rice, organic sprouted barley, and water. (See Resources on pages 247 and 249.)

The other reason I prefer brown rice malt syrup is that it works consistently in desserts that are supposed to rise or thicken, e.g. cakes, muffins, and cobbler toppings; pie, cobbler, and crisp fillings; and puddings, custards, and sweet sauces. All of these desserts call for arrowroot powder or kuzu root starch (good alternatives to cornstarch), or agar sea vegetable flakes (a nice alternative to gelatin) as the thickening agent, or aluminum-free baking powder or baking soda as the leavening agent.

By contrast, the limited and specific enzymes extracted in a laboratory leave a bitter aftertaste in the mouth from enzyme-treated brown rice syrup. Fortunately, this is most noticeable when the syrup is consumed directly, instead of in desserts where the sweet taste prevails. The color is somewhat chalky. Read the ingredients on brand name labels such as Lundberg or Aunt Pattie's. You'll see (brown) rice, water, and natural cereal enzymes or sprouted barley enzymes.

Enzyme-treated syrups are the most popular ones on the market today because of their cheaper price and wider availability. Their higher glucose content renders them sweeter than brown rice malt syrup. (See the table on page 26.)

> *IMPORTANT NOTE:* However, when used in recipes containing thickening or leavening agents, enzyme-treated syrups liquefy batters and doughs due to the starch-splitting enzymes. This is more likely when eggs are not used in a recipe as in this book. This is why you may have noticed your baking powder-leavened cake or cornbread turn to mush, or your arrowroot powder-thickened pie filling fail to thicken.
>
> Select brown rice malt syrup to avoid this problem. Or, to inactivate the enzymes so you can use the enzyme-treated rice syrups in cooked or baked desserts, boil the syrup for 5 minutes before use—3 minutes isn't long enough. Watch for foaming upon boiling and keep heat low thereafter. Note that boiling the syrup too long before use causes it to thicken into a taffy consistency as it cools. For best results, while still warm, mix syrup in with fruit (for a pie filling) or with the wet ingredients for a cake batter.

Brown rice syrup powder is also marketed as a dry sweetener. Because of the flavor and the large volume required, I don't use this sweetener.

The most endearing quality of either style of brown rice syrup is its pleasing delicate taste. Truly an elegant sweetener, it isn't cloyingly sweet like honey. Brown rice syrup doesn't compete, but rather it pairs especially well with the natural flavors of fresh and dried fruits and whole grain flours for exceptional desserts.

Rice syrup is about half as sweet as honey and can be substituted for it and other sweeteners. Rather than doubling the amount of rice syrup when substituting it for honey, include rice syrup in equal proportion and see how you like it. You may find less sweet treats are just as satisfying. For a sweeter flavor with a milder effect on the nervous system, mix some maple syrup or honey in with the rice syrup.

Malt syrups have a long shelf life and stable sweetness, but, once opened, are subject to surface molds if the room temperature is very warm or condensation takes place in the jar. If mold does form, just scrape it away; it is a surface problem and doesn't penetrate the product. Refrigeration helps retard mold formation but is not necessary.

If malt syrup becomes too thick from refrigeration, place the uncovered jar in a saucepan with two inches of water and simmer for a minute or two, or until the syrup is warm and pours easily. In these recipes, oil is always listed before the sweetener so the syrup slides out of the measuring cup easily.

Barley Malt Syrup

Barley malt syrup is thick like molasses and has a dark amber color and a deep rich flavor with a distinctly malty taste. It is lighter and sweeter than the barley malt sold for beer-making, which may impart a bitter flavor and so is not suitable for home cooking. Stronger in flavor than brown rice syrup, it is milder than molasses. See the Gingerbread (page 180), Carrot Cake (page 181) and Orange-Ginger Oatmeal Crunch Cookies (page 218) recipes for great uses of this sweetener.

Liquid barley malt is available in two forms: 100 percent barley malt and a blend of 60 percent whole grain malted barley and 40 percent corn. The higher the percentage of corn, the less expensive the product and the milder the flavor. Corn cannot be malted by itself, but when corn grits are combined with malt, the barley enzymes reduce the cornstarch to maltose. Some manufacturers mix the highly refined and chemically converted commercial high fructose corn syrup with malt syrup to form an inferior, but even sweeter product.

The brands I use, Eden and Sweet Cloud organic barley malt, contain 100 percent organic sprouting barley. It is made using traditional malting techniques. See the table on page 26 for barley malt's sugar profile.

When whole barley is soaked for two to three days in water, and allowed to sprout in temperature- and humidity-controlled chambers, the enzymes that develop change the starches and proteins in the barley into more digestible forms. After kiln-drying at 120 degrees to stop the sprouting and dry out the malt, the grains are then ground and placed in brewing vats that are filled with water and heated to make a syrup, which is drawn off, filtered, and evaporated to a thick syrup and bottled.

FruitSource (Brown Rice Syrup and Grape Juice Concentrate)

FruitSource is a fruit and grain sweetener containing organic brown rice syrup and grape juice concentrate. FruitSource is made without cereal enzymes, by a natural fermentation process. The patented natural method molecularly bonds the complex carbohydrates from whole grains to the simple sugars from fruit. While the whole rice syrup adds complex carbohydrates, most of the sweetness in this product is derived from the simple carbohydrates in the fruit concentrate.

Both FruitSource sweeteners (syrup and dry granules) have an appealing pale amber color. Dry FruitSource is not a crystal like sugar, so its ability to dissolve is slower. Therefore it is metabolized gradually, making it a more acceptable sweetener than white sugar for diabetics. Medical tests have proven FruitSource provides up to 50 percent longer-lasting energy than refined sugar (sucrose), with no dip in energy afterward beyond the starting baseline. FruitSource is ideal for celiacs, people who cannot tolerate gluten, which is present in the malted barley used to make some brands of brown rice syrup, and of course, barley malt.

In dessert cookery, FruitSource lends a very pleasing sweet taste, brighter and stronger than rice syrup, but milder than maple syrup. However, it works in some desserts better than others as is discussed throughout this book. It works brilliantly in single-layer cakes based on 1½ cups flour, but not in those made with 2 cups or more flour such as a Bundt cake. It works in arrowroot-thickened sauces in small amounts, but not when used in equal quantity as water, such as in the Fresh Blueberry Pie recipe. Dry FruitSource dissolves in hot liquids, not cool, and must be kept tightly sealed in a cool, dry environment to prevent it from hardening.

Pure Maple Syrup

For three or four weeks in early spring in New England, when the nights fall below freezing and the days just begin to get warm, the sap flows up from the roots in the sugar maples. Making syrup in this season remains one of the most American of experiences and one that links us with the Indians who, equipped with tomahawks, gashed the trunks and placed channeled pieces of wood at the lower edge of the slashes to direct sap to a container. The sap was concentrated by dropping hot stones into it, thereby boiling out the liquid. Freezing this and removing the ice that formed on top produced sugar. Native Americans taught the early settlers how to tap the maple. For many living in the northeastern United States during the nineteenth century, maple syrup or maple sugar was the basic sweetener.

To make pure maple syrup, an average of 40 gallons of clear, barely sweet sap (3 percent sucrose) are boiled down to produce 1 gallon of syrup. One tree can supply 10 to 25 gallons of sap.

There are three classifications for pure maple syrup. Grade A syrup, the most commonly available, comes in light, medium, and dark amber. Light is subtle and delicate; dark has a somewhat stronger maple flavor. Usually collected in the colder, early part of the season, Grade A has less maple flavor than Grades B or C. Grades B or C, with their full flavor, are usually reserved for baked beans. Maple sugar granules are crystalline dehydrated pure maple syrup. The complex carbohydrates and trace minerals make both syrup and granules good alternatives to cane sugar.

Most of the maple syrup sold in regular supermarkets and not labeled "pure maple syrup," is composed of corn syrup with 20 percent maple sugar syrup, artificial flavor and color, and two preservatives. You can taste the difference.

Desserts made with pure maple syrup are luxurious. I also love the intriguing flavor achieved from the more healthful mixture of pure maple syrup with brown rice syrup.

Concentrated Fruit Juice

To make concentrated fruit juice, about 5 pounds of fruit is pressed and concentrated to get 1 pint. When I have tried to use organic concentrated fruit juice as the sweetener in a dessert, the taste is not definitive enough; it tastes like apples or whatever the flavor may be, but doesn't offer a distinct, satisfying, and subtle sweet flavor. I prefer brown rice syrup or a combination of concentrated fruit juice and brown rice syrup, or FruitSource brand syrup for use as a sweetener. On the other hand, organic concentrated fruit juice works well when substituted for other liquids, such as water, juice, or soy milk in cookies, pie crusts, cobbler toppings, or cakes, in addition to the sweetener to add a stronger sweet taste.

Fruit concentrate is composed of the simple sugars fructose and sucrose, albeit from a natural source. However, according to an expert in the field, the vast majority of concentrated fruit juices on the market today, including organic concentrates, are "de-ionized" to stabilize the pH. This laboratory procedure ensures that the concentrates don't ferment and turn into wine. Unfortunately, the process also renders the concentrate devoid of any nutritional value—it contains none of the minerals or vitamins that occur naturally in a piece of fruit. Once again, we are reminded to rely on whole foods.

Sorghum Syrup

Native to Egypt where it has been grown for thousands of years, sorghum was probably introduced to North America in the 1700s. Sweet sorghum is a cereal grain similar to millet in appearance. It produces juicy stalks or canes that are topped by clusters of seeds. In the fall in the southern and midwestern states, the ripe canes are cut and pressed through rollers to extract the juice. Eight to 12 gallons of juice is boiled down to produce 1 gallon of finished syrup, a natural processing technique, but the resulting syrup is 70 percent sucrose. Both the color and the texture are like an amber honey.

Some commercial sorghum is treated with the enzymes invertase or diastase to prevent crystallization and may neutralize the effects of baking powder. Try this sweetener once in a single-layer cake, e.g. half the Basic Vanilla Cake recipe, to see the results for future use.

Date Sugar

Made from dried and granulated cosmetically inferior dates, the flavor of this gritty sweetener is not quite as nice as dehydrated sugar cane juice, but lends variety. Date sugar makes flecks in baked goods.

Honey

Honey is still the most popular natural sweetener for people wishing to make the transition to a more healthful diet. However, although honey is a relatively unprocessed natural sweetener, for several reasons it is no longer considered the best natural sweetening alternative:

1. Honey raises blood sugar levels more than sucrose (sugar), according to the Center for Science in the Public Interest. With the highest sugar content of all the natural sweeteners, honey is approximately 70 percent sweeter than sugar.

2. The amounts of vitamins and minerals in honey are so tiny as to be inconsequential.

3. Bees may be fed sugar, sulfa drugs, or antibiotics during honey production season and some big commercial producers add cane or corn syrup to light honeys.

4. The strong taste of honey may interfere with the overall taste of baked goods. I like to use it occasionally to feature its wonderful flavor.

5. For some people honey doesn't fit in with a true vegetarian approach because it is derived from insects.

Sucanat (SUgar CAne NATural) Evaporated Sugar Cane Juice

A higher-quality substitute for white sugar, Sucanat is evaporated and granulated organic sugar cane juice. The cane juice is dehydrated by spinning at a high temperature through a vacuum funnel, and is then milled into a powder. Only the water is removed. Sucanat contains more minerals, trace elements, and vitamins (though still in minimal amounts) than table sugar. It is free of anticaking agents and chemicals from processing. Laboratory analysis shows that this product consists of 88 percent sucrose with 12 percent fructose and glucose.

Sucanat has a nice taste and depth of flavor. It can be used cup-for-cup for refined sugar. It has the texture and appearance of a slightly lighter brown sugar and makes brown flecks in baked goods. Since it tends to lump, it should be passed through a strainer before use.

Organic Sugar Crystals

Although the production of sugar is largely mechanical, refined white sugar, essentially pure crystalline sucrose, receives the most processing of any sweetener other than the corn sweeteners.

To make organic sugar crystals, distributors claim that these are the basic stages used in this relatively new industry: Raw organic sugar cane is crushed and washed with water. The liquid sugar is separated from the fiber, filtered for impurities, boiled to eliminate the molasses, crystallized by evaporation, and milled to a small granular size. No additives are used in the process. The resulting sugar is 99 percent pure crystalline sucrose and is metabolized as such, containing no trace vitamins or minerals.

Unfortunately, according to an industry expert, the process is only minimally "clean" by comparison with table sugar. Chemicals and flow agents are used in the process, which is the same as for table sugar except that it doesn't go through the third of three bleaching processes. Chemicals included in the process are calcium carbonate, titanium dioxide (a paint pigment) and other whiteners, phosphoric acid for a stripping agent, and calcium and magnesium salts as flow agents.

Refined White (Cane and Beet) Sugar and Molasses

Both white and brown sugars have no nutritive value. Raw sugar cane, which contains 14 percent sucrose, is chemically processed to produce white sugar, a 99 percent pure crystalline sucrose product. It takes 3 feet of cane to make 1 teaspoon of refined white sugar.

In the sugar making process, crushed cane or sliced beet is flushed with water to extract a syrup that is heated until the sugar begins to crystallize. Then it is spun in a centrifuge to separate the crystals from the liquid called molasses. The sugar crystals are clarified with lime or phosphoric acid, then bone-black (charred beef bones or animal charcoal from the blood albumin of slaughtered animals) is used to filter or purify the table sugar, which is boiled and bleached to whiten and remove calcium and magnesium salts. Everything is removed except the sucrose.

Confectioners' or powdered sugar is made by pulverizing white sugar until it becomes a powder. Anticaking agents may be added. To make brown sugar, the molasses is separated out of the pulp and added back to white sugar to achieve the desired brown color. Or burnt white sugar, called caramel coloring, is added instead.

Molasses—light, dark, or blackstrap—is what's left over after sugar has been refined from sugar cane. Light molasses (also called Barbados molasses), the sweetest type, is the product of the first boiling, when the least amount of sugar has been removed. Dark molasses is the product of the second boiling when more sugar is removed. Blackstrap (from the Dutch word *stroop,* meaning syrup) is the bitter end, literally, because the maximum amount of sugar has been extracted after the third boiling. Blackstrap is considered a source of B vitamins and minerals— notably iron—though an average serving of 1 tablespoon contains less than a thirtieth of the RDA of B vitamins and about a sixteenth the iron and calcium.

The refining process for molasses uses sulfur dioxide to lighten the color. Molasses that has not been lightened with sulfur is called "unsulfured." The toxic substances from farming the soil are concentrated in molasses so organic brands are preferred.

Corn Sweeteners

Corn syrup, called glucose syrup in Europe, was first marketed in the early 1900s. It is made from a refined food, cornstarch (the middle part of the corn kernel), which is mixed with water and hydrochloric or sulfuric acid, then steamed to convert the starch to commercial glucose. The resulting substance is neutralized/deodorized with sodium carbonate, filtered through charred beef bones, and bleached with other chemicals to produce the odorless, clear, and tasteless liquid.

To produce high-fructose corn syrup, enzymes are added to cornstarch to produce dextrose and fructose, with the advantage to food technologists that fructose is 20 percent sweeter than sucrose and is cheaper.

Fructose

The only good source of fructose is fruits, where it occurs naturally. Fructose is a highly processed derivative of corn syrup.

SWEETENERS

Sweetener	Source	Composition
Brown rice malt syrup	organic brown rice	45% maltose, 5% glucose, 32% complex carbohydrates
Brown rice syrup, enzyme treated	brown rice, may be organic	16%–29% maltose, 35% to 40% glucose, 19% to 43% complex carbohydrates
Barley malt	malted barley, may be organic	76% maltose, 16% glucose 6% sucrose, 2% fructose
FruitSource, granular or syrup	naturally fermented organic brown rice and grape juice concentrate	20% sucrose, 20% fructose, 10% maltose, 33% to 49% complex carbohydrates
Pure maple syrup	boiled down maple tree sap	88% sucrose, 0% to 11% glucose, 1% to 2% invert sugars
Honey	nectar from flowers processed in the stomach of bees	39% fructose, 31% glucose, 7% maltose, 2% sucrose
Date sugar	dried dates	26% sucrose, 13% glucose, 13% fructose
Amazake	naturally fermented brown rice, may be organic	80% glucose, 20% maltose
Sorghum syrup	boiled down sorghum cane juice	70% sucrose
Fruit juice concentrate	fruit, from apples or grapes	15% to 20% fructose, 9% to 12% glucose, 0% to 15% sucrose
Evaporated sugar cane juice	sugar cane, may be organic	89% sucrose, 1% fructose, 1% glucose
Molasses, blackstrap and Barbados	by-product of cane sugar, may be organic	32% to 40% sucrose, 9% to 17% glucose, 9% to 15% fructose
Brown sugar	white sugar with molasses	98% sucrose
Organic sugar crystals	organic sugar cane	99% sucrose
White sugar	sugar cane and sugar beet	99% sucrose

Source: Manufacturers' analyses (see Resources on page 247).

DAIRY AND ITS ALTERNATIVES

Dairy-free milks based on grains, beans, and nuts are good choices for people who are looking for healthier alternatives to cow's milk or who are allergic to cow's milk or lactose intolerant.

Doctors associated with Physicians Committee for Responsible Medicine (PCRM)—a Washington-based group of more than four thousand physicians whose interests include both preventive medicine and alternatives to animal research—have concluded that milk is not nature's most perfect food that "every body needs." Dairy products, as they are produced today and in the quantities in which they are consumed, contribute to many of our nation's ills.

PCRM asserts that milk is an unhealthful food that produces iron deficiency anemia in infants, causes diabetes in children, and is responsible for heart disease, cancer, colic, allergies, and digestive problems. Their conclusion is that "there is no nutritional requirement for dairy products," and there are serious problems that can result from the fat, proteins, sugar, and contaminants in milk products. They assert that cow's milk should not be required or recommended in government guidelines. And government programs, such as school lunch programs and the WIC program, should be consistent with these recommendations.

Some experts have questioned the rationale behind drinking milk at any age. Milk is a transitional food that is secreted by female mammals to help their offspring adjust from the womb to the outside world. No other mammal uses milk after infancy, let alone from another mammalian species. The arrival of teeth transforms infants from a liquid to a solid state eating mammal. Adult cows don't even drink cow's milk; they get their calcium from green plants.

According to PCRM, whole milk, cheese, cream, butter, ice cream, sour cream, and all other dairy products, aside from skim and nonfat products, contain significant amounts of fat, saturated fat, as well as cholesterol, contributing to cardiovascular diseases and certain forms of cancer. According to cardiologist Dean Ornish, milk is second only to beef as the largest source of saturated fat in the American diet. Consider, for example, that one glass of 2 percent milk has as much saturated fat as three strips of bacon.

The early stages of heart disease have been documented in American teenagers. While children do need a certain amount of fat in their diets, there is no nutritional requirement for cow's milk fat. On the contrary, cow's milk is high in saturated fats, but low in the essential fatty acid linoleic acid.

Whole cow's milk contains 49 percent of its calories from fat, butter 100 percent, Cheddar cheese 74 percent, ice cream 70 percent, and part-skim mozzarella 56 percent. Even low-fat milk (2 percent) is not "low-fat" because 35 percent of its calories come from fat. And it may not be just the animal fat in milk that increases one's risk of getting heart disease. A study of diet and mortality rates from coronary heart disease in twenty-four countries has implicated milk proteins, in addition to dietary fat.

Contaminants

Milk contains frequent contaminants from pesticides to drugs. Compared to animals living freely in nature, modern farm animals are often sick and weak. They live in artificial environments, under unnaturally crowded conditions, and are fed a highly synthetic diet. In order to keep these animals alive and free of infection, they are routinely fed antibiotics. About a third of milk products have been shown to be contaminated with antibiotic traces.

Washington Post columnist Colman McCarthy jests that milk is tainted with so many drugs that it should be sold by prescription only. A 1992 U.S. government report found that the Food and Drug Administration tests for just four of eighty-two drugs that are used in dairy cows. Thirty-five of the most commonly used drugs have never been approved for use in dairy cows.

Since 1993, the controversial genetically engineered Bovine Growth Hormone (BGH) has been widely employed by commercial dairies. (According to "One Peaceful World," the newsletter of the One Peaceful World Society, a macrobiotic organization, 25 percent of all milk in the U.S. contains BGH.) Critics believe that BGH—which boosts milk production in an era of already serious milk surplus—poses grave potential health risks for consumers, including elevated antibiotic residue levels in milk. Only organic dairy foods are certified to be free of antibiotic and Bovine Growth Hormone residues. These cows eat organically grown corn, grain, and hay.

Worse still, in his book *Deadly Feasts,* the Pulitzer Prize-winning author Richard Rhodes documents the rise of BSE (bovine spongiform encephalopathy), the official name for Mad Cow Disease, which has afflicted hundreds of thousands of cows in Britain over the last decade. In 1996, British health officials announced that feeling contaminated sheep brains to British cattle gave rise to BSE and that humans who eat beef or drink milk from tainted cows are susceptible to a human strain of the disease known as Creutzfeldt-Jakob Disease (CJD). This risk to public health, however small, should be taken seriously.

Having posed the question "Will BSE come to America?" to the chairman of the Department of Animal Health and Biomedical Science at the University of Wisconsin, the chairman responded, "The answer seems to be: It's already here, in native form, a low-level infection that industrial cannibalism could amplify to epidemic scale. We still feed meat-and-bone meal to cattle. And an estimated 77 million Americans eat beef every day."

In early 1997, the U.S. government proposed banning some of these practices, but the meat industry and its allies strenuously objected. In the summer of 1997, in response to the European ban, the U.S. government banned the practice of rendering cattle, but chicken, pigs, and fish, as well as blood products, were exempted from the ban. No doubt there will be more debate on this issue.

Calcium

So where should we get our calcium, if not from milk and other dairy products? A report in the *American Journal of Clinical Nutrition* found that calcium absorbability was higher for kale (and other leafy greens such as collards, turnip greens, and broccoli, but not spinach) and soybeans than from milk. Specifically, more than 50 percent of the calcium in kale is absorbed. Only 30 percent of the calcium in milk is absorbed. Other great sources of calcium are beans, sea vegetables, nuts, sesame seeds, and canned salmon (see table).

Much research indicates that preventing calcium loss is actually three to four times more important in determining calcium balance than is calcium intake. And one of the greatest instigators of calcium loss, it turns out, is a high-protein diet.

Protein, and especially protein from animal sources, makes our blood acidic, a pH condition the body attempts to remedy by drawing calcium, an alkaline mineral, from the bones. Many North Americans typically eat twice the recommended amount of protein (50 grams for women and 60 for men in a day). Scientific studies show that when protein intake is above 75 grams per day, more calcium is lost in the urine than is retained in the body. Researchers speculate that this level of protein intake alone could account for all the bone loss commonly seen in postmenopausal women.

Meat-free diets produce less acid than those containing meat, and vegan diets (no meat, dairy, or eggs) produce less acid than those including dairy. Other calcium thieves include caffeine, alcohol, phosphate-containing soft drinks, and tobacco, along with a lack of sunshine for vitamin D, and inactivity.

Furthermore, the U.S. RDA for calcium is established higher than it otherwise would be in order to compensate for the typical, high-protein American diet. People worldwide develop and maintain strong bones on levels of calcium considerably below the 1,200-mg RDA. The World Health Organization recommends 400–500 mg daily.

For most people the RDA can quite easily be met by eating a varied diet with two or more servings of calcium-rich foods each day. (As an added bonus, these foods are excellent sources of antioxidants, fiber, folic acid, complex carbohydrates, iron, and other important vitamins and minerals you won't find in milk products.)

On the other hand, a single fast-food burger, because of its high protein and sodium and low calcium content, can cause the loss of 22 mg of calcium.

Allergies

Milk is the most common cause of food allergies. Of children with recurring middle ear infections, about one third demonstrate milk allergies. One way to reduce the number of allergies in infants is for the breast-feeding mother to avoid consuming, or make very limited use of, cow's milk.

CALCIUM SOURCES

Food	Serving Size	Milligrams of Calcium
VEGETABLES		
Broccoli, cooked	1 cup	71
Collards, cooked	1 cup	148
Dandelion greens, cooked	1 cup	147
Kale, cooked	1 cup	94
Mustard greens, cooked	1 cup	104
Turnip greens, cooked	1 cup	267
Carrots, cooked	1 cup	48
SEA VEGETABLES		
Hijiki, cooked	¼ cup	153
Wakame, cooked	¼ cup	130
Kombu, cooked	¼ cup	76
NUTS AND SEEDS		
Almonds	¼ cup	90
Carob flour	¼ cup	98
Peanuts	¼ cup	63
Pecans	¼ cup	94
Sesame seeds	¼ cup	352
Sunflower seeds	¼ cup	44
BEANS		
Beans, snap, cooked	1 cup	61
Black beans, dry, cooked	1 cup	24
Blackeye peas, fresh, cooked	1 cup	46
Chickpeas, dry, cooked	1 cup	40
Navy beans, dry, cooked	1 cup	48
Peas, split, dry, cooked	1 cup	90
Pinto beans, dry, cooked	1 cup	43
Soybeans, dry, cooked	1 cup	66
Tofu*	1 cup	86–334
FISH		
Salmon, canned with bones	3 oz.	226
Sardines, canned with bones	3 oz.	371
DAIRY		
Milk, whole, 4% fat	1 cup	291
Cottage cheese, 4% fat	1 cup	135
Yogurt, whole milk,	1 cup	274
Cheddar cheese	1 oz.	204

Sources: Nutritive Value of American Foods, USDA Handbook No 456, 1975, and Japan Nutritionist Association, 1977.

*Tofu curded with calcium sulfate has 3½–4 times as much calcium as that curded with nigari (magnesium chloride)

It wasn't until the 1960s that Western researchers discovered that the majority of the world's adults can't tolerate lactose (milk sugar), according to Harold McGee in his book *On Food and Cooking, The Science and Lore of the Kitchen*. According to the Physicians' Committee for Responsible Medicine, although 90 percent of white Americans of European ancestry can digest more than a pint of milk a day without extreme stomach upset, only 30 percent of Native Americans and Americans of African, Mexican, Jewish, and Asian ancestry can. In fact, most of the world's people lose the ability to digest milk by age three. Those who can digest it are often from northern Europe, where there is little sunshine, the natural source of vitamin D and other nutrients found in milk.

Cancer

The relationship between dairy product consumption and breast cancer is explained by Neal Barnard, M.D., president of PCRM, in his article "Women and Cancer, Opportunities for Prevention": "What is largely unknown to the American public—and sadly underemphasized in medical schools—is that breast cancer is often a preventable illness . . . There was never an organized effort to give women the information they need to make decisions about cancer prevention . . . it is known that many breast tumors are 'fueled' by estrogens, the female sex hormones . . . The principal estrogen is estradiol, and the amount of estradiol produced by the body is linked to the amount of fat in the diet . . . high-fat diets increase estrogen production apparently increasing cancer risk. Low-fat, high-fiber diets reduce estrogens to a more biologically normal level. Since meats, poultry, fish and dairy products contain no fiber, they increase the fat content and reduce the fiber content of the diet by displacing plant foods."

Dairy Milk Alternatives

Soy milk, rice milk, and almond milk are primarily among the dairy-free options to cow's milk that work well as ingredients in baking. All the dairy alternatives come in aseptic (nonrefrigerated) quart and sometimes 8-ounce containers. Once opened, the milks must be refrigerated and will stay fresh for five days to a couple of weeks. Coconut milk is another very delicious option with good color.

Natural sweeteners color the milks somewhat because they are not white like refined white sugar. FruitSource syrup lends the nicest color and taste when compared with pure maple syrup or brown rice syrup. However, it may not set up when thickened with arrowroot powder and this is why agar flakes are the chosen thickener in pudding, custard, or pastry cream recipes.

Soy Foods

Increasing in popularity in the West, soybeans have been an important human food for five thousand years. From a health perspective, the explosion in soy products is an acknowledgment that lower rates of many chronic illnesses in Asian countries may be due in part to a high intake of soy. According to Andrew Weil, "Western scientists are now discovering that soy is not just a cholesterol-free alternative to the animal proteins that Westerners typically consume—chock-full of soluble and insoluble fiber, calcium, and B vitamins—but also contains special compounds that may help reduce menopausal symptoms, lower cholesterol, prevent osteoporosis, even protect against common killers such as heart disease and cancer."

Andrew Weil gives these doctor's orders: ". . . Based on current findings, I would recommend that you consume one serving a day to reduce your risk of breast cancer, one or two to alleviate menopausal symptoms, two to four to lower cholesterol, and more than four to decrease the risk of osteoporosis. (A serving of soy is 1 cup of soy milk, ½ cup of tofu, ½ cup of tempeh, or ½ cup green soybeans.)"

From a global perspective, this extraordinarily versatile bean is central to the achievement of a hunger-free world. The soybean yields more high-quality protein per acre than any other agricultural product, and it pays back to Mother Earth by fixing nitrogen in the soil.

Soy Milk

Soy milk is by far the most popular alternative to dairy milk. To make soy milk, soybeans are soaked and then ground with water. The resulting purée is mixed with hot water and cooked for a few minutes before it is strained through a cloth bag and pressed to remove as much of the creamy white liquid as possible. It is the heat that deactivates the enzymes responsible for the formation of off-flavors. Today homogenization prevents product separation, and high heat and pressure ensure long shelf life without refrigeration. Soy milk is an excellent source of complete vegetable protein, B vitamins, iron, phosphorous, copper, potassium, and magnesium.

The brand of soy milk I have used in these recipes is Edensoy Original. However, the two other major brands, Westsoy and Vitasoy, also work well in the recipes. Edensoy ingredients include purified water, organic soybeans, malted cereal extract, Job's tears (also known as pearl barley or *hato mugi* in Japanese), organic barley, kombu (seaweed), and sea salt. Convenient and versatile, this brand contains no added fat in the form of oil, yet it adds a wonderful rich texture to baked goods such as cakes and cobbler toppings.

Soy milk is the preferred second choice in liquids (to homemade almond milk) for use in puddings, custards, or pastry cream. It has a rich creamy texture, or mouth-feel, and a delightful egg custard flavor, a bit like butterscotch pudding, that is especially noticeable when made with FruitSource syrup. Maple syrup lends its own wonderful flavor. The color is tan and there is a very slight aftertaste.

While some people feel soy milk is difficult to digest when drunk or poured cold on cereals, I have never heard of any problem when soy milk is baked in cakes or cooked in custards. Of course, if there is an allergy to soy, it should be avoided.

Tofu

Tofu is the primary source of protein for more than a billion people every day. This mild-tasting bean curd made from soy milk is easily digested, high in complete protein, free of cholesterol and saturated fat, low in calories, and immensely versatile. In this book, fresh organic tofu shines in sweet and creamy undersauces or toppings or in chocolate icing for cake.

One brand that is very popular with some natural foods home chefs is Mori Nu, particularly the silken-style tofu. This tofu has a shelf life of about six months and requires no refrigeration until opened. Ingredients include water, soybeans (not organic), isolated soy protein (a partial food), gluconolactone, and calcium chloride. It comes in small (10-ounce) aseptic packages. I don't use this brand because of its taste, but the texture is extremely smooth.

Brown Rice and Other Grain Milks

When made into pudding, all the sweet-tasting grain milks on the market, such as rice or oat or multigrain, remain thin, separate from the starch (agar, arrowroot, or tapioca) and lose their white color, turning an unattractive tannish gray color. They also have an unpleasant aftertaste.

According to a spokesperson for one of the producers, these nondairy milks are produced by the enzymatic process that converts the starches in the whole grains into the simple sugar glucose, which gives them their naturally sweet flavor. The enzymes continue to break starches down, thus preventing gelling. They advise against using the products in puddings or other products with other starches added.

Eden Foods makes a very nice, usable combination of soy milk and rice milk. The mixture is sweetened with naturally malted barley and is fat-free.

Amazake

Made from traditionally cultured (koji-fermented) organic brown rice, cereal enzymes, water, vanilla, and xanthan gum, amazake—the word means "sweet sake"—is a sweet milkshake-like beverage.

Koji is grain inoculated with the *Aspergillus oryzae* mold. It is used in the fermentation of amazake, mirin, sake, soy sauce, and miso. Koji supplies enzymes to break down the complex structure of grains and beans into readily digestible amino acids, fatty acids, and simple sugars. Grainaissance brand is the one I use.

Rich in natural sugars and enzymes, amazake has a milder effect on the body than any of the natural sweeteners. The flavor is quite sweet when drunk as a dessert beverage, but is very mild in baked goods where a sweetener is needed. It seems to act as a mild leavening agent in baked goods, but less so than soy milk. I use plain amazake to create a creamy texture in sorbets.

In my opinion, both rice milk and amazake have too distinct a flavor to work well as a pudding, or as a pastry cream base for the fresh fruit in tarts. They are best avoided for these recipes.

Nut Milks

Nut milks, like rice milk, are more watery than soy milk and so lack the luscious quality, but they may be used in place of soy milk. Homemade almond milk has the brightest white color and the freshest flavor with no chalky aftertaste in comparison with all the other milks, including commercial almond milk.

The starch-splitting cereal enzymes used nowadays in both commercial almond and rice milks (contained in the rice syrup for sweetening) may neutralize the thickener in a recipe. This may prevent the pudding, custard, or pastry cream from thickening, even with refrigeration, or may cause the mixture to separate into curds and water upon gelling with either arrowroot powder or agar flakes.

VEGETABLE OILS

On average, Americans eat the equivalent of 1½ sticks of butter a day. Fat is abundant in America's favorite foods (in descending order)—margarine, whole milk, shortening, mayonnaise, salad dressing, American cheese, ground beef, low-fat milk, eggs, butter, and vanilla ice cream.

Many food companies have stopped using animal fats, coconut oil, palm oil, or lard in response to claims by medical researchers that diets high in saturated fat have been linked to heart disease. Most specialists, and even the Department of Agriculture, say that Americans should reduce their overall intake of fats to provide no more than 30 percent of total calories. Most of us now get 35 percent to 45 percent of our calories from fat. It's the saturated fats they say we need to cut most, both the natural types (meat, eggs, butter, lard) and the manufactured types (Crisco-type vegetable shortenings).

Current studies suggest that we should go even further, and that an ideal diet might provide 15 percent to 20 percent of calories from mostly polyunsaturated fats (e.g. flax, soybean, walnut, and pumpkin oils, which all contain the essential fatty acids, omega-3 and omega-6) and monounsaturated fats, in the form of oils such as olive or canola. As with other whole foods, the most ideal source of the essential fatty acids are the nuts and seeds themselves.

The American Dietetic Association suggests we need 14 to 20 grams of fat daily. Dean Ornish, M.D., well-known champion of the low-fat diet for reversing heart disease, believes we need only 4 to 6 grams each day. To get some sense of the quantities being discussed, 1 tablespoon of oil contains about 14 grams of fat.

Kinds of Fat

The word "fat" refers to a food group that includes what you probably think of as both fats and oils. Fats come from animal and plant sources and are usually solid at room temperature; oils are produced mainly from plants and are liquid. The most common oils are extracted from seeds (safflower, sunflower, sesame, flax, and rapeseed), beans (peanut, soy), grains (corn, wheat germ), fruits (avocado, olive) and nuts (walnut, almond, and coconut).

Fats are the most concentrated source of energy in the diet. They are compounds composed of carbon, hydrogen, and oxygen, which are not soluble in water. Fats supply more than twice the number of calories per gram as carbohydrates or proteins. They stay in our digestive tract for longer periods than proteins or carbohydrates, giving a feeling of fullness. Fats protect and support vital organs such as the kidneys, heart, and liver, and a layer of fat insulates the body from cold and trauma while preserving body heat.

Calorie for calorie, no fat is better than another in terms of calorie content. A tablespoon of butter, lard, olive oil, mayonnaise, or margarine will register between 100 to 120 calories and between 11 and 14 grams of fat. A tablespoon of heavy cream has 50 calories and 6 grams of fat. Vegetable oils are, however, free of cholesterol, the waxlike substance manufactured in the human liver and also found in foods of animal origin, an excess of which can accumulate in the arteries, contributing to heart disease. And vegetable oils contain the beneficial essential fatty acids that perform a variety of key functions for the body such as transporting the fat-soluble vitamins, and are also essential components of cell membranes.

The qualities that give oils their different flavors, textures, and melting points are known as fatty acids. There are three major categories of fatty acid.

Saturated Fat

Saturated fats are present in the highest quantities in foods of animal origin—dairy products, meat, and poultry—and are usually solid at room temperature. They are also found in some vegetable oils such as coconut and palm kernel. The liver uses saturated fats to manufacture cholesterol, a fat-related substance. The more saturated fat in the diet, the more cholesterol your liver will produce.

Cholesterol, like fats, comes in two varieties—the "good" (high-density lipoproteins, HDL) and the "bad" (low-density lipoproteins, LDL). High levels of LDL cholesterol are among the primary causes of heart disease because LDL cholesterol produces fatty deposits in arteries.

Polyunsaturated Fats

Polyunsaturated fats are contained in plant foods (vegetables, nuts, or seeds) such as safflower, sunflower, and corn oils, as well as in fish like salmon and sardines. They are liquid at room temperature. Polyunsaturated fats are thought to decrease total cholesterol levels and reduce risks of clogged arteries, thus lessening danger of heart disease and stroke. Research indicates, however, that they may also reduce HDLs and eating too much may actually increase the risk of cancer.

Monounsaturated Fats

Monounsaturated fats are found mostly in vegetable and nut oils. They may be as effective as polyunsaturated in lowering LDL (bad) cholesterol without the tendency to lower good cholesterol (HDL) or produce carcinogens. Olive oil is the most concentrated source available, followed by the fats that are ideal for baking: almond, canola, sesame, and walnut.

"High oleic" is a term for cooking oils referring to safflower and sunflower oils created from new strains of oil seeds, which render the oils monounsaturated. (The original versions of these oils are polyunsaturated.) These oils are also desirable for use in baking.

Canola oil is relatively new on the American culinary scene, but for more than three thousand years rapeseed, the source for canola oil, was the preeminent culinary fat for the Indians and the Chinese. Rapeseed is a member of the cabbage family and a cousin of kale. It has been cultivated in Western Europe since the thirteenth century and has become the most popular culinary oil due to its high oleic and monounsaturated fat profile. Canola oil is history's most investigated fat and feed source for humans and animals. It is considered the most nutritionally balanced dietary fat and is known for reducing cholesterol in the body. Canola was pedigree bred (not genetically engineered) in Canada during the 1970s, hence the name "canola" for "Canadian oil."

Margarine

Some studies suggest that the manufactured saturated fats—also known as hydrogenated fats, common ingredients in processed foods and margarines—are potentially the most harmful to health. These fats contain trans-fatty acids (TFAs), a type of fatty acid that does not occur naturally but is produced in the manufacturing process. Increased dietary intake of these fats, just like animal fats, contributes to heart disease, hardening of the arteries, and elevated cholesterol levels, cancer, inflammation, aging, damage to cell membranes, and degenerative changes in tissues.

Hydrogenation is a process that pumps hydrogen gas through naturally unsaturated vegetable oils under high temperature and pressure to turn them into saturated fats in order to cause hardening. Soy margarine is a vegetable shortening that has been partially hydrogenated.

Margarine makes red blood cells stick together more than butter or cream. Hydrogenated fat prompts the liver to make cholesterol that sticks to the vessels. The fact that margarine is hard may make it hard for the body to digest. In the Nurses' Health Study of 65,000 women, it was found that women who ate four or more teaspoons of margarine a day had a 66 percent greater risk for heart disease than women who ate less than a teaspoon per month.

Crisco vegetable shortening contains 80 percent polyunsaturated soybean oil with 20 percent hydrogenated (hardened) cottonseed oil. Emulsifiers are added to the shortening to stabilize the structure of baked goods and increase their absorption of moisture. Crisco contains about half the saturated fat of butter.

Oil Production

When mass market oil is refined, research has shown that up to 1.3 percent of the fatty acids can be transformed from the natural molecular structure into trans-fatty acids, a molecular alteration that leaves them looking and acting more like saturated fat. This structural change begins to occur at 320 degrees and accelerates above 390 degrees, a good reason to toast nuts and seeds at 300 degrees. Spectrum Naturals brand oils, the ones I use most often, are not heated above 300 degrees and do not contain TFAs.

According to the expert at Spectrum, "Overheated and overprocessed oils form misshapen structures, resulting in less bioavailable nutrients. Heat stress appears to affect the oil molecules so they become more prone to adipose formation rather than structural lipoprotein formation." In other words, they are used by the body to produce fat rather than structure, e.g. tissues.

Vegetable oils are generally produced through one of three processes: solvent extraction, mechanical (expeller-) pressing, or cold-pressing. Each method generates a certain amount of heat. Heat is particularly influential in oil production because each 10-degree increase in temperature dramatically raises the rate at which the fatty acids react with oxygen, potentially destroying nutrients and promoting spoilage, as well as creating carcinogens.

Most mass market oils are obtained by solvent extraction, which involves the use of chemical solvents, some carcinogenic. These oils are also usually refined, a process during which temperatures can exceed 450 degrees.

Mechanically (expeller-) pressed oils are produced through a chemical-free, continuous mechanical process in which friction can generate temperatures of up to 220 degrees.

Cold-pressed oils are produced by a mechanical batch-pressing process in which heat-producing friction is minimized so that temperatures remain below 122 degrees. This is the European standard by law. However, the term "cold-pressed" is frequently misapplied in the United States and Canada. True cold-pressing involves the use of hydraulic presses or refrigerated in-line cooling devices on expeller presses. Under misapplication of the term, the oil could be solvent extracted and then cold-pressed.

Once produced, an oil can be left unrefined or can be put through a multistep refining procedure. Refining removes a variety of naturally occurring materials to produce an oil that can withstand high heat without burning or releasing undesirable by-products. Unlike large commercial processors, natural oil producers do not add chemical preservatives or defoaming agents during the refining process. The minimally processed refined oils are therefore healthier than the mass market equivalents, and they are always pressed without chemicals.

Oils in Baking

To create moist, satisfying texture in pastries, you must introduce a fat of some kind. In baking, chunks of fat serve as spacers in dough. As they melt in the oven, the cavities created fill with steam and gas from the leavening, causing the dough to expand and push upward, creating a flaky structure.

One's choice in fat is a matter of intention and preference. Conventional baking relies on milk, cream, butter, and margarine. Some whole foods chefs choose unrefined corn oil for imparting a "buttery" flavor. I don't like the strong taste or the heavy quality of any of the unrefined oils for baking.

The naturally sweet flavors of fresh and dried fruits, and the rich, enticing flavors and aromas of toasted nuts and seeds, as well as dessert spices, are more pronounced when the amount of fat is reduced and substituted for with minimally refined light vegetable oils. These oils have minimum color, taste, and odor and a long shelf life. The recipes in this book contain just enough oil to produce a tender crumb.

Oils that are partially or completely refined are recommended for medium-high heat use (temperatures of 320 to 375 degrees). Refined oils that are high in monounsaturated fats (50 percent or more) are best for baking. With baking, the pans exceed the maximum recommended temperature of 320 degrees for unrefined oils. A baking temperature of 350 degrees is ideal because while the outside of the dessert is carmelizing or lightly browning, the interior is actually steaming at temperatures between 220 and 300 degrees, and so the oil is not damaged.

Cooking Sprays

Cooking sprays are quite popular for the minimal amount of oil dispensed. In this book, I use baking parchment and a pastry brush to spread oil on the sides of the pans. PAM, the original nonstick cooking spray, contains canola oil, grain alcohol from corn (added for clarity), lecithin from soybeans (prevents sticking), and propellant. The label on the can states, "inhaling the contents can be harmful or fatal." Another supermarket brand has no chlorofluorocarbons that damage the ozone layer and rain forests, but still contains the dangerous propellant. One solution is the refillable nonaerosol pump available in natural foods stores that contains just canola oil and lecithin.

Storage

Spoilage in refined oils is harder to detect because these oils have had their flavor and odor bodies removed. Although their shelf life is long (usually 24 to 30 months compared with 4 to 6 months for unrefined oil), deterioration can occur. A fat or oil is rancid when it has deteriorated into bitter and toxic substances as a result of prolonged exposure to oxygen/air, heat, and light. Refrigeration is a natural antidote.

THICKENING AGENTS

Arrowroot powder, tapioca flour, and kuzu root starch are wonderful alternatives to cornstarch for delicate, glossy sauces and puddings that are quick and simple to prepare. Agar flakes substitute nicely for gelatin, eggs, and dairy products in puddings, custards, pie fillings, sorbets, and icing.

All thickeners may be used interchangeably, with slight differences in texture. After they cooled down, a taste test revealed, arrowroot, tapioca, and kuzu had clearer flavors than cornstarch, which tasted starchy. Kuzu and cornstarch had the nicest textures, more like a soft pudding, cornstarch being a little stronger than kuzu in gelling power. Arrowroot and tapioca both made a texture that was thick and somewhat viscous or thready, signifying a little less would be better.

What's nice about all these starches is that you can always thin the hot or warm mixture slightly by whisking in a little more juice, and of course, you can quickly dissolve more thickener in cool liquid and whisk it into the mixture to thicken it further. Arrowroot, tapioca, and kuzu each lend a sheen and a translucency that cornstarch doesn't. In contrast to agar flakes, the thickening power of these starches is reversed with blending.

What follows is an overview of thickening agents, natural and otherwise, for an understanding of the options in terms of quality and healthfulness.

Gelatin

Do you remember the red Jell-o with fruit and even marshmallows suspended in the translucent shimmering semisolid? You may be as surprised as I was to discover that gelatin is a slaughterhouse by-product derived from collagen, the animal protein found in the skin/hides (90 percent), bones, hooves, horns, and connective tissue of cattle, horses, and pigs. In addition to these ingredients, today's gelatin also contains sulfur dioxide, a poisonous substance.

Gelatin has a long history of use in America. Thomas Jefferson, in a recipe for wine jelly in the *Thomas Jefferson Cookbook,* begins with selecting and boiling four calf's feet for gelatin.

Cornstarch

This highly refined cooking starch is made from de-germed corn that is processed with bleaches and extractive chemicals. See introductory remarks for comparison.

Agar Flakes

Agar, also known as *agar-agar* or *kanten,* is an edible sea vegetable used as a gelling agent. The word comes from the Malayan term for gel, *agar-agar.* Commercially harvested in Japan since 1769, agar is extracted from several varieties of flat, fernlike red algae known botanically as Gelidium and called *tengusa,* "grass from heaven." This seaweed grows along the ocean floor in shallow waters. It can be harvested easily at low tide and is available anytime during the year. Its cell walls contain an abundance of complex polysaccharide starches somewhat similar to cellulose. In their wild form they are strongly flavored and somewhat foul tasting, and processing is necessary to dissolve the starchy fibers and neutralize their taste.

You may remember agar from school days when it was used in petri dishes as the substrate for bacterial culture, since only a few bacteria are capable of decomposing it. Odorless, colorless, tasteless, and calorie-free, agar is the highest in fiber of any plant product known. A great way to get the full array of minerals in sea vegetables, agar comes in four forms—flakes, strips, bars, and granules. Throughout the world agar is used as a gelling agent (or pectin substitute) in commercially prepared foods such as soups, diet foods, sausage casings, tinned fish and meats, yogurt, jam, jelly, candy, and ice cream. It is also used to keep the head on a glass of beer, and as an ingredient in toothpaste and cosmetics. In the Caribbean, agar is touted as an aphrodisiac.

According to *Cooking with Sea Vegetables,* by Peter and Montse Bradford, there are two ways to process agar. First, the modern commercial way involves the use of sulfuric and hydrochloric acids to dissolve the starches, and bleaches and dyes to neutralize the color and flavor. Most agar powder is prepared this way as are many of the thread or bar agars found in Asian stores. These are of poor quality and are best avoided.

There are two Japanese companies that supply natural foods consumers with traditional craftsmen-quality agar, Muso and Mitoku. The description of the process that follows is gleaned from information provided by Eden Foods (distributor of Muso products), Granum Inc. (distributor of Mitoku products), and *Cooking with Japanese Foods* by John and Jan Bellame.

The sea vegetables are gathered in winter and are cooked down with a little mild vinegar to soften the coarse fibers. The thick soupy mix that results is then pressed, expelling a smooth liquid. This is poured into large traylike molds and left to set.

The gelatin is then sliced into bars, which are placed outside on low bamboo frames to freeze-dry naturally. Over a period of a week or two, the cold temperatures at night freeze the bars and each day the sun melts them, eliminating their water content, until all that is left are very lightweight dry, flaky, brittle bars of starch that have been naturally bleached to a light gray color and have had their flavor neutralized.

These bars are then packaged whole or, more commonly nowadays, shaved into fine flakes to save space and expense in shipping. Flake or bar agar made by this traditional method is the type sold by most quality-conscious natural foods stores. It is more expensive than the powdered commercial product, but is a genuine natural food.

As a food for health and healing, agar cleanses the entire digestive tract, and has long been recognized for its mildly laxative properties. It bonds with toxic and radioactive pollutants and helps expel them from the body. Agar is effective in dissolving cholesterol. It contains no fat or calories and is rich in iodine, calcium, iron, phosphorus, and vitamins A, B complex, C, D, and K.

Agar dissolves when boiled for several minutes in a liquid. It sets up upon cooling for about an hour in the refrigerator or twice as long at room temperature. In contrast to gelatin, which is not meant to boil or it will lose some of its setting strength, agar may be reheated and reset.

The gelling ability varies according to the acidity or alkalinity of the food with which it is used. Acid foods require more. You may find that each batch of agar has a slightly different potency, and your personal taste may be for a firmer or softer gel. For these reasons the amount indicated in the recipes is only a guide. Try the recipes once as stated. Then, the next time you make the dessert, if you wish to check the gel quickly before it sets, take a small spoonful of the heated mix and place it on a cold surface for several minutes. You can then adjust if required by adding more agar or more liquid to the pot. Or, if the finished pudding is too congealed, simply return the mixture to the stove, reheat, and add more liquid ingredients. It will set up again.

Even without refrigeration, agar sets quickly as it cools and seals in the natural flavor and sweetness of any fruits used. Blending the set gel produces a whipped mousse consistency. Light and refreshingly cool, a more natural Jell-O made from fruit juice, fresh fruit, and agar is especially welcome in summer.

The gelled texture of agar can be made creamier with the addition of dissolved arrowroot, tapioca, or kuzu. When combined with the other thickeners, agar gives more body and firmness, contributing to a texture with terrific mouth-feel.

One-quarter cup of agar flakes, one bar of agar, or 1 to 1½ tablespoons agar powder with 3 cups liquid is the standard range to achieve a suitable gel. The recipes in this book use agar flakes as these are most healthful and are commonly available and easy to use. If you are using agar bars, first break the bars into small pieces and soak them for an hour. Squeeze out the excess liquid, the proceed as indicated for the flakes.

Arrowroot Powder

This white powder comes from the starch of a tropical rhizome that is derived by peeling, washing, grating, and sifting in repeated operations followed by drying, according to the *Oxford Book of Food Plants*. Almost the whole world supply is provided by the island of St. Vincent in the West Indies.

Arrowroot is used exclusively by people seeking better quality thickening agents for their cooking. Some are unaware of kuzu root starch as a thickener with historic healing powers as well. Others, like myself, rely on kuzu more for medicinal purposes, but use arrowroot powder for culinary purposes because it is cheaper than kuzu. My research showed prices ranging from $1 to $3.50 per pound for arrowroot and $20 to $24 per pound for kuzu.

Then there's the relative ease of using arrowroot over kuzu. Arrowroot powder dissolves instantly compared with the white chalky chunks of kuzu root starch, which must be whisked a few seconds longer. For thickening the juices in an apple pie or a peach cobbler, it's less fuss to sprinkle the fruit with arrowroot powder than to dissolve the chunks of kuzu in water or juice and then drizzle it over the fruit.

When working with arrowroot (and tapioca) starch, wait until the mixture reaches a gentle boil before deciding to add more starch. In contrast to agar, once the starch gel has set up and is firm, stirring or blending will thin or completely dissolve it. Be sure to stir flavorings into the thickened mixture while it is still hot, before it sets. When storing starches, remember to keep them very dry in an airtight container. Stored this way, each of these thickening agents keeps indefinitely.

Regarding health, my own experience confirms what *Oxford* says about the starch: "It is in very fine grains which are easily digestible and is thus particularly suitable for invalid diets." Once when I was teaching cooking classes in Tortola in the British Virgin Islands, a spirited native black woman named Patsy was assisting me. She told me that arrowroot is revered by the islanders for the same reasons kuzu is respected by the Japanese. She said all the West Indian mothers feed their children puddings made with arrowroot on a regular basis, and especially when sick. Her family was rarely ill and both she and her children had no cavities, a healthy state that may also be attributed to their traditional plant-based diet.

Tapioca Flour

Tapioca (also known as cassava root, manioc, and yucca) is obtained by crushing the swollen tuberous root of Brazilian cassava with water. After settling, the starch is separated and dried, then crumbled by forcing it through a metal sieve or plates. The particles are then tumbled in rotating barrels or cylinders to form either the pearl or flake form and dried for export to temperate countries for use in puddings, cookies, and candies. Tapioca flour is just as fine in texture as arrowroot powder or cornstarch.

Kuzu (or Kudzu) Root Starch

According to *The Book of Kuzu,* by William Shurtleff and Akiko Aoyagi, and information supplied by Eden Foods, importer of high-quality artisanal Japanese foods, kuzu (pronounced KOO-zoo in Japan and KUD-zoo in the southern U.S.) is extracted from the leguminous vine plant that has been used in China and Japan for more than a thousand years.

Kuzu grows as a wild vine in the mountains of Japan and the American South. In Japan, kuzu is harvested from December to March when the sap, rich in starch and trace minerals, is concentrated in the root. The traditional labor-intensive and chemical-free processing involves digging the huge and extensive roots, which are then cut into chunks using a power saw and crushed into fibers. The fibers are soaked and rinsed. A crude fibrous paste is formed, which is washed, filtered through cloth, and allowed to settle out in broad, shallow settling ponds. The process may be repeated up to fifty times to obtain the pure white starch.

Kuzu contains compounds called flavonoids that inhibit the craving for alcohol. These substances also have the capacity to relax and dilate blood vessels and to loosen stiff muscles, resulting in improved circulation, reduced high blood pressure, and relief of angina pectoris and rheumatism.

Kuzu is soothing to the digestive system and very easy to digest. As a kitchen remedy, when made into a hot beverage with a little natural soy sauce or umeboshi plum, kuzu alleviates intestinal problems from diarrhea to acid stomach, nausea, and ulcers, and can prevent or relieve the symptoms of the common cold or flu (fever, headaches), hangover, weakness, jetlag, and inability to concentrate. Kuzu helps create the slightly alkaline blood condition that is necessary for restoring and maintaining vibrant health. I rely on it.

Used in desserts, kuzu's alkalinity balances the acidity of sweets and fruits. Figure 1 heaping tablespoon of the chunks or 2 level tablespoons of the powder (crush the chunks in a mortar or food processor to make powder) per cup of liquid to be thickened. The chunky starch must be thoroughly dissolved in cool water (hot water will clump it) before adding the milky mixture to the liquid ingredients to be thickened. Bring the mixture to a boil, stirring occasionally with a whisk until a thick and shiny sauce forms upon boiling, about 2 minutes when starting with just 1 cup cool liquid, 15 seconds with hot liquid.

Not all brands of kuzu are the same. Costs vary widely, usually as a reflection of how it was grown and processed. The less expensive brands sold in Asian food stores may be mixed with potato or another vegetable starch, diluting its purity and therefore altering its healing and culinary qualities.

LEAVENING AGENTS

Leavening agents include eggs, yeast, or chemicals (baking powder and baking soda). Today's health-conscious home chef may be looking for recipes and products that substitute egg whites or egg replacers for whole eggs and nonfat milk for whole milk, and that cut down or eliminate all butter and shortening. Generally, though, most products sold in supermarkets haven't yet reduced or eliminated preservatives and artificial flavors and colors from their list of ingredients. And while these ingredient changes show awareness of the need for change to meet customer demand, they do not address the quality of the eggs and dairy products.

Eggs

Many people choose to eliminate eggs from their diet. According to Physicians Committee for Responsible Medicine, "about 70 percent of the calories in eggs are from fat, and a big portion of that fat is saturated. They are also loaded with cholesterol—about 215 milligrams for an average-sized egg." That's more than two thirds of the suggested daily cholesterol limit of 300 milligrams. So eating an egg doesn't leave much room for other cholesterol-containing foods in the day's diet. "And because egg shells are fragile and porous and conditions on egg farms are crowded, eggs are the perfect host to salmonella—the bacteria that is the leading cause of food poisoning in this country. An increase in the number of outbreaks of salmonellosis has been traced to contaminated eggs."

Eggless egg replacers are available in many natural foods stores. Ener-G Egg Replacer is the brand name for a combination of starches and leavening agents that bind and leaven cooked and baked foods. Ingredients include potato starch, tapioca flour, leavening (calcium lactate, calcium carbonate, citric acid), and carbohydrate gum. Note that calcium lactate is dairy-free. I haven't found a need for this product, but you may want to try it. The recipes on the box for muffins and cake include baking powder as an ingredient in addition to the leavening in the product.

On another note, lightness without eggs can be achieved with light handling as well as proper leavening. Whip together the liquid ingredients used in the batter (oil, sweetener, and liquid), mixing well with a wire whisk, or in a food processor or blender.

Baking Powder and Baking Soda

I choose to use aluminum-free baking powder (specifically Rumford brand baking powder) and baking soda to replace eggs, yeast, and regular baking powder because they are quick and convenient. Commercial yeast is slow compared with baking powder, and people with allergies or candida cannot tolerate yeast. Aluminum-free baking powder and baking soda create delicate cakes and prevent cookies from being brittle or heavy, making them crisp-tender and light, even when thick and substantial.

According to *Shoppers Guide to Natural Foods,* in the mid-nineteenth century an alkaline salt was developed from soda ash treated with carbon dioxide. Soda, used with an acidic food (sweeteners, lemon juice, cocoa, spices) or as a basic component of baking powder, opened the door to a new level of cake and pastry making.

Today baking soda is produced by the Solvay method, by which a brine solution is run into saturation tanks where it mixes with ammonia gas. This ammonia brine combination is then injected with carbon dioxide and bicarbonate of soda (also known as baking soda and sodium bicarbonate) is created. It is dried and milled into the fine white powder.

Cream of tartar, a by-product of the wine-making industry, was the acid companion to baking soda in the earlier formulas for baking powder. However, today's bakers prefer instead the more complex and powerful formulas that produce "double-acting" reactions, activating both in the mixing bowl and in the oven.

To make your own cream of tartar-based baking powder, mix together two parts cream of tartar (may be purchased in the bulk herb section of natural foods stores or in any supermarket), one part baking soda, and two parts arrowroot powder. The rise with this homemade baking powder is as good as with commercial brands.

Because potassium bicarbonate is not sodium-based like sodium bicarbonate (baking soda), those concerned with their salt intake may prefer it. Potassium bicarbonate is available over the counter in pharmacies, and potassium-based baking powder is now available in some natural foods stores.

Rumford brand baking powder is a simple double-acting acid powder containing calcium phosphate (extracted from phosphate rock), bicarbonate of soda, and cornstarch to prevent too early action.

Other brands of baking powder contain not only sodium bicarbonate, cornstarch, calcium phosphate, calcium sulfate, and often calcium silicate (to keep it free-flowing), but also sodium aluminum sulfate. One piece of cake made with aluminum baking powder has 5 to 15 milligrams of aluminum, a little in every bite. Studies have shown that aluminum salts can be absorbed from the intestines and concentrated in various human tissues, and that high aluminum levels are found in the brains of patients with Alzheimer's and Parkinson's diseases. In addition, aluminum is linked to bone degeneration and kidney dysfunction.

It's safe to say that it's not a good idea to include leavening agents on a daily basis. Baking soda has been shown to decrease blood flow as well as the body's oxygen use by 25 percent and to cause lactic acid levels in the blood to rise. Both baking soda and baking powder deplete B vitamins and interfere with vitamin C absorption.

Store baking powder tightly sealed in a cool, dark place for no longer than six months. To tell if your baking powder is still viable, combine 1 teaspoon baking powder with ½ cup hot water. If it bubbles vigorously, it is still usable.

Flax Seeds

Flax seeds are referred to in the Bible. Also called linseeds, in today's nutrition-minded times they are known for their omega-3 content, being the richest of all food sources. Also known as linolenic acid, this essential fatty acid lowers cholesterol. Another good quality of flax seeds is their high soluble and insoluble fiber contents, even higher than oat bran. And components of flax seed fiber called lignins are converted by the body into lignans, which have been associated with reduced risk of colon and breast cancer.

Flax seeds are rich in mucilage, which works as a binder and a leavener in baked goods. The only perceptible difference is the specks of flax throughout the baked good, which give it a nice tweedy look. For a recipe for Flax seed slurry, see the Linen Cake recipe on page 163.

Tofu

Tofu is used as a binder in baked goods. It doesn't act as a leavener. One-quarter cup or 2 ounces of tofu has about the same protein, fat, and moisture as one egg. Blend tofu smooth with the liquid ingredients before they are added to the dry ingredients. I prefer soy milk, which is simpler to include in desserts with great results.

SALT

Salt is truly a precious, life-giving natural element and, unfortunately, is sorely misunderstood. As it turns out, the quality of salt is as important as the quantity consumed. A food is more than the sum product of its nutrients. The place from which it came, the consciousness with which it was harvested and processed, are all factors that contribute to its quality and long-term health-fulness. Our choices determine the well-being of our bodies as good salt serves to remineralize our blood on a meal-to-meal basis.

Health Considerations

Today, some fifty million Americans have high blood pressure, which increases the risk of stroke, heart disease, and kidney disease. In industrialized countries, where salt intake is high, blood pressure tends to rise with age.

A number of medical studies have found that raising the salt content of a vegetarian diet has little or no effect on blood pressure. On the other hand, a 1981 study at Harvard suggests that the real villain in hypertension (abnormally high blood pressure) is not salt, but protein- and cholesterol-rich animal foods, meat and dairy. As reported in "Salt: Some Concerns" by Don Matesz (*Macrobiotics Today,* May/June 1992), macrobiotic persons eating miso soup every day and cooking with unrefined sea salt and tamari soy sauce had among the lowest normal blood pressures ever recorded in modern society. However, when given 250 grams of beef per day for four weeks, their blood pressure rose significantly, along with their cholesterol levels (*Journal of the American Medical Association,* 246: 640–44).

The attitude of moderation rather than deprivation was furthered by the Intersalt research project, published in the *British Medical Journal.* In this study of more than ten thousand men and women, scientists from thirty-two countries concluded that "Cutting back would have a minimal effect on lowering blood pressure," according to Dr. William Bennett, editor of the *Harvard Medical School Health Letter.*

Decreasing fats in the diet, lowering alcohol intake, and increasing whole grains, vegetables, and fruits high in potassium also help to lower blood pressure, experts say. Potassium must be present in sufficient amounts to remove sodium from the blood.

Salt has become victim to the peculiarly American overreaction: if too much is bad, then less is better, and none is best of all. What is clear is that the reason the elimination of salt is advised is not because we oversalt in the kitchen, but because most people consume snack foods, fast and processed foods, all of which contain large amounts of salt or sodium. In addition to a diet laden with pizza, frozen dinners, canned soups, breakfast cereals, potato and corn chips, pretzels, crackers, and nuts, smoking and eating a lot of fatty foods such as meat and dairy products, dulls the senses, including taste.

Moreover, research scientists usually make no distinction among types of salt, nor do they take into consideration the rest of the diet. The connection between salt and disease might be less clear-cut if we looked at a low-fat, whole foods, primarily vegetarian (plant-based) diet in conjunction with minimally refined, natural sea salts, rather than at the conventional modern diet, which is high in saturated fats, refined foods, and refined and kiln-dried salts.

In a diet of whole foods, the level of salt is often relatively low compared to the average modern diet containing, according to *Nutrition Almanac,* between 2 and 6 grams and often up to 15 grams per day. The 1977 report, "Dietary Goals," from the U.S. Senate Select Committee on Nutrition and Human Needs, and now the federal government as well, recommends a limit of 2,400 milligrams of sodium a day, the amount in 6 grams of salt or just a bit more than a teaspoon.

Kinds of Salt

Sea water contains about 75 percent sodium chloride. The rest is mainly magnesium and calcium compounds and there are at least seventy-five other chemical elements in very small amounts, most of them, it would seem, vitally required for the human body to function. The normal saline count in body fluids is about 1 percent. This is less than the 3 percent salt proportion in sea water, but it does indicate the briny origins of human life. Longtime macrobiotics teacher and author of *Acid and Alkaline,* Herman Aihara, spoke to the value of salt in preventing infection ("Learning from Salmon, Again," *Macrobiotics Today,* June 1987): "If our body fluid loses its salt, falling below the level of a 0.85 percent salt solution, then we lose control of microbe growth and we will have an overgrowth of yeast, mold, bacteria, and viruses."

Table Salt

Today's table salt is highly refined to 99 percent sodium chloride, 39 percent sodium, and about 60 percent chloride by weight. It is essentially void of other minerals and trace elements. Any substance this pure may no longer be considered a food, but rather a chemical like refined white sugar. Refined salt is also comparable to white bread or white rice in that most nutrients are removed and then a few are returned to create a semblance of healthfulness. Such a refined product may actually deplete the body of the store of minerals necessary to neutralize and digest refined foods.

Only 14 percent of our domestic salt supply comes directly from the sea, from sea salt factories around the San Francisco Bay. The remaining land salt is, however, technically sea salt, for it was deposited by the ocean that covered the earth three hundred million years ago. Of the remaining salt supply, 60 percent comes from salt springs and 26 percent from salt mines.

Salt is extracted from the earth or sea by three methods: shaft mining, solution mining, and solar evaporation. The first and second processes produce land-mined salt. In terms of health, over long periods of time, rain will have leached out some important minerals and trace elements in land salt deposits.

According to Jacques de Langre, founder of The Grain and Salt Society, who is my salt teacher, most salt is processed to meet the worldwide requirements of the Codex Standard for Food Grade Salt. "The salt refining industry removes almost all of the minerals for profit. Trace elements such as magnesium, bromine, and sulfur are extracted from sea salt in the refining stage. They are sold to the chemical industry or to pharmaceutical companies to make dietary supplements."

Only 5 percent of the salt produced worldwide goes for human consumption. The Codex specifies that food grade salt (also called "table salt" or "cooking salt") should not be less than 97 percent sodium chloride (NaCl). Or, salt must not have more than 3 percent trace minerals, but can legally contain up to 3 percent chemical additives such as bleaches, anticaking agents, and conditioners, all for cosmetic purposes.

The uniformly fine crystals are created by subjecting the salt to a heat of 1200 degrees during the kiln-drying process. According to de Langre, heating salt by boiling, kiln-drying, or vacuum-flash recrystallization causes loss of minerals due to precipitation.

To make salt free-flowing, most large commercial processors, such as Morton's and Leslie's, add anticaking agents (magnesium carbonate) and crystal modifiers such as sodium ferrocyanide and green ferric ammonium citrate, which coat the salt crystals and prevent them from attracting moisture. Iodized salt generally includes added potassium iodide (twenty times the naturally-occurring amount of iodine is added to refined salt), dextrose (sugar) to stabilize the iodine, and sodium carbonate to stop the mixture from turning purple.

Rock, Solar, and Kosher Salt

This big crystal salt contains no more minerals than table salt, just the usual 97 percent of sodium chloride, the remainder existing chiefly of minor amounts of naturally occurring components. Kosher salt is produced under rabbinical supervision for use in kosher foods.

Sea Salt

It's ironic that because of the Codex's dictums, only refined sodium chloride can bear the name "sea salt." Most sea salt is the same as commercial table salt without the added sugar and anticaking agents. Much of the sea salt sold in the bulk bins at natural foods stores is supplied by the Leslie company, which does not market any sea salt directly, but does supply salt that is marketed by others as such.

Processing is the reason for the reduced mineral content. Most sea salt today is produced on an industrial scale by leaving vast lakes of sea water to slowly evaporate, then collecting the salt on a concrete surface by bulldozer. The salt accumulates impurities and pollutants during this slow and rather crude process and therefore needs to be washed. Unfortunately, the washing process not only cleans the salt, it also strips out many of the essential minerals and trace elements, leaving a depleted and refined product.

Sea salt manufacturers try to distinguish their salt from table salt mainly by claiming greater levels of minerals. There are higher levels of minerals in natural sea salt, but they comprise possibly 3 percent with trace elements comprising a minute portion of this. This is certainly not close to the amount claimed by some suppliers, but it is higher than the 0.5 percent or less in commercial salts like Morton's or Leslie's.

There are at least several brands of good sea salt that I am aware of: SiSalt, Gold Mine's Natural Solar-Dried Sea Salt, and Amashio Japanese Natural Sea Salt. See Resources, page 247, to contact these companies.

Unrefined Sea Salt

Unrefined sea salt differs from both common table salt and sea salt. This salt contains essential macro- and micro-nutrients. The price is higher, but considering the method of harvesting, the nutrient value, and how little is used, especially in desserts, it's worth the price.

There are varying opinions in the macrobiotic health community as to which sea salt is truly the best based on its magnesium content. This seems to me like a non-issue because magnesium is a mineral that is needed for many functions in the body, and salt is not a major source. For example, 1 teaspoon of salt has 33 milligrams of magnesium, compared with 1 cup of cooked brown rice containing 89 milligrams. The Recommended Daily Allowance for magnesium is 280 milligrams for women and 350 milligrams for men.

The beauty of unrefined sea salt is that it is a natural whole food containing all the ingredients necessary for its digestion. This is real sea salt obtained from the evaporation of the ocean's water. No synthetic mineral supplement can equal the wealth of minerals, regardless of how rich its content or how precisely it is formulated.

The macro- and micro-nutrients (also called magnesium salts, mother liquor, bitterns, or *nigari* in Japanese) are contained in the wet part of the salt. These moist salts are not free-flowing. Salt naturally attracts moisture from the air and is best stored in a container with a lid, both made of glass, ceramic, or wood to avoid corrosion.

Celtic Sea Salt

This unrefined sea salt is the salt I use most often. Celtic Sea Salt supplies more than eighty vital minerals and trace elements including magnesium, sulfur, potassium, calcium, silica, iron, manganese, phosphorous, and iodine. Founder of The Grain and Salt Society, Jacques de Langre says his teacher and a founder of macrobiotics, George Ohsawa, stated that Celtic Sea Salt "is the only kind of salt that macrobiotic people should use."

Celtic Sea Salt comes from the pristine salt marshes of Brittany, the northwestern region of France. The method used for gathering these nutritional salts follows a two-thousand-year-old Celtic tradition and is supported by modern quality-control standards. Each salt field is lined with a layer of clay that not only isolates the salt from sand and earth, but also filters any pollutants that might be present in the water, and serves to ionize the many minerals in the salt, making it richer in electrolytes.

The light gray Celtic Sea Salt, harvested in the late summer, is light gray in color because of the pure food- and cosmetic-grade clay beds and should not be confused with dark gray industrial crude salts from Europe. The salt is harvested by hand by lightly skimming the surface of the clay beds just below the water level with long wooden hand tools. Over a three-month period, the salt is exposed to sun and wind allowing water to evaporate. This centuries-old technique produces salt that contrasts sharply with the white salt extracted by bulldozers from concrete beds at the Mediterranean coastline, which is more polluted than the San Francisco Bay.

Laboratory analyses are done annually. Light gray Celtic Sea Salt has the highest mineral content of the unrefined sea salts. It contains 83 percent sodium chloride (31 percent sodium and 52 percent chloride), the remaining 17 percent includes other nutrients.

Atlantic Fine Sea Salt

Eden Foods (see Resources) imports and distributes this unrefined sea salt. Harvested in the North Atlantic off the coast of Brittany, it is sun-dried and stone milled. Mineral content is 93 percent sodium chloride and 7 percent other minerals and trace elements.

Salt in Cooking

Cooking with salt instead of using it "raw" at the table allows the salt to dissolve completely so the myriad minerals and trace elements marry with the other ingredients in a truly alchemical union. In this way, the sum is truly greater than its parts in terms of taste and digestibility.

In regard to desserts, most baked goods taste flat and unappealing without a little salt. And salt serves to neutralize the acid quality in fruit, enhancing and balancing its sweetness. Salt also draws out the delicious fruit juices from the fruit during cooking. So seek out the best quality salt you can find and enjoy this precious staple in quantities associated with seasoning for great taste and for preservation of both food and of vibrant health.

FRUIT

You don't need to desert desserts just because you want to eat healthy. Sweet treats can be healthy if you use fresh fruit and fruit juice to replace excess sugar and fat. With whole fruits, you can enjoy your sugar in the healthiest form, with the fiber attached. So follow the seasons, noticing which fruits are available as the year unfolds, thereby preparing your body to survive healthfully during that season. Winter is the only time the variety stops, time to enjoy the winter keepers, apples and pears. Apples, in particular, are blood cleansing because of the nonnutritive substance pectin, which is transformed during digestion into an acid that combines with heavy metals and is excreted.

Or include the dried varieties of summer's bounty. Their sugars are concentrated. Did you know that a handful of dried figs contains as much sugar as two whole cantaloupes? Organically grown and sun-dried fruits are best. Timbercrest Farms from California is one good brand.

Avoid commercial brands that are sprayed with sulfur dioxide before being dried to ensure that the fruit maintains a bright color and looks succulent. Golden raisins—also known as yellow or white raisins and sultanas—are often treated with sulfur dioxide to lighten them further. Choose organic unsulfured golden raisins that are just slightly darker in color than those that are sulfured.

Fruit juices are highly concentrated foods—1 cup of apple juice contains the juice of 3 or 4 apples without the fiber. So for a lighter effect and taste, especially for young children whose taste buds and sweet tooths are just being established, dilute juice with water, a quarter or more of the total volume. Buy organic when possible. If they aren't organic, the apples used for apple juice can be highly chemicalized.

When making fresh fruit gels, the clarity of filtered juices and apple cider serve as a beautiful medium to display the colorful jewel-like berries and other seasonal fruit.

Citrus zest adds a tangy zip to desserts. Zest is the colored part of the skin of citrus fruits where the most concentrated flavor oils are found. It differs from the peel or rind, which refer to the whole skin. The white part, or pith, just under the skin, is bitter and should not be used. Because pesticide residues are found mainly on the peels, it is best to use only organic fruits for zesting. The proper (and fun-to-use) tool for this purpose is a zester, which is available in cookware shops. Otherwise, a sharp knife or a potato peeler works (use a sawing motion) to cut zest, then mince it, or use the fine holes of a grater to remove the zest.

Choose fruit spreads made from organic fruits sweetened with fruit juice concentrate. Since Colonial times, apple cider jelly has been simply made from evaporated apple cider. One gallon cider yields just 2½ cups (20 ounces). It's so concentrated that it requires no refrigeration.

SEASONINGS

Sweet seasonings round out the flavors and add excitement to desserts much the same way that fresh herbs and savory spices spark a main dish. In addition to exotic spices, freshly zested citrus zests and freshly grated ginger, vanilla and almond extracts, the fresh green leaves of scented geraniums and mint family plants lend a gentle lift to the look, aroma, and taste of dessert.

Pure vanilla extract contains water, 35 percent alcohol by volume, and the extractives from vanilla beans. Pure vanilla flavor contains less alcohol and has the same taste components, but is less concentrated. The alcohol is used for extracting and holding the flavoring matter in suspension. Organic vanilla extract is also available.

According to the *Whole Foods Encyclopedia,* "Imitation vanilla is—at best—made from vanillin, a sulfite waste by-product of the paper industry. At worst, vanillin is a totally synthetic product. Neither is recommended. Vanillin does simulate the flavor of pure vanilla but is harsh, abrasive, and lacks the well-rounded, sweet real vanilla flavor and aroma. By law, any product containing vanillin must be labeled as imitation."

Read the label to avoid synthetic additives such as propylene glycol, caramel coloring (to stabilize color since each batch is different), and preservatives as well as sugar and corn syrup.

The almond extract carried in many supermarkets is labeled "imitation" and contains water, 36 percent alcohol, and benzaldehyde, and may also contain propylene glycol and sugar. One producer's spokesperson told me, "Propylene glycol is a water soluble food grade oil used as a carrier to extract the flavor from the almonds." One good natural version, Cook's Choice natural almond extract, contains oil of bitter almond, natural flavorings, alcohol, and water.

Grain coffee granules or powders make great caffeine-free flavoring agents in desserts or serve as caffeine-free beverages to serve with dessert. A wide variety is available in natural foods stores.

One of my favorites is Roma roasted grain beverage, containing roasted malt barley, roasted barley, and roasted chicory. Another called Yannoh is the original instant coffee substitute created by George Ohsawa and the early proponents of macrobiotics. It contains organic barley, malted barley, rye, chicory, and wild acorns.

CHOCOLATE AND CAROB

Chocolate is the most tempting of all foods for many people. A survey done by *Natural Health* (September, 1993) summarized that chocolate is the hardest food for readers to give up. The passionate craving for chocolate is so intense that "chocoholic" has become part of our lexicon. Besides the sensory properties of its attractive aroma and exquisite taste, the mouth-feel further enhances chocolate's seductive appeal. Cocoa butter, the fat naturally occurring in cocoa beans, is solid at normal room temperature but melts at body temperature . . . in your mouth.

If you have a feeling chocolate isn't good for you, but you aren't sure exactly why, here is some intellectual food to chew on. What is chocolate made of and how does it compare with carob, the beloved natural foods substitute for chocolate?

Cocoa beans contain about 55 percent of a saturated fat from the oil called cocoa butter. In the manufacture of cocoa powder (the form most often used in this book), this fat is largely removed, but in making chocolate candy, extra cocoa butter is added back in, along with up to 40 percent sugar (to counteract the remaining natural bitterness) and milk.

Chocolate also contains the psychoactive ingredients, caffeine and phenyethylamine (called PEA). A piece of chocolate cake has less caffeine than a cup of coffee, but enough to give you a buzz. It is PEA that has led to chocolate's reputation as an aphrodisiac and antidote for unrequited love, as well as an antidepressant. According to an article from *New Scientist* reported in *Spectrum—The Wholistic News Magazine,* some scientists feel that chocolate is a sex substitute because every 100 grams of it contains up to 660 milligrams of PEA, an amphetaminelike substance closely related to the body's own dopamine and adrenaline. By affecting the involuntary nervous system—raising blood pressure, heart rate, glucose levels, and heightening sensations—a fair amount of this chemical induces a euphoria similar in kind to the emotion of love or sex. However, there's no evidence that the PEA in chocolate actually has any mood-altering or libido-enhancing effects.

A related alkaloid called theobromine, a chemical cousin of caffeine, is chocolate's main stimulant. Its wake-up effect isn't as strong as caffeine, but it's an even more powerful diuretic. These stimulants are linked to the headaches, heartburn, intestinal distress, and allergic reactions some people experience after eating chocolate.

From a health standpoint, regular chocolate consumption is linked to almost every disease of our time from general fatigue, headaches, and herpes to diabetes, heart disease, and cancer. Certainly chocolate is best saved for special occasions rather than eaten as part of the day-to-day lifestyle of one who aspires to greater health.

Cocoa Powder

In reduced-fat baking, unsweetened cocoa powder is a very handy product. It imparts the intense taste of chocolate with only a trace of its saturated fat. Cocoa powder provides the chocolate impact without the bother of melting, chopping, or grating. It also costs less, has a longer shelf life, and contains less fat and cholesterol than solid chocolate.

When available, I use organic unsweetened cocoa powder or one that is low in fat (a maximum of 9 percent), made from partially defatted cocoa beans, and is 99.7 percent caffeine-free. (WonderFree cocoa powder is one such product. The caffeine is extracted by pressing; no alkali or emulsifiers are used.)

Chocolate Chips

Look for chocolate chips that are grain-sweetened with whole-grain malted barley and corn, and that contain no refined sugars, no dairy products (e.g whey powder and nonfat milk powder), and no hydrogenated tropical oils (e.g. fractionated palm kernel oil) and therefore no saturated fat. For example, Sunspire brand contains only unsweetened chocolate, the above mentioned sweetener, cocoa butter, soy lecithin, and pure vanilla.

Carob

The natural foods movement has promoted carob powder as a naturally sweet whole food substitute for chocolate. However, *The Wellness Letter—The Newsletter of Nutrition, Fitness and Stress Management* from the University of California at Berkeley, reports that carob is no more a health food than chocolate. In its pure form, carob contains a tenth the fat of chocolate and no caffeine. But carob has considerably more sugar, as well as another possibly undesirable ingredient.

Carob, like chocolate, comes from a bean, from the long, brown, and leathery pod of a Mediterranean evergreen tree. The sticky pulp that comes from the carob pods has a high content of vegetable tannins, naturally occurring substances that reduce the absorption of protein through the intestinal wall. Children should go easy on carob because tannins have been shown to depress the growth rate of young rats.

Unprocessed carob powder has 2 percent fat but up to 48 percent natural sugar. Cocoa powder is about 23 percent fat according to *Shopper's Guide to Natural Foods*—and 5 percent natural sugar. Carob also contains 8 percent protein and is a good source of vitamins and minerals, especially calcium.

However, when either of the two powders are processed into solids such as candy or chips, the differences between them are largely erased, since both are mixed with saturated fats such as butter and additional sugar. In fact, some carob bars contain more saturated fat than a Hershey bar; others have more sugar than a serving of ice cream.

Carob candies and carob chips, sweetened or unsweetened, contain partially hydrogenated (and sometimes fractionated) palm kernel oil, an oil that is more than 80 percent saturated fat, or coconut oil, milk powder, soya lecithin, and refined sugar (white, brown, or turbinado sugar, fructose, corn syrup, or honey) or malted corn and barley.

In conclusion, for the emotional satisfaction and pleasure this comfort food brings, for relatively healthy people and especially on festive occasions such as birthdays, it seems that the best choices to make are the pure forms of either unsweetened cocoa or carob powder—without the added saturated fat, cholesterol, and refined sugar in the candy bars and some of the chips. By adding a good quality sweetener, and perhaps a bit of oil, to these powders in cakes, cookies, or puddings, you can control the quality of the ingredients and thereby the overall quality of the dessert.

EDIBLE FLOWERS

To add drama to dessert presentations from cakes to sorbets, include whole flowers or flower petals from edible wild or organically cultivated (or, at least, pesticide-free) plants. Colors range from the quiet pastel shades of rose petals to the splashy hues from orange nasturtiums, yellow or orange calendulas (also called pot marigolds), maroon and pink pansies or Johnny Jump-ups, purple violets or chive flowers, red or purple sage flowers, and blue star-shaped borage flowers. Other edible flowers include day lilies, dandelion, red and white clover, and berry blossoms.

APPLIANCES, COOKWARE, AND SUPPLIES

Food Processor

This appliance saves enormous time and energy, whether for grinding nuts or making a creamy smooth purée. Food processors are quieter and quicker than blenders.

Mixing Bowls

A set of stainless steel and glass mixing bowls in graduated sizes does it.

Baking Dishes and Pans

Glass baking dishes of 1½- and 2-quart capacity are most practical. The imported and domestic colorful stoneware baking dishes available in fine kitchen shops hold the same capacities and make great presentation.

For pies, a standard glass 9-inch pie pan holds 4 cups, while a 9-inch deep-dish pie plate holds 5 cups. Have an 8- and a 10-inch pie pan on hand as well.

Baking sheets, muffin tins, and basic 9-inch cake pans made of stainless steel are best. Springform and tart pans, 9- and 10-inch, may be made of tinned steel or aluminum. Pans for fun cake shapes usually come in aluminum, and the Bundt pan I prefer is Teflon-coated for easy removal.

Measuring Cups

Measure ingredients carefully. There are two different types of measuring cups: one for liquid and one for dry ingredients. Pyrex glass measuring cups with pouring spouts are for liquids. Stainless-steel cups, where the ingredients can be leveled off with a knife, are for measuring dry ingredients. Both types hold the same amount. The difference is a matter of convenience.

Strainers

Use a small flat strainer for lifting fruits from hot liquids, and a large strainer for sifting cocoa and carob powders or chestnut flour, which tend to form lumps or, if desired, for ensuring even distribution of all dry ingredients.

Oven Thermometer

Check your oven for temperature accuracy with a mercury oven thermometer kept standing in the center of the oven at all times.

Cooling Rack

Cool all cakes, cookies, pies, and tarts on a rack so that air can circulate completely around them. This prevents moisture from accumulating on the bottom.

Zester

A zester, also called a citrus zester, is a fun and very handy tool for grating the aromatic oils from the surface of citrus fruits. Available at any kitchen store.

Baking Parchment

Lining cake pans and cookie sheets with parchment ensures getting the cake out safely, helps to prevent overbaking, and makes clean-up easy. Although waxed paper does serve the purpose and works in a pinch, it's a mistake to substitute it for parchment, because the wax will melt and may leave an odd taste. Both white and unbleached (brown) parchment are available.

Other Useful Items

Citrus juicer (manual or electric for large volumes), kitchen scale, timer, wooden mixing spoons, large and small wire whisks, rubber spatula, pastry brush, serrated knife for cutting cake, apple corer, and cherry pitter.

Fresh Fruit Desserts

Some of the healthiest people on earth are the Mediterranean cultures among whom, until recently, elaborate desserts were rarely served. Fresh seasonal fruits were, and still are, abundant and highly regarded. A heaping basket of various fruits is often placed on the table after the main course is cleared. Dried fruits replace fresh ones in the winter and are often stewed.

Fresh fruit compotes and salads are wholesome desserts by their very nature, based on seasonal fruit and prepared without fat save for the occasional garnish-size portion of rich and crunchy nuts and seeds. Easy to prepare with virtually no cooking involved, these colorful desserts are perfect for today's busy cook.

Although compotes are defined as "fruit cooked or stewed in syrup," fresh fruit compotes broaden the possibilities for ending carefully orchestrated menus with simple fruit desserts. Each recipe has its own unique character, marked by the addition of a special syrup, or a particularly colorful blend of colors and shapes. A warm-weather combination of nectarines, blueberries, and green grapes is a charming, jewel-like finale to any meal.

One of the best things about poaching fruit is that the fruit need not be completely ripe. In fact, fruit that is a little hard will hold its shape better during poaching than fully ripened fruit. Because the poaching liquid is sweetened and infused with flavorful ingredients, fruit that is overly tart will become sweeter when poached, and fruit that lacks flavor will improve. When poaching, keep the liquid below a simmer so the outside of the fruit doesn't overcook before the interior has softened.

These recipes use new ingredients to create syrups as intriguing as those based on refined white sugar, wines, and liqueurs. The delicate tastes of brown rice syrup and pure maple syrup, compared with other natural sweeteners such as honey and some fruit concentrates, combine beautifully with fresh fruits without overpowering their natural flavors. The brands of brown rice syrup that taste the best in these desserts are those without a cereal enzyme in their list of ingredients. FruitSource syrup, sorghum, or honey may be substituted.

In addition to choosing mild sweeteners to complement the fruit's natural flavor, include interesting flavors from wine, citrus juice, or vinegar to give the fruit sparkle.

When it's possible to procure them, organic fruits are always the best choice, especially when the fruit will be eaten fresh. Rinse the fruits by swishing them in a bowl of cool water. Adding salt to the rinsing water—1 teaspoon of salt per quart of water—is an especially good idea if the fruit is not organically grown, as salt may help to neutralize the chemicals.

Although both fresh and cooked fruit compotes are great by themselves, you may choose to serve them on top of plain vanilla cake or vanilla nondairy ice cream, or with a cookie on the side for a nice textural contrast.

For making large amounts, increase the volume of fruit in a recipe proportionately, but increase the syrup by half.

Fresh Strawberry Compote with Orange-Ginger Syrup

This recipe was chosen to appear in the cookbook Cooking with the Stars, *published by Center for Science in the Public Interest.*

Orange-Ginger Syrup **(makes ½ cup)**

¼ cup strawberry-apple juice or strawberry cider

¼ cup brown rice syrup, FruitSource syrup (brown rice syrup and grape juice concentrate), or part honey

1 teaspoon orange zest

1 teaspoon peeled and grated fresh ginger root

Few grains of sea salt

Fruit and Garnish

1 pint strawberries, 2½ to 3 cups, halved or quartered

Fresh mint or lemon balm sprigs for garnish

1. In a bowl big enough to hold the strawberries, whisk the syrup ingredients together. Add the strawberries and allow them to marinate for at least 1 hour. As the fruit releases its juices, the strawberries become submerged in the syrup and the flavors marry. Stir occasionally.

Makes 2 to 3 servings, or about 2⅓ cups

Calories: 140

Protein: 1g

Saturated Fat: 0

Fiber: 3g

Carbohydrate: 33g

Fat: 1g

Cholesterol: 0

Sodium: 27 mg

Calories from Carbohydrate: 91%

Calories from Fat: 6%

Calories from Protein: 3%

Citrus and Apple Compote with Five-Spice Syrup

Makes 4 to 8 servings, or 4 to 5 cups

Calories: 147

Protein: 1g

Saturated Fat: 0

Fiber: 3g

Carbohydrate: 36g

Fat: 1g

Cholesterol: 0

Sodium: 20mg

Calories from
Carbohydrate: 93%

Calories from Fat: 4%

Calories from Protein: 3%

The combination in this recipe pleases with variations made according to what's in season and is organically grown—navel, Valencia, mandarin, temple, or blood oranges for their spectacular color. Tangerines have too many seeds and the sections are too small to be desirable here.

A grapefruit knife is an inexpensive and timesaving investment for separating grapefruit or orange sections from the rind and membranes.

Five-spice powder is a Chinese combination of powdered fennel (or anise or star anise), ginger, licorice root, cinnamon, and cloves. It may also include coriander or lemon balm. One company, Frontier Herbs, ensures that no radiation is used in its ingredients, which are a little different—cinnamon, fennel, cloves, star anise, and white pepper.

Syrup

½ cup apple cider or juice

½ cup brown rice syrup or FruitSource syrup

Zest of half a lemon, chopped

½ teaspoon five-spice powder

Few grains of sea salt

Fruit

1 navel or Valencia orange

1 mandarin orange

1 pink (ruby or star) grapefruit

1 Red Delicious apple

1 Gala apple

2 tablespoons pomegranate seeds for garnish (optional); 1 fruit yields 1½ cups seeds

Mint sprigs or scented geranium leaves for garnish

1. Combine the syrup ingredients in a small saucepan. Whisk the mixture as it comes to a boil. Turn the heat off and allow the syrup to cool while you cut the fruit.

2. After removing fruit segments, squeeze the rind to save the flavorful fruit juices. Discard seeds. For apples, halve and core them. Cut each half into 8 slices, then crosswise into thirds.

3. Place fruits and their juices in a bowl and pour the syrup over all. Marinate all day or overnight in the refrigerator. Stir a couple of times. Serve with syrup and garnishes. Compote lasts several days refrigerated.

Fresh Peach Compote with Almond-Orange Syrup

See the photo of this dessert.

Makes 6 servings, or 4½ to 6 cups

Calories: 190
Protein: 2g
Saturated Fat: 0
Fiber: 3g
Carbohydrate: 42g
Fat: 3g
Cholesterol: 0
Sodium: 15mg
Calories from Carbohydrate: 83%
Calories from Fat: 3g
Calories from Protein: 4%

¼ teaspoon almond extract

½ cup orange juice

½ cup brown rice syrup, FruitSource syrup (brown rice syrup and grape juice concentrate), or sorghum syrup

Zest of an orange

Zest of a quarter of a lemon

Few grains of sea salt

Fruit and Garnishes

2 pounds peaches, 4 peaches, or 6 cups, halved and cut into ½-inch slices, then in half crosswise

¼ cup sliced almonds, toasted and chopped

Fresh mint sprigs for garnish

1. In a bowl big enough to hold the peaches, whisk the syrup ingredients together. Add the peaches.

You may serve this compote immediately or allow it to marinate. A lot of liquid comes out of the peaches as they sit—fruit is submerged in syrup after an hour—adding volume and a greater depth of flavor to the syrup. Gently stir occasionally with a rubber spatula.

2. Serve both fruit and syrup. Garnish with almonds and mint.

Melon Compote with Lemon-Sesame Syrup

Makes 3 servings, or 3 cups

Calories: 197
Protein: 2g
Saturated Fat: 0
Fiber: 2g
Carbohydrate: 44g
Fat: 3g
Cholesterol: 0
Sodium: 38mg
Calories from Carbohydrate: 85%
Calories from Fat: 3g
Calories from Protein: 4%

2 tablespoons lemon juice

⅓ cup brown rice syrup

3 cups one or more melons (watermelon, honeydew, and cantaloupe is
   a good combination) cut into cubes or balls, juice reserved

Few grains of sea salt

1 tablespoon sesame seeds, toasted

Edible flowers for garnish such as nasturtiums or pansies (optional)

1. In a bowl big enough to hold the melon(s), whisk together the lemon juice, sweetener, juice from the melon(s), and the salt. Add the melon pieces. Serve right away or marinate for an hour or longer in the refrigerator.

2. Grind the sesame seeds until half are ground. Just before serving, stir in the seeds and garnish.

Variation

Gingered Melon Compote: Omit the sesame seeds. Include ½ teaspoon peeled and grated fresh ginger.

Early Autumn Mixed Fruit Compote in Lime Syrup

Makes 6 servings, or 6 cups

Calories: 216

Protein: 2g

Saturated Fat: 0

Fiber: 4g

Carbohydrate: 51g

Fat: 2g

Cholesterol: 0

Sodium: 19mg

Calories from Carbohydrate: 91%

Calories from Fat: 6%

Calories from Protein: 3%

Lime Syrup (makes 1 cup)

¼ cup light white wine

¼ cup apple cider or pear juice

½ cup brown rice syrup

Zest of a lime

Juice of 2 limes, about ¼ cup

Few grains of sea salt

Fruit

3 nectarines, peaches, or pears, cut in bite-size pieces

2 cups seedless green grapes, or part small red Champagne grapes

1 cup each blueberries and raspberries or blackberries

2 kiwi, peeled, halved lengthwise, and cut into bite-size pieces

Fresh mint sprigs for garnish (optional)

1. Whisk syrup ingredients together in a large bowl.

2. Add nectarines, grapes, and blueberries and toss gently. Chill, stirring once or twice. Just before serving, stir in raspberries or blackberries and kiwi. Garnish if desired.

Italian Fresh Fruit Salad

Makes 4 servings, or 4 cups

Calories: 127
Protein: 2g
Saturated Fat: 0
Fiber: 4g
Carbohydrate: 32g
Fat: 1g
Cholesterol: 0
Sodium: 2mg
Calories from Carbohydrate: 90%
Calories from Fat: 6%
Calories from Protein: 4%

I love the name of this dessert in Italian (note that "c" is pronounced "ch" when it precedes "e")—macedonia di frutta fresca.

1 apple
1 pear
1 peach
2 cups, or about ¾ pound, assorted fruit (apricots, nectarines, plums, cherries, seedless grapes, melon balls, berries)
1 to 1½ cups orange juice, or part light white wine or sparkling wine
zest of ½ a lemon
1 tablespoon lemon juice
Few grains of sea salt

1. Cut fruit into small bite-size pieces. Gently mix all ingredients in a large bowl.

2. Marinate at cool room temperature or in the refrigerator for several hours to overnight, mixing a couple of times.

Variation

Lightly toasted walnuts, almonds, and/or pine nuts, as well as raisins, may be added as other authentic recipe ingredients. Add nuts before serving to preserve crunch.

Brandied Peaches

Makes 5 cups

2 pounds peaches

1 cup brandy

1 cup brown rice syrup

1. To peel peaches, add them to a large pot of boiling water and simmer for 2 minutes. Remove and run cool water over peaches.
2. Peel, slice, and transfer peaches to a quart jar and a half-pint jar.
3. Whisk brandy and syrup and pour over peaches. Refrigerate to meld flavors, at least overnight. Brandied peaches keep well for a week in the refrigerator.

Calories: 408

Protein: 2g

Saturated Fat: 0

Fiber: 3g

Carbohydrate: 89g

Fat: 2g

Cholesterol: 0

Sodium: 11 mg

Calories from
Carbohydrate: 87%

Calories from Fat: 3%

Calories from Protein: 2%

Strawberries in Vinegar

Makes 2 or 3
servings, or 2 cups

This recipe (Fragole all'Aceto) and the next one, both Italian in origin, serve as examples of how the simplest of fruit desserts can offer satisfaction. The vinegary taste loses its bite with chilling. The raspberry vinegar I use is based on white wine vinegar. Either wet or dry sweeteners work well, except dry Fruit-Source, which doesn't dissolve easily.

2 tablespoons raspberry, strawberry, or balsamic vinegar

2 to 3 tablespoons FruitSource syrup, maple syrup granules,
 or evaporated sugar cane juice

1 pint strawberries, halved

1. Mix vinegar and sweetener (start with less) in a bowl or glass jar big enough to hold the berries, then add the berries.
2. Refrigerate for at least ½ hour, stirring or turning the jar over once. Taste to adjust for balance of tart and sweet flavors and add more sweetener, if necessary. Lasts for a couple of days.

Calories: 79

Protein: 1g

Saturated Fat: 0

Fiber: 3g

Carbohydrate: 19g

Fat: 0.4

Cholesterol: 0

Sodium: 6mg

Calories from
Carbohydrate: 92%

Calories from Fat: 4%

Calories from Protein: 4%

Peaches in Port

Makes 4 to 6 servings, or 4 cups

Calories: 179

Protein: 1g

Saturated Fat: 0

Fiber: 3g

Carbohydrate: 40g

Fat: 0.1

Cholesterol: 0

Sodium: 11mg

Calories from Carbohydrate: 89%

Calories from Fat: 1%

Calories from Protein: 3%

½ cup port wine

½ cup FruitSource syrup

¼ teaspoon almond extract (optional)

2 pounds peaches, 5 to 6 medium, sliced and then slices cut in thirds

1. Mix wine, sweetener, and extract in a bowl or glass jar big enough to hold the peaches, then add the peaches.

2. Refrigerate until serving, stirring or turning jar over occasionally. Peaches are completely submerged in their own juices and the flavors meld beautifully when left for eight hours. Lasts several days.

Variation

Peaches in Mirin: Substitute 1 cup mirin (Japanese sweet cooking liqueur) for red wine and 1 teaspoon vanilla for almond extract.

Cherries Jubilee

**Makes 4 servings,
or 2 cups**

This sauce—originally made with sweetened and preserved cherries, brandy, and kirsch—is served hot on vanilla ice cream and is often ignited for drama. Great fun!

Note that the fruit must be heated before serving so the fumes that waft from the alcohol cause the fire to ignite when a match is held close by.

Calories: 299

Protein: 3g

Saturated Fat: 0

Fiber: 3g

Carbohydrate: 57g

Fat: 6g

Cholesterol: 0

Sodium: 77mg

Calories from

Carbohydrate: 78%

Calories from Fat: 18%

Calories from Protein: 4%

I pound cherries, fresh or frozen, about 2½ cups fresh, stemmed
   and pitted, or 2 cups frozen cherries with the (⅓ cup) juice

Zest and juice of half a small orange, ¼ cup juice

¼ cup granular FruitSource

I tablespoon arrowroot powder

2 to 4 tablespoons brandy

Vanilla nondairy ice cream

I. Place cherries (and the juice if frozen), zest, and sweetener in a 2-quart saucepan and bring to a boil. Simmer for 5 minutes.

2. Stir arrowroot into orange juice until dissolved and add it to the pan. Stir until a sauce forms, in about a minute. Turn heat off.

3. Drizzle brandy on top of hot fruit. Ignite and pour over vanilla ice cream.

Variation

Kirsch is the liqueur most often used in this recipe, but an organic honeyed fruit wine or an orange muscat would be appropriate, too. If desired, drizzle in some liqueur after flame has died down.

Peach Melba

Makes 4 servings

Calories: 416

Protein: 5g

Saturated Fat: 1g

Fiber: 7g

Carbohydrate: 78g

Fat: 11g

Cholesterol: 0

Sodium: 72mg

Calories from
Carbohydrate: 72%

Calories from Fat: 23%

Calories from Protein: 5%

The temporal nature of fruit crops is part of what makes them so precious. Of all the stars of summer, peaches and berries shine the brightest, with their contrasting sweet and tart flavors and their blaze of rainbow colors.

The great chef Georges Escoffier's most famous culinary creation is the classic pêches Melba. *He invented it while chef at the Savoy restaurant in London and named it for Australian opera star Nellie Melba. According to the cookbook* Le Cordon Bleu at Home, *the original version was served without a sauce, in a silver bowl hidden between the wings of a swan carved in ice. Escoffier later simplified the presentation by adding the raspberry sauce. According to his obituary in the* New York Times, *pêches Melba deserves credit for igniting America's passion for the ice cream sundae.*

This dessert is normally made up of a sugar syrup-poached peach perched on top of a ball of ice cream blanketed in a pool of raspberry sauce or coulis and sprinkled with almonds.

By substituting gentler sweeteners and nondairy ice cream, you can create a more healthful, modern version of the classic. This simple dessert is so gorgeous, you just have to make it!

Peaches

4 small ripe peaches

2 cups apple juice

¼ cup brown rice syrup

Juice of half a small lemon

Pinch of sea salt

Raspberry Sauce (makes ¾ cup)

1½ cups raspberries, about 6 ounces

¼ cup brown rice syrup

½ teaspoon vanilla

Topping and Ice Cream

½ cup sliced almonds

1½ tablespoons granular FruitSource

4 scoops vanilla nondairy frozen dessert

1. In a 3-quart saucepan, poach whole peaches in juice with syrup and lemon juice until tender when pierced with a small sharp knife, 3 to 10 minutes depending on the ripeness of the fruit. Turn fruit once or twice. Leave the skins on until you finish cooking so that the fruit will pick up the rosy hue.

2. Let the peaches cool in the syrup in the refrigerator, or remove peaches and reduce the poaching liquid by slow boiling for about 20 minutes, uncovered, until you have about ½ cup. Peel, halve, and pit peaches.

3. Meanwhile, to make the raspberry sauce, purée the berries in a food processor or food mill. Strain through a fine strainer to remove the seeds. Whisk in the sweetener and vanilla and chill.

4. To prepare almonds for garnish, spread them on an oiled baking sheet and sprinkle with the sweetener, or a little of the fruit syrup. In a 300° oven, bake until lightly browned, 10 to 12 minutes.

5. To serve, divide reserved poaching liquid among dessert dishes or large wine or saucer champagne glasses. Add a scoop of nondairy ice cream and place a peach half on either side of the ice cream. Spoon the raspberry sauce in a wide band overlapping both the peach halves and the ice cream. Garnish and serve immediately.

Dried Fruit Compote

Makes 6 to 8
servings, or 4 cups

Calories: 186
Protein: 3g
Saturated Fat: 0
Fiber: 5g
Carbohydrate: 49g
Fat: 0.3g
Cholesterol: 0
Sodium: 11mg
Calories from
Carbohydrate: 94%
Calories from Fat: 1%
Calories from Protein: 5%

Served in New England inns to this day, compotes have been enjoyed historically by many cultures from the Chinese to the Germans and the Spanish. This
simple winter compote is made from dried fruit that is stewed in water. Dried
fruit is so much sweeter than fresh fruit that any extra sweetener, even substituting apple juice for water, makes the dessert seem overdone.

This recipe was chosen to appear in the cookbook Cooking with the Stars,
published by Center for Science in the Public Interest.

4 cups dried fruit, single or mixed fruit (1 pound mixed dried fruit)
1 quart water
2- or 3-inch stick cinnamon
Zest of half a lemon

NOTE
For large amounts, add just
enough water to cover the fruit.
On one occasion, 20 cups of
dried fruit called for 16 cups of
water. The resulting compote
served 36 guests nicely.

Place all the ingredients in a saucepan and bring to a boil. Turn the heat
down, cover, and simmer until the fruit is plump and juicy and the liquid has become syrupy, 15 to 30 minutes.

Variations

Serve the compote garnished with ½ cup toasted, chopped nuts.

Chinese Fruit Compote: add 1 teaspoon Chinese five-spice powder to
the fruit in the last few minutes of cooking.

Dried Fruit Spread, Fruit Butter, or Turnover Filling: For great sweet
spreads, especially nice spread on warm bread during the cold season,
cook together 1 cup dried fruit with 1 cup water, then purée. Makes ¾
cup.

Cranberry and Dried Fruit Compote: Add 8 orange slices to cook with
the dried fruit. When done, stir in ½ cup cranberries. Simmer until
berries are cooked but still retain their shape, about 5 minutes more.

Baked Apples

A tried-and-true favorite in the U.S. since Colonial times and in the former Soviet Union as well, stuffed baked apples are a plump, succulent dessert that can be made in a jiffy while diners enjoy their meals. Make extra for a quick snack or dessert later.

4 apples (Golden Delicious, Granny Smith, Gala, Gravenstein), cored

Stuffing

¼ cup nut butter (almond, hazelnut [filbert], or sesame butter)

¼ teaspoon cinnamon

Up to 3 tablespoons apple juice or cider

¼ cup currants or raisins

1. Preheat the oven to 400°F.

2. With a fork, mix the nut butter and cinnamon. Only if nut butter is stiff, add the juice gradually to achieve a smooth texture. Stir in the currants or raisins. Transfer the apples to a cake pan or baking sheet. Insert the filling with a teaspoon. Pack it in with a chopstick, allowing filling to mound on top. Mix up more filling if apples, or the holes you've made, are particularly large.

3. Bake the apples until they are soft enough to be pierced easily all the way to the middle, 20 to 45 minutes depending on the variety.

Variations

Nutty Raisin-Miso Stuffing: Add a teaspoon of any variety of miso to the stuffing ingredients for added depth of flavor and nutrition.

For another filling, include ¼ cup each toasted and chopped nuts and fruit preserves. Almonds with strawberry jam or apricot preserves make nice combinations.

Calories: 256

Protein: 3g

Saturated Fat: 1g

Fiber: 7g

Carbohydrate: 43g

Fat: 10g

Cholesterol: 0

Sodium: 3mg

Calories from Carbohydrate: 62%

Calories from Fat: 33%

Calories from Protein: 5%

NOTES

Pippin apples tend to get mushy faster than some others, so watch for them to be done earlier. McIntosh apples bake in just 25 minutes. Hard green apples like Mutsu take the longest. I've enjoyed Jonathan, Jonagold, Cortland, Winesap, and Blushing Gold apples prepared this way, too.

Don't cover the apples with foil unless you want them to fall apart and turn into delicious applesauce.

Baked Apples with Shortbread Topping

Makes 2 servings

Calories: 322

Protein: 3g

Saturated Fat: 0

Fiber: 3g

Carbohydrate: 70g

Fat: 4g

Cholesterol: 0

Sodium: 214mg

Calories from

Carbohydrate: 84%

Calories from Fat: 12%

Calories from Protein: 4%

Filling

2 small to medium Golden Delicious apples, peeled,
   quartered, and thinly sliced crosswise

2 tablespoons raisins

2 tablespoons dry sweetener (FruitSource, maple syrup granules,
   or evaporated sugar cane juice)

1 tablespoon arrowroot powder

1 teaspoon lemon juice

Shortbread Topping

¼ cup whole wheat pastry flour

¼ cup unbleached white pastry flour

2 tablespoons dry sweetener

¾ teaspoon aluminum-free baking powder

Few grains of sea salt

1½ tablespoons vegetable oil

1½ to 2 tablespoons soy milk, water, or apple juice

1 teaspoon natural sugar crystals for garnish (optional)

1. Preheat the oven to 400°F.

2. Mix filling ingredients and transfer to 2 ramekins or other ovenproof bowls that may also be used as serving containers. Cover and place on a cake pan or baking sheet to catch drips. Bake until apples test barely tender when poked with a fork, 30 to 45 minutes.

3. To make shortbread topping, mix dry ingredients, then work in oil. Add soy milk to form a smooth pliable dough. Add a little more flour if necessary. Divide dough in half and roll or pat into two round shapes large enough to cover the ramekins. Remove covers and put shortbread topping in place. Sprinkle with natural sugar crystals if desired.

4. Return ramekins to oven to bake until topping is golden, 10 to 15 minutes more. May be served hot, warm, or at room temperature.

Baked Apples with Streusel Filling

Makes 4 servings

Richly delicious! Golden Delicious apples work best in this dessert—sweet and tender.

4 apples (Golden Delicious, Pippin, Rome Beauty, or Granny Smith), cored
About 1½ cups apple juice or cider
Zest and juice of 1 small lemon

Streusel Filling

½ cup whole wheat pastry flour
¼ to ½ cup granular FruitSource
¼ teaspoon cinnamon
Few grains of sea salt
3 to 4 tablespoons walnut oil or another light oil, start with less

1. Preheat the oven to 400°F.

2. Cut a thin slice from the bottom of each apple so that it will sit securely. Transfer to a pie pan.

3. To make filling, in a medium mixing bowl combine flour, sweetener, cinnamon, and salt. Work in oil until mixture is crumbly. Loosely fill apple cavities with streusel mixture just level with the tops.

4. Pour apple juice into pan to come about a quarter of the way up the sides of the apples. Add the lemon zest and juice. Sprinkle remaining streusel around the apples, saving enough to garnish the tops.

5. Bake until apples are soft but still retain their shapes, 45 to 50 minutes. Garnish tops with reserved streusel in the last 10 minutes of baking. Serve warm with the thickened juices spooned around the apples.

Variation

Baked Apples with Buckwheat Streusel Filling: Substitute buckwheat flour for pastry flour. Color is darker, but flavor works nicely with apples.

Calories: 341
Protein: 2g
Saturated Fat: 1g
Fiber: 5g
Carbohydrate: 62g
Fat: 12g
Cholesterol: 0
Sodium: 23mg
Calories from Carbohydrate: 69%
Calories from Fat: 29%
Calories from Protein: 2%

Oven-Poached Pears with Hazelnuts

Makes 4 servings

Calories: 175

Protein: 2g

Saturated Fat: 0

Fiber: 3g

Carbohydrate: 32g

Fat: 5g

Cholesterol: 0

Sodium: 19mg

Calories from
Carbohydrate: 71%

Calories from Fat: 26%

Calories from Protein: 3%

2 pears (Bosc, Comice, Bartlett, D'anjou, or French Butter pears),
   peeled if desired, halved lengthwise and cored

1 tablespoon arrowroot powder

½ cup apple juice or cider

¼ teaspoon of one or more of the following powdered spices: cinnamon,
   ginger, cloves, nutmeg and/or cardamom, or Chinese five-spice

Few grains of sea salt

¼ cup liquid sweetener (brown rice malt syrup, FruitSource syrup,
   or pure maple syrup)

¼ cup hazelnuts, toasted, skinned, and chopped for garnish

Mint sprigs or scented geranium leaves for garnish

1. Preheat the oven to 400°F.

2. Place the pears in a 2-quart baking dish, cut side down. Mix the arrowroot with enough of the juice to barely cover and set it aside. Mix the spices and salt with the remaining juice and sweetener and pour it over the pears. Cover and bake until pears test tender, 20 to 30 minutes.

3. Stir the thickener mixture and drizzle it into the liquid around the pears. Gently tilt the dish in a circular motion to mix the thickener with the hot liquid. Return dish to oven until liquid becomes bubbly, shiny, and thick, about 5 minutes more.

4. Spoon the syrup over the pears to serve. Sprinkle with nuts and place mint or geranium leaf where the stem of the pear would be. (Note: A scented geranium leaf imparts an incredible amount of flavor to the sauce even when used only as a garnish.)

Variations

Sweetener-Free Oven-Poached Pears: Omit sweetener, substituting that much more juice.

Vanilla Poached Pears: Add a vanilla bean, slit in half lengthwise, to baking dish with pears. Or add 1 teaspoon vanilla extract to arrowroot-juice mixture before adding it to the pot. Remove vanilla bean before serving.

Wine-Poached Mixed Fruit

Makes 4 servings, or 4 cups

A simple yet impressive finale to a lovely supper, wine-poached fruit may be served alone or with nut bread, plain cake, or over nondairy ice cream. May be made a day or two in advance to allow the fruit to soak up and become infused with the fragrant, spicy sauce.

1½ cups dry red (Burgundy, Cabernet) or light or fruity white wine

½ cup orange juice

½ cup brown rice syrup or FruitSource syrup, or fruit-sweetened jam or jelly

8 black peppercorns

1 teaspoon fresh rosemary, separated from stem

1 vanilla bean, split lengthwise

6 pitted prunes

2 peaches, peeled, halved, and each half quartered

2 pears, peeled, halved, and each half quartered

4 rosemary sprigs for garnish

¼ to ½ cup Cognac Cream for garnish (optional)

Cognac (or Rum) Cream   (makes 1 cup)

½ pound tofu, fresh, medium, or silken/soft

¼ cup pure maple syrup or FruitSource syrup

2 tablespoons Cognac (or rum)

1½ teaspoons vanilla

1. In a 2-quart saucepan, bring the first 7 ingredients to a boil. Turn off heat while you prepare the peaches and pears.

2. To peel the peaches, submerge them in boiling water for 1 minute, then drain. When cool enough to handle, gently peel off skin.

3. Add peaches and pears to pot and return to a boil, then simmer until tender, about 15 minutes.

4. To make Cognac cream, purée ingredients until creamy smooth.

5. Garnish to serve. Or allow fruit to cool somewhat before transferring to a glass jar to refrigerate.

Calories: 298

Protein: 3g

Saturated Fat: 0

Fiber: 4g

Carbohydrate: 67g

Fat: 2g

Cholesterol: 0

Sodium: 12mg

Calories from
Carbohydrate: 90%

Calories from Fat: 6%

Calories from Protein: 4%

Variations

Add fresh cherries, raspberries, or strawberries just before serving if desired.

Flavor with other seasonings such as whole cloves, allspice, or star anise, or thyme, summer savory, or mint.

Wine-Poached Pears with Cognac Cream: Include all the ingredients from the above recipe except the fruit. Substitute 4 pears.

Peel the pears, leaving the stem intact. Use a melon baller or a tablespoon to cut out the cores from the bottom end. Cut a thin slice off the base of each pear so they stand upright.

Place other ingredients in a saucepan large enough to hold the pears. Bring to a boil. Add pears on their sides. Reduce heat and poach until the pears are tender when pierced with the point of a knife, about 5 minutes on each side. Turn four times. Cooking time varies with size and ripeness of pears.

Transfer pears to a heatproof bowl. Remove seasonings from poaching liquid and bring to a boil until liquid has reduced by half to ¾ cup, about 15 minutes. Allow to cool to thicken further.

To serve, spoon some syrup on a dessert plate or bowl, then set a pear on top. Spoon 1 or 2 tablespoons Cognac cream over one side of each pear. May be served warm or at room temperature.

Sorbets

According to the classic French culinary encyclopedia Larousse Gastronomique, sorbets were the first iced desserts. They were originally made of fruit, honey, aromatic substances, and snow. They originated in China in the eighth century B.C. in chambers constructed to conserve naturally formed winter ice, which was then mixed with sweetened fruit juice. The Chinese passed the practice to the Persians and Arabs, who introduced it to the Italians. The word "sorbet" derives from the Italian sorbeto, *derived from Turkish* chorbet *and Arab* charah, *which simply means drink.*

It wasn't until the sixteenth century in Florence that frozen desserts became an art. Their popularity quickly spread throughout Europe. It was a century or two later that ice cream, the dessert of the aristocracy in the French court, became available to more common folk.

Whether served as an intermezzo, a palate refresher between courses in a big dinner, or for dessert, sorbets vary widely. French recipes call for adding Italian meringue to the half-frozen mixture. Nowadays, recipes may also contain milk, yogurt, buttermilk, heavy cream, whipped cream, egg white, or gelatin.

INGREDIENTS

These days many people prefer iced desserts that are less rich than ice cream, hence the growing popularity and sophistication of sorbets. By contrast, ice cream is laden with fat, which can actually make us hotter. So when you want to cool off or quench your thirst and satisfy your sweet tooth all at the same time, the natural choice is elegant, easy homemade sorbets containing next to no fat, no cholesterol, no refined sugar, no artificial color, and few calories.

With only 5 to 10 minutes preparation time, these new sorbets are light and refreshingly easy nondairy frozen desserts. Based on whole fruits, fruit juices, and natural sweeteners, they are intensely flavored and sometimes tart and sweet at the same time with textures ranging from satiny smooth to crunchily crystalline. For the most concentrated color and flavor, choose the fruits that are sweetest and most perfumed.

Sugar syrup—containing an average of a little less than a cup of refined white sugar cooked with a cup of water, and sometimes with a little corn syrup added for consistency—is traditionally added to the fruit. My sweetener of choice is malted brown rice syrup, although enzyme-converted rice syrup will work well. It is higher in quality than sugar syrup, e.g. there is no refinement nor chemicals used in processing. With brown rice syrup there is no need to mix and heat a syrup. All the recipe ingredients can be mixed together in one step, and the very pleasing fruity flavors are enhanced because brown rice syrup doesn't compete with their delicate sweetness. Other liquid sweeteners such as FruitSource syrup and pure maple syrup may be substituted. (Include less maple syrup as its flavor is sweeter.)

I have made the original (plain flavor) amazake rice nectar an optional ingredient in the recipes because I know it may not be available in some parts of the country. The benefits of adding amazake are that it makes for a smoother texture with a hint of sweetness, especially with berries, and the volume is increased. The flavor of the sorbets made with amazake is luscious but not as saturated, more mellow in quality. I find that ½ to 1 cup amazake per 4 cups fruit works well.

Some people incorporate egg whites into the sorbet. This is an unnecessary step and, according to recent studies, uncooked eggs may not be safe since they may carry salmonella.

For excitement, in addition to citrus, vanilla, or leaves of scented geraniums or mint family plants, some of the recipes include fillips such as wine (bubbling Champagne, light fruity white wine, or dry red wine). The wine makes a creamier sorbet because its alcohol doesn't freeze.

TECHNIQUES AND COOKWARE

The three freezing techniques that may be used depend on the equipment you have on hand. The old-fashioned technique is to whisk the ingredients by hand when a ring of crystals about half an inch wide has formed around the outside edge of the mixture. Laborious instructions call for stirring every half hour or so, until the dessert is icy but not completely frozen.

Nowadays sorbets are easy to make at home if you have a food processor or, as a second choice, a blender. In addition, the old-fashioned ice-cream maker that demanded half an hour or more of laborious hand-cranking has been replaced by convenient electric models that stir the sorbet until ready to serve.

For serving, stainless steel ice cream scoops are a good choice, but the best tool is a classic ice cream scoop, the original of which dates back to 1935. Modern-day Teflon-coated nonstick versions have handles that are filled with a self-defrosting solution or antifreeze that makes them perfect for cutting through frozen desserts with ease, forming neat balls that release instantly.

The simple food processor method is the one I use. Some recipes call for freezing the fruit first, but some fruits such as raspberries and blueberries are hard as bullets when frozen separately, making them difficult to purée. For the greatest ease, thoroughly purée all of the ingredients together (fruit, sweetener, flavoring agent such as citrus juice or zest, and amazake rice nectar or wine, if included), then freeze the mixture in a freezerproof container.

When solidified, allow to thaw for 15 minutes or so, then break sorbet into 1- or 2-inch chunks and process again until smooth but not completely melted. This process, called churn-freezing, ensures ice crystals remain small and air is drawn in for a finer texture.

Return sorbet to freezer until it firms up enough to serve; 8 hours or longer is the best on average. Even if I have made a sorbet a month ahead of serving, I purée it about 8 hours before serving for the smoothest texture. You may wish to present the frozen dessert in well-chilled dishes to minimize melting.

Strawberry Sorbet

Makes 4 to 6 servings,

or 3 ¼ to 4 ½ cups

Calories: 168

Protein: 1g

Saturated Fat: 0g

Fiber: 3g

Carbohydrate: 2g

Fat: 1g

Cholesterol: 0

Sodium: 7mg

Calories from

Carbohydrate: 92%

Calories from Fat: 6%

Calories from Protein: 2%

Pretty light pink and luscious, this sorbet is a personal favorite. It can be referred to as the master recipe for a straightforward sorbet made the easiest way, without agar sea vegetable flakes for texture as explained in the next recipe.

In designing this recipe I tried milky liquids other than amazake to impart a somewhat creamy texture. Amazake is by far the most effective. By comparison, soy milk, rice and other grain milks, and almond milk are each quite thin in texture. The resulting sorbet is not quite as sweet nor as smooth as when amazake is included. But each has a satisfying flavor and works nicely should amazake be hard to come by in some areas of the country.

2 pints strawberries, 4 cups or 1¼ pounds, hulled; or 2 10-ounce packages frozen
    unsweetened strawberries (yields 2 cups soft/thawed berries including juice)

¾ cup FruitSource syrup

1 tablespoon lemon juice

½ cup plain amazake rice nectar, soy milk, rice or other grain milks, or almond milk

1. In the food processor, purée all ingredients until smooth. Pour mixture into a freezerproof container. Cover and freeze until set, at least 8 hours.

2. Take sorbet out of refrigerator to thaw for about 15 minutes. Break sorbet into 1- or 2-inch chunks with a fork or spoon and purée in food processor until smooth.

3. Return to container and freeze until mixture sets up to desired texture, at least 4 hours in a shallow container. Serve. If mixture becomes too hard, simply reprocess a few hours before serving.

Variation

Add 2 to 4 tablespoons orange muscat dessert wine in addition to or in place of amazake.

Raspberry Sorbet

Makes 3 to 6 servings, or 3 to 4 cups

Calories: 235

Protein: 1g

Saturated Fat: 0g

Fiber: 5g

Carbohydrate: 55g

Fat: 2g

Cholesterol: 0

Sodium: 8mg

Calories from

Carbohydrate: 92%

Calories from Fat: 6%

Calories from Protein: 2%

Strikingly beautiful, this sorbet is light and creamy with a crystal clear berry taste. The combination of agar sea vegetable flakes and amazake makes for the most luscious texture in a sorbet. Consider this recipe a master recipe for incorporating these three ingredients.

The leaves of scented geraniums have been used historically to add aromatic flavoring to teas, jams, cakes, and punches. They go especially well with berries. Shepherd's Garden Seeds carries several plant varieties that come with recipes.

To extract the delicate flavors from lemon-, rose-, or ginger-scented geraniums, the leaves (2 per cup of liquid) and flower petals (1 teaspoon per cup of liquid) may be simmered with liquid, then strained for custard or iced desserts such as the variation on this recipe. Fresh leaves and flowers make nice garnishes as well.

2 pints raspberries, or 2 10-ounce packages frozen unsweetened
   raspberries (4 cups thawed berries with juice)

1 tablespoon agar sea vegetable flakes

½ cup orange juice

1 cup brown rice syrup

1 cup amazake (optional)

1. Purée the berries in a food processor. Press through a strainer with a rubber spatula to remove seeds. Makes 1½ to 2 cups. Return purée to rinsed processor.

2. Sprinkle agar flakes over juice in a 1-quart saucepan. Bring to a boil, then simmer until dissolved, about 3 minutes. Purée with berries, brown rice syrup, and amazake, if included. Freeze solid, at least 8 hours or overnight.

3. Break sorbet into pieces and process until light and smooth. Return to covered container and freeze until texture is suitable for serving.

Variations

Blackberry Sorbet: The color of this sorbet is a gorgeous deep red. Blackberries, like raspberries, are a type of bramble berry. Varieties include olallieberries, boysenberries, loganberries (a blackberry-raspberry cross), youngberries, and nectarberries.

Substitute blackberries for raspberries. Include four 6-ounce flats of fresh berries (yield is 6 cups berries or 1½ cups purée.) A 1-pound bag of thawed frozen blackberries contains 1⅔ cups berries with juice and yields 1¼ to 1½ cups purée. This amount works fine in the above recipe.

If desired, substitute ¼ cup orange marmalade for that amount of brown rice syrup.

To add an intriguing flavor, add 1 large or 2 small rose geranium leaves to the pot with the juice. Strain geranium out. Garnish individual servings with small rose geranium leaves.

Recipe yields 2¼ to 3 cups without amazake, 3½ to 4 cups with amazake.

Blueberry Sorbet: Blueberry Sorbet is milder in flavor and the color is more subdued.

Include 2 pints fresh blueberries (each basket contains 11½ ounces or 1¼ cups berries) or 2 10-ounce packages thawed frozen blueberries in place of raspberries. (Each package contains 1½ cups berries and juice.) Process berries, then strain to remove skins. Makes 1½ cups. If desired and available, add lemon geranium leaves as in the preceding recipe.

Proceed as above, including just ¾ cup brown rice syrup and adding both 1 tablespoon lemon juice and 1 teaspoon vanilla. Yield is same as above.

Berry Sorbet Parfait: Layer alternate stripes or scoops of strawberry sorbet with blackberry or blueberry sorbet in tall dessert or wine glasses. Place glasses on a baking sheet and return to freezer until firm. To serve, garnish each with fresh berries and a sprig of mint.

Makes 3 to 6 servings, or 2½ to 4½ cups

Champagne Peach Sorbet

The velvety texture of fresh peaches makes them the perfect choice for use in sorbets. A refreshing finale to any meal, this combination of peaches, Champagne, and fresh ginger makes for a complex flavor with an exciting, crisp bite.

1 pound ripe peaches, 3 peaches or 3½ cups, quartered

½ cup Champagne

½ to ¾ cup brown rice syrup or peach jam, less without amazake, more with it

1 tablespoon peeled and grated fresh ginger

1 cup amazake (optional)

1. Purée ingredients until smooth.

2. Pour mixture into a freezerproof container. Freeze, then process again. Freeze until serving.

Variation

Peach Sorbet with Red Wine: Substitute dry red wine (Cabernet, Merlot) for Champagne for an intriguing flavor that is even richer-tasting prepared as an ice, without the amazake. Substitute ¼ cup pure maple syrup with ¼ cup orange juice for brown rice syrup. Makes 3 cups.

Calories: 140

Protein: 1g

Saturated Fat: 0

Fiber: 1g

Carbohydrate: 36g

Fat: 1g

Cholesterol: 0

Sodium: 6mg

Calories from
Carbohydrate: 94%

Calories from Fat: 4%

Calories from Protein: 2%

Plum Sorbet with Red Wine

**Makes 3 to 4
servings, or 3 cups**

Red wine extends the light pink color of the plums even further and, along with the five-spice powder, adds an exotic depth of flavor. Ingredients in five-spice powder include cinnamon, fennel, cloves, star anise, and white pepper.

1 pound ripe plums, 2½ cups, chopped

½ cup orange juice

1 tablespoon agar flakes

¾ cup brown rice syrup

½ cup red wine, dry or fruity

½ teaspoon five-spice powder

1. Process plums.

2. In a 1-quart saucepan, bring orange juice to a boil with agar flakes and simmer until dissolved, about 3 minutes. Add to processor with remaining ingredients and purée until smooth.

3. Freeze, purée again, and return to freezer until serving time.

Calories: 299

Protein: 2g

Saturated Fat: 0

Fiber: 2g

Carbohydrate: 66g

Fat: 2g

Cholesterol: 0

Sodium: 10mg

Calories from
Carbohydrate: 92%

Calories from Fat: 6%

Calories from Protein: 2%

Cranberry-Persimmon Terrine

Calories: 181

Protein: 1g

Saturated Fat: 0

Fiber: 2g

Carbohydrate: 45g

Fat: 1g

Cholesterol: 0

Sodium: 6mg

Calories from

Carbohydrate: 95%

Calories from Fat: 3%

Calories from Protein: 2%

The stunning colors—vibrant red and dazzling orange—and the satiny smooth texture of the combination of these two sorbets make this terrine ideal for serving during the holiday season.

Persimmon trees are members of the ebony family, with their barks made striking by a checkered alligator pattern and deep color. Commenting on the fruit's astringency, Captain John Smith wrote: "If it not be ripe, it will drawe a man's mouth awrie with much torment. When it is ripe it is as delicious as an apricock."

Persimmons were popular with the earliest Americans as they are to today's Japanese, Chinese, and Koreans, who love the Oriental persimmon, called kaki, *which is grafted onto native persimmon.*

The two categories of persimmons are the pointed, tapered, red-orange fruits called hachiya, *which are inedibly astringent unless soft-ripe. They ripen nicely and the black streaks on the otherwise deep orange skin pose no problem. The other kind is the rounded, flat-bottomed, lighter-colored fruits called* fuyu, *which are nonastringent and can be eaten hard (great in salads) to soft. Both ripen from October into December. It's recommended to pick only the softest ripe persimmons from the tree or on the ground. Either variety will ripen at room temperature in two or three days. Freezing softens Hachiya persimmons in 24 hours. Eat them out of hand, or discard the leaves, wash and peel the fruit, and purée the flesh to use in fresh fruit desserts such as this one, or in baking, or to freeze for later use.*

Cranberry-Orange Sorbet **(makes 4 to 5 cups)**

¾ pound fresh or frozen cranberries, 3 to 3½ cups

2 cups orange juice

1 tablespoon lemon juice

½ cup pure maple syrup

½ cup brown rice syrup

2 tablespoons agar flakes

Persimmon Sorbet **(makes 2 to 3 cups)**

1½ pounds ripe hachiya persimmons, 3 to 5 pieces of fruit, or 1½ to
  2¼ cups, peeled

⅓ cup orange juice or apple cider, or part of each

3 tablespoons pure maple syrup

2 tablespoons brown rice syrup

1 teaspoon vanilla

Garnishes

Sprigs of mint

Slices of persimmon

1. To make Cranberry-Orange Sorbet, sort through cranberries and discard any damaged ones. Rinse and drain.

2. Put all ingredients in a 3- or 4-quart saucepan. Cook until cranberries pop and agar dissolves, about 5 minutes. Purée in a processor or blender until light and foamy.

3. Freeze in a shallow container for at least 4 hours.

4. To make Persimmon Sorbet, purée ingredients until creamy smooth. Freeze in a shallow container for at least 5 hours.

5. Line two 6-cup loaf pans with plastic wrap. Don't worry if it doesn't lie completely flat; it doesn't show in the end.

6. Allow sorbets to thaw about ½ hour for ease in puréeing. Chop the cranberry mixture into pieces and transfer to a food processor to purée. Place half the purée in the lined pans, smoothing it out with a rubber spatula. Return to freezer to harden for about 20 minutes.

7. Purée the persimmon sorbet and spread all of it evenly over the cranberry sorbet in each of the loaf pans. Freeze until somewhat solid, about 20 minutes. Purée and spread the other half of the cranberry sorbet on top of persimmon sorbet, three layers in all. Return to freezer to harden completely, at least 2 hours.

8. To serve, pull back plastic wrap and invert the terrine onto a platter. You may need to tug a bit on the plastic. Unwrap and cut into ½- to 1-inch slices, dipping the knife into hot water and wiping it off between slices. Garnish.

NOTE

If serving sorbets separately (not in terrine), allow to thaw for 20 to 30 minutes for ease in serving.

Lemon-Lime Sorbet with Raspberry-Balsamic Coulis

Makes 4 servings, or 2 cups

Calories: 324

Protein: 1g

Saturated Fat: 0

Fiber: 3g

Carbohydrate: 77g

Fat: 2g

Cholesterol: 0

Sodium: 13mg

Calories from
Carbohydrate: 93%

Calories from Fat: 6%

Calories from Protein: 1%

This dessert makes a beautiful presentation, and it's sweet and creamy with that zingy flavor only citrus can impart. Should you come upon some Meyer lemons, which have a sweet flavor, you may still want to include some common lemon juice for tartness.

¼ cup fresh lemon juice, 2 to 3 lemons

1 tablespoon fresh lime juice, 2 to 3 limes

¾ cup FruitSource syrup or brown rice malt syrup

1½ cups water

Zest of half a lemon, minced

2 tablespoons white Riesling or agar flakes

Raspberry-Balsamic Coulis   (makes ¼ cup)

¼ cup FruitSource syrup or brown rice syrup

1½ cups raspberries, about 6 ounces

½ teaspoon vanilla

Up to 1 tablespoon balsamic vinegar

Garnishes

Fresh raspberries in season

Lemon balm or mint sprigs, or pansies of appropriate color

Lemon and lime zest

1. Place juices with sweetener, water, and wine, if using, in food processor container. In a 1-quart saucepan, bring water to a boil with agar, if included. Simmer until agar dissolves, about 3 minutes. Add to processor and purée.

2. Transfer to a freezerproof container. Cover and freeze until firm.

3. Process coulis ingredients, except balsamic vinegar, until smooth. Pass through a strainer and discard seeds. Gradually add vinegar for an added punch. Cover and chill.

4. Reprocess sorbet and return to freezer until firm. To serve, spoon 2 or 3 tablespoons of coulis on top of each serving of sorbet. Garnish.

Banana-Berry Sorbet

This sorbet is berry pink and fragrant of sweet banana.

4 bananas, about 1½ pounds or 3 cups, peeled and cut into 1-inch pieces

3 cups strawberries, stemmed

½ to ¾ cup brown rice syrup, to taste

1 tablespoon lemon juice

1 cup amazake (optional)

3 to 6 slices strawberry for garnish

1. Purée ingredients until smooth in a food processor. Freeze, then purée again. Return to freezer for at least 4 hours.

2. Serve garnished.

Variation

Substitute raspberries for strawberries.

Makes 5 to 7 servings, or 5 to 6 cups

Calories: 158

Protein: 1g

Saturated Fat: 0

Fiber: 3g

Carbohydrate: 38g

Fat: 1g

Cholesterol: 0

Sodium: 5mg

Calories from Carbohydrate: 92%

Calories from Fat: 5%

Calories from Protein: 3%

Mango Coconut Sorbet

Makes 4 to 6 servings, or 4¾ cups

Calories: 389

Protein: 2g

Saturated Fat: 11g

Fiber: 3g

Carbohydrate: 68g

Fat: 14g

Cholesterol: 0

Sodium: 19mg

Calories from Carbohydrate: 69%

Calories from Fat: 30%

Calories from Protein: 2%

This is the richest and the creamiest of all the sorbets in this book because of the coconut milk, which is first-press premium grade from fresh, ripe coconut meat and naturally processed without chemical additives or preservatives. I used Thai Kitchen brand (Epicurean International Inc., P.O. Box 13242, Berkeley, CA 94701). The regular coconut milk derives 9 grams of fat per 2-ounce serving, 7 grams being saturated fat. The light version (which is creamy and tastes great) counts 3 grams of fat per 2-ounce serving, 2.5 grams saturated. Both contain 0 cholesterol since they are from a plant instead of an animal, e.g. cream or butter. Either may be used here.

Ripe mangoes have a yellow skin in comparison with the green and red skins of the underripe fruit.

2 ripe mangoes, 1½ pounds, or 2½ to 3 cups, peeled and flesh cut from seed

1½ cups pure coconut milk, a 14-ounce can regular or light coconut milk

1¼ cups brown rice syrup

3 tablespoons lime juice

2 tablespoons peeled and grated fresh ginger

Fresh shaved coconut or toasted coconut flakes for garnish (optional)

In a food processor, purée ingredients until creamy smooth. Freeze in a covered container, then purée again. Return to freezer. Garnish, if desired.

Piña Colada Sorbet

**Makes 5 to 6 servings
or 4 to 5½ cups**

Calories: 194

Protein: 1g

Saturated Fat: 7g

Fiber: 0

Carbohydrate: 29g

Fat: 8g

Cholesterol: 0

Sodium: 12mg

Calories from
Carbohydrate: 60%

Calories from Fat: 38%

Calories from Protein: 2%

Luscious, white, and so very refreshing, coconut milk adds richness to the taste of this sorbet while the optional rum enhances the texture, which is very icy without it.

The various brands of pineapple coconut juice may contain water, concentrated pineapple juice, coconut, natural vegetable stabilizer or gums (xanthan, carrageenan, sodium alginate, and locust bean), and perhaps some concentrated white grape juice or honey. Coconut fat will naturally separate from coconut milk, so be sure to shake well before using and if fat remains separate, strain the mixture before freezing.

1 quart pineapple coconut juice

3 tablespoons agar flakes

1 cup coconut milk

¼ cup FruitSource syrup

¼ cup rum (optional)

1. In a 1- or 2-quart saucepan, bring 2 cups juice to a boil with agar flakes. Watch for foaming over upon boiling. Allow to simmer until agar dissolves, 3 to 5 minutes.

2. Mix with remaining juice, coconut milk, syrup, and rum if included and transfer to a freezerproof container. Freeze.

3. After a thaw, purée in a food processor. Freeze again. If rum is included, sorbet may be served straight from the freezer. Otherwise, allow to thaw for 20 minutes before serving.

Mocha Sorbet

**Makes 2 to 3 servings,
or 2 to 2½ cups**

Calories: 239

Protein: 8g

Saturated Fat: 1g

Fiber: 1g

Carbohydrate: 45g

Fat: 4g

Cholesterol: 0

Sodium: 102mg

Calories from
Carbohydrate: 74%

Calories from Fat: 14%

Calories from Protein: 12%

This soy milk-based sorbet tastes great and is surprisingly creamy. I prefer Roma instant grain coffee granules (see page 247), but the other brands available in natural foods stores will have an equally nice result.

2 cups plain soy milk

¼ cup brown rice syrup

2 tablespoons pure maple syrup

2 tablespoons cocoa powder

4 teaspoons instant grain coffee powder or granules

½ teaspoon vanilla

1 tablespoon agar flakes

Malt-sweetened chocolate, shaved for garnish

1. Whisk ingredients together in a 2-quart saucepan. Bring to a boil (watch for foaming over), then simmer until agar is completely dissolved, 3 to 5 minutes.

2. Freeze. After a thaw, purée in a food processor and return to freezer. Allow to thaw 20 to 30 minutes before serving.

Variations

Coco Mocha Sorbet: Fold in ¼ cup shredded coconut, plain or toasted, to sorbet after second puréeing and before freezing again.

Almond Mocha Sorbet: Add 2 to 4 tablespoons almond butter to purée.

Mocha Chip Sorbet: Fold in ½ cup malt-sweetened chocolate chips or chunks.

Pies & Tarts

There's nothing like a freshly baked pie! Making one is a form of self-expression and love shared. And, of course, eating a piece can be sheer delight.

Pies have a long history dating back to Roman times. They were common in England by the Middle Ages. In Colonial days in America, New England housewives baked a hundred pies at a time. They stacked them in big jars and stored them in a shed where they'd freeze. Before serving, a pie was placed in the pie cupboard in the fireplace chimney to thaw out.

According to a Gallup Poll, Americans rate pie (along with cake and ice cream) as their idea of the perfect dessert. Pillsbury research tells us that the most popular flavors year-round are apple, pumpkin, cherry, and pecan. In the spring and early summer, they are apple, lemon, and peach. And a survey done by Natural Health magazine showed that fresh fruit pie with a nut crust was the choice for dessert of most of the respondents from a selection of fifty-six dishes to include in a dinner for a group of friends.

Tarts are French versions of single-crust pies. As you'll see in the recipes, free-form tarts (no pans) are the easiest kind to make. New classic versions of panned tarts are made with a sweet whole grain pastry layered with a dairy-free pastry cream filling, or jam or chocolate, then topped with fruit and brushed with a glaze based on jam or juice.

The following recipes are designed to fit a standard 9-inch pie or tart pan, although any size from 8 up to 11 inches will do. The filling will just be a bit thicker or thinner.

These homespun pies look and taste as if they came from Grandma's kitchen. Most of the recipes rely on the naturally sweet flavors derived from fresh and dried fruits and juices or sweet vegetables such as winter squash, parsnips, or yams.

Pie apples and other fruits are usually peeled for the uniformity of texture or mouth-feel. (Cooking time does not differ one way or the other.) But for color and for nutrient value, I sometimes leave the skins on or peel just half the fruit.

Two methods of cooking the filling are covered in these recipes. The advantage of a precooked filling is that baking time is reduced considerably. The advantage of baking the filling in the pastry is that you omit the step of precooking.

PASTRY

Most recipes for pastry are based on the classic French pâte brisée, which is high in fat—often calling for half as much fat as flour—and low in nutrients, calling for adulterated white flour, shortening (lard, butter, or margarine), refined salt, and sometimes refined white sugar and egg.

In contrast, what follows is a pastry recipe that yields a rich and delicate crust that is easy to work with and is low in fat. Organic whole wheat pastry flour and unbleached white pastry flour are the main ingredients. Pastry flour is milled from soft wheat, which has less gluten and more starch than the hard wheat used to make bread flour, making it a better choice for a light flaky pie crust. Pastry flour is also lighter in color and texture than bread flour: it brings a lovely golden color to the crust, making it an integral part of the pie rather than merely a container for the filling. Unbleached white flour is included for a more familiar looking pastry, lighter in color and a bit lighter in texture. White pastry flour is preferred over white bread flour, but either will work. And, should you choose to make all whole wheat pastry flour crusts, they will be wonderful.

Light vegetable oils such as walnut, canola, sesame, sunflower, and safflower give the dough a flaky texture when baked. They add a satisfying quality of richness without the cholesterol or high volume of saturated fat that comes from animal fats, such as butter or lard, or from the vegetable shortenings. I prefer these light vegetable oils over unrefined corn oil, used by some natural foods chefs, which has a strong flavor and heavy texture. Too much oil produces a pastry that is crumbly and falls apart. The amount of oil called for in these recipes is perfect—relatively low in fat, yet light and flaky in texture.

Compared with most dessert recipes, these call for sweeteners that are of the highest quality, and less of them is needed. People's tastes vary greatly on the amount of sweetener they prefer, so feel free to alter the recipes ¼ cup in either direction after following the recipe as it stands the first time you make a dish.

The water or other liquid called for in recipes serves to hold the flour together. The amount needed varies because the absorbency rates of flours vary, so look for the point at which the flour comes together into a dough with a smooth, pliable texture. Too much water produces a heavy, dense pastry. To avoid this result, follow the instructions to add the oil first, and then add the water to create the desired texture. Purified water is always the best choice for use in food and drink.

Arrowroot powder or tapioca flour replaces cornstarch as the thickening agent in the fillings, and are just as easy to use in the same amounts. Kuzu root starch may also be substituted.

The recipe for a pastry glaze based on a wet sweetener adds a nice touch for a shinier surface, usually derived from milk or egg.

TECHNIQUES

In the classes I've taught, it seems the biggest mistake people make in creating pastry is adding too little liquid. It's always better to start with a slightly wet dough rather than one that is too dry. You can always work in more flour for the perfect texture—soft and moist, the kind of pastry that rolls out easily. Save yourself frustration by simply discarding a dry dough, because it's difficult to work liquid into a dry dough without making the dough dense and tough in the process.

Handle the dough as little as possible during preparation. Do not knead it, which develops the elastic quality of the gluten and makes the pastry tough. Instead, simply shape it into a mass with your hands before rolling.

Many people prefer to use chilled ingredients (oil and liquids, even flour) in their pastries because it makes pastries based on standard ingredients flakier. Chilling allows the fat to firm up, but this doesn't happen with oil, so I omit that extra step. If my flours and oil are in the fridge, I use them cold, but if they're on the counter due to use or because I just brought them home from the market, I use them at room temperature. I once made two pastries, one with cold ingredients and one with room temperature ingredients. There were no noticeable differences in appearance, texture, or taste. Both were great—light, flaky, and rich tasting. Be sure not to use chilled wet sweeteners or you will need to exert much effort in working the thick sticky mass into the dough. Store them in the pantry.

Rolling out the dough between sheets of waxed paper (or parchment) works better for most people than does rolling on a floured surface or a pastry cloth, especially for people who are unfamiliar with pastry making. With waxed paper you can relax, knowing the pastry will roll out successfully every time. Waxed paper requires a generous sprinkling of flour on the bottom sheet and on top of the dough to allow the dough to roll, while parchment calls for the smallest bit. With rolling, replenish the flour on both sides when you notice it's vanished; flip the pastry over, peel off the paper, and sprinkle on more flour.

In contrast to traditional pastries based on hard fats, balls of dough made with oil do not roll out easily after either refrigeration or freezing. However, rolled dough that has been set in place in the pan may be refrigerated or frozen until you are ready to use it. Wrap in a loose plastic bag to avoid damaging the edge, then seal.

The technique of placing a handful of uncooked beans over the pastry to prevent puffing is unnecessary because, even when this happens, which is rarely, the dough falls back in place soon after baking. I usually omit the other technique of poking the pastry with the tines of a fork for the same purpose because sometimes the holes remain after baking, allowing wet filling ingredients to seep through.

Press a cookie cutter in the center of the top crust for decoration and to mark a place to check for doneness. For a whimsical effect, animal cookie cutters such as a large goose, a duck, or a butterfly are pretty as well as fun. Bake the pie until you no longer see the thickener—arrowroot powder, tapioca flour, or wheat flour—on the fruit. This shows the fruit has softened and released its juices enough to be absorbed by the thickener.

Another way to make top pie crusts with cute designs is the Pie Topper, a plastic dish with designs stamped in it such as hearts, apples, or Christmas trees. Roll the dough over the dish and it punches out the design. Or cut out appropriate seasonal or holiday designs with cookie cutters and bake them separately to place on individual servings of a single-crust pie for decoration.

I prefer using three strips of foil over pie crust shields for preventing the rim from burning.

Roll extra pie dough thin for cookie-crackers. Sprinkle the dough with flavorful seeds (sesame, sunflower, pumpkin, cumin, or anise), other seasonings (cinnamon or nutmeg, herbs, or salt and pepper), or nutmeal (toasted and ground pecans, walnuts, almonds, or hazelnuts). Cut the dough with a knife or a pastry wheel—its wavy design lends a pretty effect—or with cookie cutters. Bake the crackers along with the pie, but check them in 5 to 8 minutes; they may take 12 to 15 minutes to bake completely, depending on the thickness.

I'll never forget the pastry crackers our acupuncturist-M.D. friend Michael Volen used to make for us when we visited him at his home. Michael loved to make summer fruit pies from the trees in his orchard. He would make extra pastry, which he rolled out and transferred whole to a baking sheet. We would sit around the kitchen table talking, laughing and breaking off pieces of the giant cracker until it was a memory. Then we ate the pie.

SWEETENERS

IMPORTANT NOTE: While brown rice malt syrup or pure maple syrup are most often called for as sweeteners, the enzyme-treated rice syrups work if you simmer the desired amount in a small saucepan for 5 minutes before use to inactivate the enzymes. Without this step, the pie will taste great but often the juices won't thicken and the texture will be watery. After heating the rice syrup, gingerly drizzle and immediately stir it into the filling ingredients when it is still warm to prevent lumping or hardening into a taffy consistency upon contact with cool or room temperature fruit. Even if this should happen, the syrup will melt again with baking and then thicken into a sauce, offering good flavor. Also, in comparison with the other sweeteners, enzyme-converted rice syrups leave a dull sheen on some fruits such as the Fresh Blueberry Pie.

Both FruitSource sweeteners, granular and the syrup, are included in some of these pie recipes. It is not absolutely clear to me why these sweeteners are not consistent in their ability to set up. For instance, in the Fresh Blueberry Pie recipe the syrup fails to thicken into a sauce or to solidify into a gelled pie filling that can be cut and served. This is true even when the lemon juice is omitted and the sweetener is not cooked, but simply folded in with the other filling ingredients. On the other hand, the syrup sets up nicely in the Mango-Key Lime Pie filling, where it is not cooked with the starch. Granular FruitSource works beautifully in the Free-Form Berry Pie, the Bramble Berry Pie, and in the Blueberry Nut Crumb Pie.

Single-Crust Pastry 1 and Tart Pastry with Glaze

¾ cup whole wheat pastry flour

¾ cup unbleached white flour

⅛ teaspoon sea salt

¼ cup light vegetable oil (walnut, canola, sesame, almond, sunflower, safflower, etc.)

Up to ¼ cup wet or dry sweetener, e.g. 1 to 4 tablespoons brown rice syrup, FruitSource syrup, pure maple syrup, barley malt, sorghum syrup or honey; or granular FruitSource, maple syrup granules, or evaporated sugar cane juice (optional)

Up to ½ cup water, apple juice or cider, or soy milk, less (none to ¼ cup) with wet sweeteners, more (¼ to ½ cup) with dry sweeteners

Glaze (optional)

Pastries are sometimes brushed with milk or egg wash for a shiny surface. This new glaze creates a golden sheen. Glazing the pie before it is baked is not as effective as doing so toward the end of baking because the glaze virtually disappears.

Alternately, dry sweeteners may be sprinkled on the pastry after brushing it with soy milk or water so they stick. As with the wet sweeteners, do this at the end of baking. The nicest looking ones are organic sugar crystals and granular FruitSource. Maple syrup granules and evaporated sugar cane juice are too dark and don't melt properly for this purpose.

1 tablespoon brown rice syrup or FruitSource syrup

1 teaspoon water

1. Preheat the oven to 350°F.

2. Mix the dry ingredients—flours, salt, and dry sweetener if included. Stir in the oil until lumps or beads of dough form, or until it resembles coarse meal. Add wet sweetener if desired—be sure the syrups are at room temperature for ease in handling—then add the liquid (water, juice, or soy milk) gradually. Mix quickly until you have a somewhat soft, pliable ball in the center of the bowl. Add a little more flour if necessary.

Gather the dough together with your hands and lightly form it into a smooth flattened disk. The mixture can be rough, not fully mixed, so that the dough appears marbled when it's rolled out, indicating that the crust will be flaky.

I sometimes use a food processor to make the pastries for several pies consecutively. To do this, place the dry ingredients in the container and pulse a few times to mix. Add the oil and pulse briefly, then the sweetener. Pulse again. Add the liquid gradually. Work quickly, taking care not to overmix and thereby toughen the dough.

3. Roll dough in a circular shape between sheets of waxed paper; sprinkle flour over the bottom sheet and on top of the dough. Use light, short strokes in the beginning, starting from the center outward in each direction. You may choose to rotate or spin the dough around to do this. Then use longer strokes, applying more pressure to ensure an even crust.

4. Peel off the top piece of waxed paper and invert rolled dough into oiled pan—an oiled 8-, 9-, 10-, or 11-inch pie or tart pan. Peel off other layer of waxed paper. With your fingers or scissors, trim off the excess dough to within a finger's width of the rim, leaving enough to fold over toward the inside of the pan to form a rim. If the dough tears, patch it with a small disk of dough—the reliable cut-and-paste technique.

5. For a pie, crimp the edges by pressing dough between the fingertips (thumbs and forefingers) of both hands. Use the thumb and first finger of your left hand to hold the edge of the crust and push the thumb or the right index finger between these two fingers toward the center of the pie. Or simply score the edges with a fork. Continue rotating the pan as you go.

For a tart, press the folded dough against the flutes (the scalloped edges) of the pan.

6. To refrigerate the dough for future use, roll it out and shape it in the pie pan and wrap it in plastic to store for several hours or overnight, or freeze it.

Otherwise, bake the pastry, alone or filled, in the bottom third of the oven until just about done, 12 to 20 minutes alone or with a precooked filling, 15 to 90 minutes with an uncooked filling.

7. If desired, mix the glaze ingredients and brush over the rim of the pastry, starting from the inside edge. Take care not to let glaze run be-

tween rim and pan where it could stick. Return the pie to the oven until golden, about 5 minutes more.

Variations

Nutted Pastries (e.g. **Hazelnut Pastry, Walnut Pastry,** or **Pecan** or **Almond Nut Crust**): Add ¼ to ½ cup nutmeal—nuts toasted, then finely ground in a food processor or blender, or finely chopped. Nuts must have a powdery consistency or they will tear the pastry. See page 241 for a guide to cooking times for toasting nuts and seeds.

Vanilla-Nut Pastry: Add 1½ teaspoons vanilla.

Spiced Pastries: For apple pies, add at least 1 teaspoon spices such as cinnamon, nutmeg, and ginger or cardamom.

Lemon or Orange Pastry: Include the zest and juice of half a lemon or half an orange, substituting the juice for that amount of water or other liquid in the pastry.

New Classic Tart Pastry/Sweet Nutted Tart Pastry: Based on the French pâte sucrée, make the pastry a sweet cookie-like dough by including the largest amount of sweetener called for in the recipe, e.g. ¼ cup wet or dry sweetener. This volume is less than in a traditional tart pastry, and is still plenty sweet. Nuts may also be included.

Single-Crust Cutout Pastry: Pinch off a quarter of the dough for making pastry cutouts. Roll out the bigger portion for the bottom crust and transfer it to the lightly oiled pie plate.

Roll out the other portion of dough and, with cookie cutters, cut out 10 shapes, one for each serving, or enough shapes to partially cover the surface of the filling. Bake cutouts on a parchment-lined baking sheet and arrange on filling after pie is baked. A medium-large autumn leaf cutter is delightful used this way. Arrange the cutouts in different directions like falling leaves. (See the photograph.)

Or place smaller cutouts such as leaves or hearts on the rim of the pastry, overlapping them for a decorative effect. For this you'll need to keep the rim flat, simply folded over and pressed thin.

Baking Powder Leavened Pastry: Add ½ teaspoon aluminum-free baking powder for a slightly more buoyant pastry.

Wheat-Alternative Pastry: Both whole grain and white spelt flours stand in very nicely for whole wheat pastry flour and white wheat flour.

Wheat-Free Pastry: All of the other flours make a decent pastry that will shape and roll out easily. However, with the exception of rye flour, the other flours are difficult to flute. The solution to this is to form the dough in a tart pan where you can simply press the dough against the sides of the pan to shape the rim. In addition to rye, other flours to use include oat, barley, and buckwheat (you may need to double the volume of water).

Gluten-Free Pastry: Chestnut flour has a wonderful sweet taste. Sift it first. Other flours include rice, millet, and quinoa. Rice and millet flours require more water.

Single-Crust Pastry 2 and Lattice Pastry with Glaze

1 cup whole wheat pastry flour

1 cup unbleached white flour

¼ teaspoon sea salt

⅓ cup light vegetable oil (walnut, canola, sesame, almond, sunflower, safflower, etc.)

Up to ⅓ cup wet or dry sweetener, e.g. 1 to 5 tablespoons brown rice syrup,
    FruitSource syrup, pure maple syrup, barley malt, sorghum syrup, or honey;
    or granular FruitSource, maple syrup granules, or evaporated sugar cane
    juice (optional)

Up to ½ cup water, apple juice or cider, or soy milk, less (none to ¼ cup) with
    wet sweeteners, more (⅓ to ½ cup) with dry sweeteners

Glaze *(optional)*

2 tablespoons brown rice syrup or FruitSource syrup

2 teaspoons water

1. Preheat the oven to 350°F.

2. Mix the flours with the salt. Stir in the oil until lumps or beads of dough form, or until it resembles coarse meal. Add some sweetener if desired—be sure the syrups are at room temperature for ease in handling—then add the liquid gradually. Mix quickly until you have a somewhat soft, pliable ball in the center of the bowl. Add a little more flour if necessary.

3. Gather the dough together with your hands and lightly form it into a flattened disk. Prepare as Single-Crust Pastry I or as lattice pastry. For the latter, divide dough into two portions, two thirds for bottom crust and one third for lattice.

4. Roll both portions of dough in circular shapes between sheets of waxed paper; sprinkle flour over bottom sheet and on top of dough.

5. For shell, peel off top piece of waxed paper and invert rolled dough into an oiled 8-, 9-, 10-, or 11-inch pie or tart pan. Peel off other layer of waxed paper. With your fingers or scissors, trim off the excess dough to within a finger's width of the rim, leaving enough to fold over toward the inside of the pan to form a rim. If the dough tears, patch it with a small disk of dough. Fill.

6. Roll out and cut the smaller portion of dough into 8, 10, 12, or 14 strips, ½ to 1 inch wide. Use a knife or a pastry wheel for a wavy design. Lay the strips over the filling, half in one direction. Interlace or weave the remaining strips in the other direction, perpendicular or at an angle from the first set of strips. Trim strips even with pastry shell edges. Fold edges up over strips, roll edges, and crimp.

7. Bake the pastry until done. If desired, mix the glaze ingredients and brush over the rim and latticework. Return the pie to the oven until golden, about 5 minutes more.

Variations

Twisted Lattice Pastry: Twist each strip just before you lay it down. There's no need to interlace these strips.

See the variations for the Single-Crust Pastry on page 98. Volumes may remain the same or may be increased slightly.

Double-Crust Pastry with Glaze

1½ cups whole wheat pastry flour

1½ cups unbleached white flour

¼ teaspoon sea salt

½ cup light vegetable oil (walnut, canola, sesame, almond, sunflower, safflower, etc.)

Up to ½ cup wet or dry sweetener (brown rice syrup, FruitSource syrup, pure maple syrup, barley malt, sorghum syrup, or honey; or granular FruitSource, maple syrup granules, or evaporated sugar cane juice), optional

Up to 1 cup water, apple juice, or cider, less (none to ½ cup) with wet sweeteners, more (½ or 1 cup) with dry sweeteners

Glaze (optional)

2 tablespoons brown rice syrup or FruitSource syrup

2 teaspoons water

For 10 servings, per serving:

Calories: 211

Protein: 3g

Saturated Fat: 1g

Fiber: 0.03g

Carbohydrate: 25g

Fat: 11g

Cholesterol: 0

Sodium: 54mg

Calories from Carbohydrate: 47%

Calories from Fat: 48%

Calories from Protein: 5%

1. Preheat the oven to 350°F.

2. Mix the dry ingredients. Stir in the oil, then the sweetener. Add the liquid gradually to form a pliable dough.

3. Divide the dough in half and roll out each half separately between sheets of waxed paper. Lay the bottom pastry in place and trim the pastry so it barely extends over the rim of an oiled 9- or 10-inch pie pan. Fill the pie. Invert the top crust onto filled pie shell. Trim the top pastry so it extends ½ inch beyond the rim of the pan. Fold excess top pastry under the bottom pastry to form a rim. Crimp or flute with your fingers or press with a fork to seal. With a fork or knife, poke holes in the top crust to serve as air vents.

4. For a pie with a precooked filling, bake the pie until the top and edges of the crust are golden brown, 15 to 25 minutes. Let the pie cool for at least an hour before serving for the filling to firm up.

For a pie with an uncooked fruit filling, cover the rim with foil. Place a baking sheet or a piece of foil on the shelf under the pie pan to catch any dripping juices.

Bake until the juices bubble and come up through the air vents, 45 to 75 minutes. Remove the foil. If desired, glaze the surface and rim and return the pie to the oven for 5 minutes more. Transfer to a rack to cool.

Variations

Double-Crust Cutout Pastry: For decorative air vents, press a cookie cutter through the dough in the center of the pie or to mark individual serving portions. This is best done when the dough is rolled out on the waxed paper.

See the variations for the Single-Crust Pastry on page 98, doubling ingredients.

PHYLLO PASTRY

Old-world phyllo is a fragile, tissue-thin strudel-like pastry dough made of high-gluten flour, water, a dash of salt, and in some instances, a small amount of oil. Most of us know phyllo by its use in baklava, the flaky, moist, and crunchy Middle Eastern confection. Phyllo originated in Turkey more than five hundred years ago.

Whole wheat phyllo is available in well-stocked natural foods supermarkets. The one I use (Papa Cristo's; see Resources) contains enriched wheat flour, whole wheat flour, water, cornstarch, vegetable oil, and salt.

Both brands of phyllo found in most supermarkets, Apollo and Athens Foods Fillo Doughs, contain these ingredients: enriched, non-bromine bleached wheat flour (malted barley flour, niacin, iron, thiamin mononitrate, riboflavin), water, cornstarch; and may contain 2 percent or less of the following: vegetable oil (corn and/or soybean), salt, potassium chloride, preservatives (sodium and/or calcium propionate, potassium sorbate), xanthan gum, and citric acid.

BAKING WITH PHYLLO

The best phyllo to work with is the flexible and moist refrigerated fresh phyllo from a Middle Eastern or an Italian deli. But most of us must rely on frozen phyllo dough. Don't worry if the layers stick together in places, making them a bit difficult to separate, or if they tear. You will use about four layers, and by the time the layers are set in place with the filling, small tears will either not show at all or will appear crispy with baking. If you are making several pastries, buy two packages of phyllo to be sure you'll have enough.

One must be organized and work quickly with phyllo. Keep the remaining pieces covered with a dry kitchen towel to keep them from drying out. A dampened towel may cause them to stick together.

Oil may be substituted for butter with good results. In fact, some chefs have noticed that baked phyllo stays crisp a lot longer when brushed with oil instead of butter.

Some chefs prefer to cut down on the volume of oil by using nonstick cooking spray. The most popular of these aerosol spray oils is PAM. PAM contains canola oil, grain alcohol from corn, lecithin from soybeans, and propellant. This is a wonderful idea except for the aerosol design, which is linked to destroying the planet's ozone layer. Try a nonaerosol alternative (such as California Naturals' Eco Pump). Fill it with your favorite oil and pump the cap.

PUFF PASTRY

I prefer phyllo dough to puff pastry because of its more healthful ingredients. Freshly made puff pastry may contain flour, butter, water, and salt, and sometimes milk and eggs. Commercially available Pepperidge Farm Puff Pastry contains unbleached wheat flour, partially hydrogenated vegetable shortening (soybean and cottonseed oils colored with beta carotene), water, salt, corn syrup, and mono and diglycerides.

APPLE PIES AND TARTS

And every seed I sow
Will grow into a tree
And someday there'll be apples there
For everyone in the world to share.

—*J. APPLESEED*

In a cookbook that celebrates the bounty of the seasons, it seems fitting to start this chapter with some discussion of the premier fruit of the fall and winter seasons and a fruit that is such a keeper it is also available year-round, the all-American apple. The complex of acidity, sweetness, and bitterness, together with the scent, makes up the flavor of the fruit. The texture of the flesh may be soft and mealy, or hard and crisp.

Apples are the most important and most widely cultivated fruits of the temperate regions, successful in a wide range of climates and soils. They have been grown for at least three thousand years, and are valued especially for their good keeping qualities. Until the twentieth century, hardly any other fresh fruit was available in winter.

Charcoal remains of apples have been found by scientists in the ruins of Stone Age villages in Europe. By the 300s B.C., the Greeks were growing several varieties. Ancient Romans spread various kinds of apples throughout much of England and other parts of Europe. The early American colonists brought both apple seeds and trees from England. The first recorded apple orchard was planted in what is now Boston's Beacon Hill in 1625. The settlers dried their apples or used them in making cider or apple butter. They saw that the Indians had already brought seeds from trees in the East and had planted them around their villages. From Europe and North America the seeds traveled to the southern hemisphere, India, China, and Japan.

All our cultivated apples were parented by the wild crab apple (*malus pumila,* a member of the rose family), which is native to southeastern Europe and southwestern Asia according to *Encyclopedia Brittanica.* And the handbook *Fruit Trees and Shrubs* says all apples with fruits two inches or less in diameter are classified as crab apples.

In the United States, more than 80 percent of the apples are used as fresh fruit; 10 percent of the crop is used for vinegar, juice, jelly, and apple butter. Another 10 percent is canned as pie stock and applesauce.

Apples provide about 100 calories per large fruit. They consist of 85 percent water and contain vitamins A and C as well as potassium and pectin.

Today, of the thousand apple varieties in cultivation in America, only twenty make up 75 percent of our nation's crop with Red Delicious accounting for 20 percent of the total production, followed by McIntosh, Winesap, Jonathan, Rome Beauty, and Stayman. Some of the earlier apples have been revitalized as heirlooms.

The best time to buy apples is in the late summer and autumn, when harvesting occurs and they are most fresh, firm, and fragrant. As for classifying them according to use (eating, baking, cooking, and all-purpose), experts disagree on several counts. In general, eating apples are crisper and sweeter than cooking apples. Rome apples are generally favored for baking and Gravenstein apples for both eating fresh out of hand or for use in cooking. All that considered, I've never served an apple dessert everyone didn't eat, even when a pie filling came out a little tarter or softer than usual because I tried a different variety or used whatever type was available organically grown, sometimes using a combination.

Like no other dessert, apple pie has earned a special place on our tables as well as in our hearts. The quintessential American dessert for generations, apple pie is presented in each of the following recipes with a distinctive twist.

Classic Apple Pie

Calories: 384

Protein: 3g

Saturated Fat: 1g

Fiber: 3g

Carbohydrate: 68g

Fat: 12g

Cholesterol: 0

Sodium: 110mg

Calories from

Carbohydrate: 69%

Calories from Fat: 28%

Calories from Protein: 3%

History tells us that the most patriotic of American desserts evolved from the "Olde English pyes," early creations that had thick crusts and heavy fillings of meat and dried fruit. The early American colonists put salt pork and sugar in their apple pies and lots of shortening in the crust. It was our Pennsylvania Dutch ancestors who perfected the classic apple pie as we know it today.

We've come a long way from the simplicity of those early days. For example, on a recent visit to a supermarket I jotted down the ingredients in Mrs. Smith's apple pie: apples, water, wheat flour, corn syrup, lard, sugar, and margarine (partially hydrogenated soybean oil and/or lard, water, salt, may contain nonfat dry milk, lecithin, mono- and diglycerides, sodium benzoate, BHT or citric acid, preservative, artificial color and flavor, vitamin A palmitate). And although apple pie has a natural image, commercial apple pie may have twice as much fat and twice as many calories as French fries, and a higher dose of both than even chocolate cake because of the fat in the crust.

Here's a recipe for real old-fashioned apple pie. Favorite pie apples, alone or in combination, are Granny Smith, Pippin, Golden Delicious (which soften faster and more completely than Granny Smith), Rome, and McIntosh, but good pies can also be made with Gala, Spartan, Gravenstein, Jonathan, Jonagold, Braeburn, and Winesap.

This recipe appeared in MacroChef *magazine, Fall 1994.*

Filling

3 pounds apples, 6 to 8 apples or about 9 cups, peeled
  and sliced (each half cut into eighths)

¼ cup arrowroot powder

1 teaspoon cinnamon

½ teaspoon nutmeg

¼ teaspoon sea salt

¾ cup brown rice malt syrup, or part pure maple syrup

1 tablespoon lemon juice

Double-Crust Pastry with Glaze (see page 101)

1. Preheat the oven to 350°F. Brush a 9- or 10-inch pie plate with oil.

2. To prepare the filling, in a large bowl, mix apples with dry ingredients, then mix in wet ingredients.

3. Prepare the pastry and fill. Poke air vents in the top pastry with a fork, or cut the words "Apple Pie" into the pastry with a sharp knife. To prevent excessive browning, cover the rim with foil. Place a baking sheet or a piece of foil on the shelf under the pie pan to catch dripping juices.

4. Bake the pie until the fruit tests tender when pierced with a small sharp knife, 50 to 90 minutes, depending on apples. Remove the foil. If desired, mix the glaze ingredients and brush it over the surface and rim of the pie. Return the pie to the oven for 5 to 10 minutes more. Or brush crust lightly with water or soy milk and sprinkle with a tablespoon of organic sugar crystals.

5. Transfer pie to a rack to cool for at least 1 hour before serving for the juices to become saucy. If desired, serve with a scoop of vanilla nondairy ice cream.

Variations

Vermont Apple Pie: For the sweet tooth, include pure maple syrup for the sweetener in both the filling and the pastry.

Sweetener-Free Apple Pie: Substitute thawed apple juice concentrate for sweetener in filling and pastry. Or include ½ to 1 cup raisins with ½ cup apple juice or cider in place of sweetener.

Apple-Berry Pie in Double-Crust Cutout Pastry (see page 102): Berries make a striking contrast in color, shape, and flavor to the apples in this pie. Raspberries are available through the early fall season when apples are in their prime.

Include a pint basket of berries (red raspberries, huckleberries, etc.) and ½ teaspoon combined nutmeg, mace, and cardamom in addition to cinnamon. Gently fold berries into apple mixture last to retain their shapes.

Deep-Dish Apple Pie with Streusel Topping

Calories: 267

Protein: 2g

Saturated Fat: 1g

Fiber: 3g

Carbohydrate: 46g

Fat: 9g

Cholesterol: 0

Sodium: 136mg

Calories from
Carbohydrate: 67%

Calories from Fat: 30%

Calories from Protein: 4%

This scrumptious pie features a precooked filling and a streusel topping. This combination of apples is especially nice to use in precooked fillings because the shapes hold up well.

Dry sweeteners burn easily when they melt in the pan over direct heat, even with oil, but when sprinkled over hot cooked fruit and simply covered as in this recipe, they melt nicely.

Deep-dish pie pans vary in shape and size, so feel free to improvise with whatever dish works for holding an especially abundant volume of fruit. A 9½-inch deep-dish glass pie pan with a 2-inch-high rim works nicely. (Most pie pans are 9 or 10 inches wide and have a rim that is 1½ inches high.)

Filling

2 tablespoons light vegetable oil (walnut, canola, etc.)

4 pounds combined Granny Smith and Golden Delicious
    or Pippin apples, 12 cups, peeled and sliced

½ teaspoon sea salt

1 cup dry sweetener (granular FruitSource and/or maple syrup granules
    or evaporated sugar cane juice)

1 teaspoon cinnamon

1 teaspoon nutmeg

½ teaspoon cardamom, or ¼ teaspoon each cardamom and coriander

Zest of a lemon

2 teaspoons vanilla

Single-Crust Pastry with Glaze (see page 96)

Streusel Topping

½ cup whole wheat pastry flour

½ cup unbleached white flour

¼ cup dry sweetener

Pinch of sea salt

¼ cup light vegetable oil

¼ cup pecans, toasted and chopped

1. Preheat the oven to 350°F. Brush a deep-dish pie pan with oil.

2. To make the filling, heat the oil in a large pot. Add the apples and sprinkle them with salt. Cover to cook over medium-low heat until fruit is barely tender and holds its shape, about 10 minutes, stirring occasionally.

3. Sprinkle sweetener and seasonings over apples—do not stir—and cover to cook until sweetener has melted and apples are completely tender, about 5 minutes more. Stir gently.

4. Prepare the pastry and crimp the edges. Prebake it for 10 minutes.

5. Mix topping ingredients, except nuts, until crumbly. This is most easily done by rubbing mixture between your palms. Add a little more flour if necessary. Toss in nuts.

6. Transfer filling to pie shell. Sprinkle topping over filling.

7. Bake pie until topping and crust are golden, 15 to 20 minutes. Glaze the rim in the last 5 minutes of baking, if desired.

Variation

Substitute 2 teaspoons Chinese five-spice powder for seasonings listed.

Apple Strudel

Makes 4 to 8 servings

Strudels come in many shapes: a rectangle folded in three sections like a sheet of paper ready to insert in an envelope; rolled in a tubular shape; or cut and shaped to look braided or latticed like this one. My Austrian friend Vilma says you must have bread crumbs in a proper strudel, and the pastry must be very thin to be delicate and crisp. Apple strudel also makes a nice breakfast pastry.

Filling

1¼ pounds Pippin apples, about 4½ cups, peeled and thinly sliced

¼ cup currants (optional)

¼ cup walnuts, toasted and finely chopped

3 tablespoons dry sweetener (granular FruitSource)

2 tablespoons whole wheat bread crumbs

Calories: 268

Protein: 3g

Saturated Fat: 1g

Fiber: 2g

Carbohydrate: 39g

Fat: 12g

Cholesterol: 0

Sodium: 107mg

Calories from Carbohydrate: 56%

Calories from Fat: 39%

Calories from Protein: 5%

1 teaspoon cinnamon

1 teaspoon minced orange zest

⅛ teaspoon sea salt

Lattice Pastry (see page 100)

1. Preheat the oven to 350°F. Line a baking sheet with parchment or lightly brush with oil.

2. Mix the filling ingredients reserving 1 tablespoon sweetener to sprinkle on top later.

3. Prepare the pastry. Roll it out to a large, thin rectangle between sheets of waxed paper. Transfer pastry to the baking sheet so you don't have to move it later after it's filled. Trim the edges by cutting along the inside edge of the baking sheet with a knife, or use a pastry wheel for wavy or zigzag edges.

N O T E

Should you decide to use a combination of apples such as Granny Smith and Rome Beauty, add 2 tablespoons more sweetener to enrich the taste of the blander Romes.

4. Arrange the filling lengthwise on the central one third of the dough. Cut the side portions of dough into 1-inch strips on the diagonal with a knife or pastry wheel. Fold these strips over the filling, alternating one side and then the other in crisscross fashion.

5. Cover pastry with foil and bake until fruit is soft when tested with a thin sharp knife and you can hear and see the juices, 40 to 50 minutes. Remove foil and sprinkle the top with reserved tablespoon dry sweetener. Return to oven until golden brown, 10 minutes more.

Variation

Apple Strudel in Phyllo: Prepare the filling with 1½ times the volume of ingredients. You may choose to presoak the currants in rum.

Very lightly brush or spray 4 layers of phyllo dough (made from either whole wheat or white flour) with light vegetable oil; you'll need 2 to 3 tablespoons for brushing. Layer sheets on top of each other. Shape strudel letter-style or in a roll.

For letter-style, place the filling lengthwise across the middle of the dough and fold both shorter sides in toward the center. Fold the long edges over on top of each other. Turn package over so the seam side is down.

For a roll shape, place the filling across the end of the dough nearest you, then roll it up. Arrange the package seam side down. In either case, brush the surface with oil and score it in 2- or 3-inch sections. Sprinkle with sweetener. Cover strudel lightly with foil and bake until fruit is soft, 30 to 40 minutes depending on variety of apples. Remove foil and bake for 5 minutes more, if desired.

Nouvelle Tarte Tatin

Makes 8 to 10 servings

Calories: 350

Protein: 4g

Saturated Fat: 1g

Fiber: 4g

Carbohydrate: 63g

Fat: 10g

Cholesterol: 0

Sodium: 38mg

Calories from

Carbohydrate: 71%

Calories from Fat: 25%

Calories from Protein: 4%

Tarte Tatin (pronounced tah-TAN) is a caramelized upside-down apple tart. A creative variation on the apple pie theme, it's relatively easy to make.

This recipe is adapted from a classic tarte Tatin recipe by Anne Willan, founder and president of L'Ecole de Cuisine La Varenne in Burgundy, France, and at The Greenbrier in West Virginia. The recipe appeared in the magazine Taunton's Fine Cooking.

As the story goes, more than a hundred years ago the Tatin sisters made a business of baking the apple dessert their beloved and deceased father had enjoyed so much. They ran the Hotel Tatin in the tiny railroad junction of Lamotte-Beauvron in Sologne near Orléans in central France, where you can still enjoy tarte Tatin today.

The French use a specially designed copper pan lined with tin or stainless steel, but an ovenproof skillet works nicely as well. The principal technique is to cook firm apples in a buttery caramel made with generous amounts of sugar cooked with butter—actually a butterscotch—so the flavor penetrates the apples and they are almost candied on the outside.

Golden Delicious is the traditional apple of choice because it is firm enough to retain its shape with cooking. Granny Smith is the next most popular apple for this dessert, and Willan also suggests Braeburn, Jonathan, and Jonagold varieties.

To make the caramel with more natural sugars, I tried both granular FruitSource and maple syrup granules, but both tasted burnt.

The original filling calls for ½ cup butter (¼ pound) and 1 to 1½ cups sugar. The pastry usually called for is a puff pastry, or a pâte brisée in the La Varenne recipe consisting of 1½ cups flour, 5 tablespoons butter, 1 egg yolk, 2 tablespoons sugar, ½ teaspoon salt, and water. The basic Single-Crust Pastry works very nicely here with less overall fat and no cholesterol.

Filling

4 pounds Golden Delicious apples, 8 or 9 apples, peeled

2 tablespoons light vegetable oil (walnut, canola, etc.)

¾ cup FruitSource syrup or brown rice syrup or part pure maple syrup

Juice of half a lemon, about 2 tablespoons

Single-Crust Pastry (see page 96)

Tofu Chantilly Cream (makes 1 cup)

The traditional version of this recipe consists of whipped cream flavored with sugar and vanilla or brandy.

½ pound tofu, fresh, medium or silken/soft

¼ cup pure maple syrup

2 tablespoons brandy

1½ teaspoons vanilla

1. Core the apples, or to continue the nice generous round shape of the apples, follow the La Varenne technique. Use a melon baller to scoop out the ends. Halve the apples and core them with the melon baller.

2. To caramelize apples, heat the oil, sweetener, and juice in a large ovenproof skillet (9 to 11 inches in diameter). Stand the apples upright and pack them tightly in the pan in concentric circles starting from the outside. If you have too much or too little space in the pan, tuck in or take out an apple. They will shrink. Once the liquids start bubbling, cook uncovered over medium-low heat so the juices that come from the apples combine with the caramel ingredients and apples start to soften, about 20 minutes. Turn apples upside down and continue cooking until apples are tender and juice has evaporated somewhat, perhaps 20 minutes more. (Apples will caramelize more with baking.) Allow apples to cool to lukewarm while you prepare the pastry.

3. Preheat the oven to 350°F. Include maximum amount of sweetener (¼ cup) in pastry. Roll the pastry a little thicker than normal, perhaps ⅛ inch thick. With scissors, trim the pastry ½ inch larger than the pan. Transfer pastry to the pan to cover the apples and, with the help of a rubber spatula, tuck edges down around apples. Brush inner rim of pan with oil to prevent sticking. Bake tart until pastry is lightly browned, 25 to 30 minutes.

4. Allow tart to cool for an hour before turning it out. This time allows the juices to thicken further and to be reabsorbed by the apples and the pastry.

5. To unmold the tart, first run a sharp knife around the edge to be sure pastry is separate from pan. Place a large platter over the top crust and skillet and quickly flip both over. Lift the skillet. Scoop and re-arrange any apples that stick to the pan. (This is unlikely.) Voila! C'est magnifique!

6. To make Tofu Chantilly Cream, purée ingredients until silky smooth.

7. Serve tart as is, with a generous drizzle of the cream, or à la mode with vanilla nondairy ice cream.

Variation

With sliced apples, total cooking time is still about ½ hour over medium heat.

OTHER FRESH FRUIT PIES AND TARTS

It seems fitting to start this section with an easy tart that's a joy to make any time. Galettes are French country-style pies with free-form pastries that don't need to be shaped or fluted. Rather, the rolled pastry is simply flipped or folded over the fruit. Galettes can also be easily prepared in phyllo dough, as you can see in the recipe for Pear Tart in Phyllo Pastry.

I tried both wet and dry sweeteners for this recipe. The free-form shape definitely calls for a dry sweetener as wet ones soften the dough and cause the filling to leak through the pastry. Choose granular FruitSource or maple syrup granules for the filling for these tarts. Both sweeteners melt to a pretty bright color with a nice light sweetness. Evaporated sugar cane juice melts to look like molasses, making it unattractive for use in a tart, and the taste is overpowering, canceling out the more delicate fruit flavors.

The recipe for a new version of classic fresh fruit tarts is great, but more time-consuming and inappropriate for the novice or weekend baker who just wants to make an exquisitely simple, tasty dessert that celebrates the season.

Free-Form Berry Pie

Filling

½ cup dry sweetener (granular FruitSource or maple syrup granules)

2 tablespoons arrowroot powder

Pinch of sea salt

3 cups assorted berries, such as blackberries, blueberries, and
raspberries, about 1 pound

Single-Crust Pastry with Glaze (see page 96)

1. Preheat the oven to 350°F. Line a baking sheet with parchment or lightly brush with oil.

2. Mix dry ingredients for filling. Rinse and drain berries in a strainer, then transfer to a towel and carefully blot dry. Leave dry ingredients and berries separate until pastry is ready, to avoid sweetener clumping on moist berries.

3. Make pastry, including sweetener. A texture that is supple and moist works best. Roll pastry out to a thin circle and transfer to baking sheet.

4. Gently mix dry filling ingredients and berries with a rubber spatula. Distribute fruit evenly over pastry, leaving a 2-inch border around the perimeter. Fold pastry border over filling to form a pleated ruffle effect like a drawstring purse that is open in the middle.

5. Bake until fruit is juicy and pastry is done, about 20 minutes. To glaze pastry, brush surface with 2 teaspoons oil, then sprinkle with 2 teaspoons granular FruitSource, or brush surface with a glaze made with FruitSource syrup (or brown rice syrup) diluted with a little water. Either way, return to oven for 5 minutes more.

6. Transfer baking sheet to a cooling rack and allow to cool for at least 15 minutes. Using a cake lifter or 2 large spatulas, move pastry to a serving platter or cutting board.

Variations

Fig and Berry Galette: Substitute fresh figs, quartered, for some of the berries. Mission figs are beautiful with their dark purple skins around the rosy red flesh.

Calories: 222

Protein: 2g

Saturated Fat: 1g

Fiber: 3g

Carbohydrate: 38g

Fat: 7g

Cholesterol: 0

Sodium: 49mg

Calories from

Carbohydrate: 67%

Calories from Fat: 29%

Calories from Protein: 4%

N O T E

Should you find golden raspberries, which are less acidic and more delicate than red raspberries, sprinkle a few on top just before serving to preserve their beautiful color and shape.

Peach and Berry Galette: Substitute peaches, sliced, for some of the berries.

Fresh Plum Galette

Makes 8 to 10 servings

The idea for this galette comes from our local newspaper. The fat and calories are cut in half in this version. Please note that this pie filling did not thicken when sweetened with granular FruitSource.

Single-Crust Pastry (see page 96)

Calories: 239

Protein: 4g

Saturated Fat: 1g

Fiber: 2g

Carbohydrate: 42g

Fat: 8g

Cholesterol: 0

Sodium: 34mg

Calories from Carbohydrate: 68%

Calories from Fat: 28%

Calories from Protein: 4%

Filling

2½ pounds plums, 6 to 7 cups, cut into quarters or eighths, depending on size

Zest and juice of half a lemon

⅔ cup maple syrup granules or evaporated sugar cane juice

3 tablespoons arrowroot powder

½ teaspoon cinnamon

⅛ teaspoon each cloves and nutmeg

¼ teaspoon sea salt

Topping

1 tablespoon light vegetable oil (e.g. walnut, almond, canola)

1 tablespoon granular FruitSource

1. Preheat the oven to 350°F. Brush a 9-inch pie pan with oil.
2. Prepare the pastry, adding baking powder as in the variation. Transfer pastry to pan. Leave the overhang as is or trim edge even with scissors.
3. In a large bowl, mix fruit with lemon. In a smaller bowl, mix dry filling ingredients, then gently toss with fruit. Mound filling onto pastry and flip overhang up over the plums. Brush top of pastry with oil and sprinkle with sweetener.
4. Bake until center is bubbling, about 1 hour.

Try other stone fruits such as peaches or apricots.

Makes 8 servings

Apple Galettes in Lemon Pastry

Calories: 291

Protein: 2g

Saturated Fat: 1g

Fiber: 2g

Carbohydrate: 48g

Fat: 11g

Cholesterol: 0

Sodium: 107mg

Calories from

Carbohydrate: 64%

Calories from Fat: 33%

Calories from Protein: 3%

These rustic French free-form pies, based on precooked apples, make great break-fast pastries. See the photo.

Filling

2 tablespoons light vegetable oil (walnut, canola, etc.)

2 pounds combined Granny Smith and Golden Delicious or
    Pippin apples, 6 cups, peeled and sliced

¼ teaspoon sea salt

1 teaspoon 5 spice powder

½ cup dry sweetener (granular FruitSource and/or maple syrup granules)

Single-Crust Lemon Pastry with Glaze (see page 98)

1. Preheat the oven to 350°F. Line two baking sheets with parchment or brush with oil.

2. Heat the oil in a large pot. Add apples and sprinkle with salt and 5 spice powder. Cover and cook over medium-low heat until fruit is barely tender and holds its shape, 10 to 15 minutes, stirring occasionally.

3. Sprinkle sweetener over apples—do not stir—and cover to cook until sweetener has melted and apples are completely tender, about 5 minutes more. Allow filling to cool, uncovered, while you prepare the pastry.

4. Include ¼ cup dry sweetener in pastry along with lemon zest and juice. Divide pastry in two pieces and roll each into circles. Transfer to baking sheets. Place half of filling in the center of each pastry round and flip the edges up over the pastry by pulling up on the parchment paper.

5. Bake until pastry is golden, about 20 minutes. If desired, brush top with glaze and return to oven for 5 minutes more.

*Fresh Peach Compote with
Almond-Orange Syrup and
Cardamom Cookies*

Parfait of Fresh Fruit with

Almond Cream

Peach and Berry Gel with

Fresh Peach Coulis

Tri Berry Pie—
with small cutouts strewn

Blueberry Pie with Nut Crumb Topping

Apple Galette in Lemon Pastry

Pear Tart in Phyllo Pastry

Lavender Shortbread

Almond Orange Cake with
Tofu-Almond Cream

Chocolate-Pecan Bourbon Bundt
Cake with Raspberry Coulis

Basic Vanilla Cake with
Minted Strawberry Sauce and Tofu Cream

5 Nut Tart

Pumpkin Pie

Chocolate-Dipped Biscotti

Orange-Ginger Oatmeal Crunch Cookies

Hazelnut Hearts, Wheat-free Vanilla Cookies

Peanut Butter Fudge Cookies

Gingerbread Cookies

Pear Tart in Phyllo Pastry

See the photograph of this dessert.

2 to 3 tablespoons canola oil

4 sheets whole wheat phyllo dough

4 large pears, peeled, halved, and thinly sliced lengthwise

2 tablespoons sliced almonds, lightly toasted

¼ cup maple sugar granules or granular FruitSource

½ teaspoon cinnamon

Mint leaves or small sprigs for garnish

1. Preheat the oven to 350°F. Lightly oil a baking sheet.

2. Lightly brush or spray oil on one side of each sheet of phyllo, stacking one on top of another on the baking sheet. (Don't worry about phyllo that rips terribly. It won't show in the finished dessert, and it will look and taste great.) Roll up the edges to form sides.

3. Arrange pears in 3 or 4 barely overlapping rows down length of phyllo. Sprinkle with half of the almonds. Mix sweetener and cinnamon and sprinkle over pears.

4. Cover with parchment and bake until pears are tender and sweetener has melted, about 20 minutes, then uncover and bake 5 to 10 minutes more.

5. Garnish with remaining almonds and mint.

Makes 12 to 16 servings

Calories 76

Protein: 0.4g

Saturated Fat: 0.2g

Fiber: 1g

Carbohydrate: 12g

Fat: 4g

Cholesterol: 0

Sodium: 25mg

Calories from
Carbohydrate: 59%

Calories from Fat: 39%

Calories from Protein: 2%

New Classic Fresh Fruit Tart

**Makes one 9- or 10-inch
round or square tart or
6 tartlets**

Calories: 329

Protein: 3g

Saturated Fat: 1g

Fiber: 1g

Carbohydrate: 57g

Fat: 10g

Cholesterol: 0

Sodium: 88mg

Calories from
Carbohydrate: 69%

Calories from Fat: 28%

Calories from Protein: 4%

Delightful and dazzling in appearance, open-faced fresh fruit tarts are tempting desserts at lunch, teatime, or dinner. They are especially fun to make during the summer and fall, when fresh fruit is in abundance. Everyone can participate in creating his or her own work of edible art.

Mixing fruits is the way to get the benefit of multicolors and contrasting flavors. Include joyful color combinations and arrangements. Ideas include your choice of: strawberries or raspberries with blueberries or boysenberries and kiwi and/or peaches or apricots; small melon balls or grapes with raspberries and kiwi slices; or place the kiwi slices to form a border around a circle of mandarin orange sections with a red berry in the middle. Berries are nice arranged in concentric circles or in neat rows depending on the shape of the tart pan. Peaches, nectarines, and kiwi slices look beautiful overlapped in a circle or in rows. Or feature single fruits such as blueberries, raspberries, strawberries, or apricot or peach halves.

Classic tarts may be prepared in large pans or small individual tartlet pans. French tart pans made of tinned steel with fluted or scalloped edges and removable bottoms offer a wide range of choice among various sizes of the classic round shape as well as square and rectangular shapes.

These tarts consist of a sweet pastry shell, which may first be spread with a pastry cream or custard filling, nut paste or cream, or sometimes a layer of jam or chocolate, and then topped abundantly with the jewel-like fresh fruit, which is glazed. For the best texture and appearance, assemble the tarts close to serving time, or at least on the same day.

Compared with other tart recipes, the fat and calories are cut by a third and there is no cholesterol in this version.

New Classic Tart Pastry (see page 98)

¼ to ⅓ cup Chocolate (or Carob) Sauce II (see page 217) or jam, optional

1 cup Pastry Cream (see page 234) or Nut Paste or Cream (see page 243)

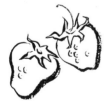

Fruit

1½ to 3 cups fresh fruit in season—berries (strawberries, raspberries, blackberries, blueberries), grapes, cherries, peeled and sliced kiwi, stone fruits such as apricots and peaches, or hard fruits such as apples and pears

Jam Glaze (makes ¼ to ½ cup)

Glaze acts like an edible lacquer that makes the fruit glisten. It also prevents the fruit from drying out. This recipe makes a glaze that is spreadable with a pastry brush or spoon, very unlike the thick, gelatinous toppings found on fruit pies in many bakeries.

Apricot jam and orange marmalade are appropriate for use on any fruits, especially the bright ones. Raspberry jam makes for a darker glaze that is suitable for dark fruit such as red or black grapes.

½ cup fruit-sweetened apricot jam, orange marmalade, or
  raspberry jam (a 10-ounce jar contains about 1 cup)
2 tablespoons lemon, orange, or apple juice, sweet Japanese
  cooking wine (mirin), rum, brandy, or water

Or Fruit Juice Glaze (makes a little less than 1 cup)

Filtered apple juice or apple cider contributes to the clarity of this glaze for both fresh and dried fruit tarts. Substitute raspberry juice for apple juice when using this glaze for blueberries, as apple juice mars their color.

1 tablespoon arrowroot powder
1 cup filtered apple juice or cider
3 tablespoons pure maple syrup, brown rice malt syrup or
  FruitSource syrup, or part of each
1 teaspoon lemon or lime juice (optional)
1 tablespoon agar flakes
⅛ teaspoon sea salt
Fresh mint sprigs for garnish

1. Preheat the oven to 350°F. Prepare the pastry in a tart pan and bake it. Allow to cool.

2. If desired, pour and spread sauce made from melted chocolate or carob chips into baked pastry shell. Refrigerate to set for about 15 minutes. Or spread jam to cover pastry.

3. Prepare the pastry cream (allow to cool for 10 minutes) or almond paste or cream and pour or spread evenly over bottom of tart shell or over chocolate or jam layer. Refrigerate to set, about 10 minutes. Meanwhile, prepare stone fruits by blanching them to remove their skins. To prepare apples or pears, peel, slice, and sauté fruit until just tender. Artfully arrange fruit on top of pastry cream, or chocolate or jam.

4. To prepare jam glaze, whisk together jam and liquid, then press through a strainer to remove any pulp or seeds. Brush the glaze onto the surface of the fruit and over the rim of the pastry.

Or prepare fruit juice glaze by placing arrowroot powder in a small bowl with enough of the apple juice to barely cover it. Place remaining juice in a 1-quart saucepan with the rest of the ingredients. Bring to a boil, then simmer until the agar completely dissolves, 3 to 5 minutes. Stir arrowroot mixture and add it to the pot. Stir until mixture thickens slightly and simmering resumes. Allow juice to cool about 15 minutes before pouring a little of it over fruit. Refrigerate tart.

Cranberry-Currant Tart

This very simple no-sweetener fruit pie is as elegant as it is naturally delicious.

Single-Crust Pastry with Glaze (see page 96)

Filling

½ cup currants

1½ cups filtered apple juice or cider

3 tablespoons agar flakes

¼ teaspoon sea salt

2 cups cranberries

1 tablespoon arrowroot powder

Water

1. Prepare pastry and bake it in a tart pan, glazing the rim.

2. In a 2-quart pot, bring currants, juice, agar, and salt to a boil. Simmer until agar is completely dissolved, 3 to 5 minutes.

3. Sort through cranberries to discard soft ones along with any stems. Rinse, drain, and add cranberries to pot. Cook until tender but not mushy, 2 to 5 minutes more.

Makes 6 to 8 servings

Calories: 214

Protein: 2g

Saturated Fat: 1g

Fiber: 2g

Carbohydrate: 36g

Fat: 7g

Cholesterol: 0

Sodium: 104mg

Calories from Carbohydrate: 66%

Calories from fat: 30%

Calories from Protein: 4%

4. Stir arrowroot in a little cool water to completely dissolve and add to pot. Stir gently until mixture thickens slightly, in a few seconds. Transfer filling to tart shell. Allow filling to cool and gel before serving, about 1 hour at cool room temperature.

Variations

Cranberry Tart: Omit currants and substitute ½ cup sweetener (¼ cup each brown rice malt syrup and maple syrup is nice) for ½ cup of juice.

Cranberry-Fruit Tart: Thanks to cookbook author Lorna Sass for this great idea. Include just 1 cup of cranberries and ¼ cup of currants. Add 1¼ cups combined fresh diced apples and pears and 1 tablespoon orange zest.

Pear Pie in Walnut Pastry

Makes 8 to 10 servings

Calories: 390

Protein: 4g

Saturated Fat: 1g

Fiber: 4g

Carbohydrate: 61g

Fat: 16g

Cholesterol: 0

Sodium: 165mg

Calories from
Carbohydrate: 60%

Calories from Fat: 35%

Calories from Protein: 4%

Filling

3 pounds pears (pears don't need to be fully ripe), about 6 to 7 pears
or about 8 cups, peeled and thinly sliced

3 tablespoons arrowroot powder

1½ teaspoons nutmeg

¾ teaspoon ginger

½ teaspoon cardamom

½ teaspoon sea salt

¾ cup brown rice malt syrup or pure maple syrup

Double Crust (Lemon-) Walnut Pastry

1 cup whole wheat pastry flour

1 cup unbleached white flour

1 cup walnuts, toasted and finely ground

¼ teaspoon sea salt

⅓ cup light vegetable oil (walnut or canola)

2 tablespoons brown rice syrup or pure maple syrup (optional)

¼ to ⅓ cup water, or 3 tablespoons lemon juice

1. Preheat the oven to 350°F. Brush a 9-inch pie pan with oil. To prepare filling, with a rubber spatula mix fruit with dry ingredients, then stir in sweetener.

2. To prepare pastry, mix dry ingredients, then stir in oil until mixture is pebbly. Drizzle in sweetener and stir. Add liquid as necessary to form a smooth pliable dough.

3. Roll half portions of dough between sheets of waxed paper. Sprinkle flour liberally over bottom sheet of paper and on top of dough before rolling out thin. Add more flour as needed to make rolling easy, taking care not to add so much as to mar the surface.

4. Transfer one portion of dough to pie pan. Fill and lay other pastry on top. Pinch off excess dough and press edges together to flute. Poke holes in surface with a fork. To prevent burning the rim, cover it with foil.

5. Bake until filling is soft in the middle, 1 hour and 15 minutes. Allow pie to cool for at least 1 hour before serving for filling to set.

Makes 10 servings

Calories: 254

Protein: 3g

Saturated Fat: 1g

Fiber: 2g

Carbohydrate: 45g

Fat: 8g

Cholesterol: 0

Sodium: 83mg

Calories from
Carbohydrate: 69%

Calories from Fat: 27%

Calories from Protein: 4%

Fig and Almond Tart

The plump fresh figs in this special tart glisten from the lemon- and vanilla-infused syrup. The idea came from a recipe in Bistro Cooking *by Patricia Wells.*

Fig Compote Filling and garnish

3 pint baskets figs, about 2 pounds or 7 to 8 cups, stem ends trimmed

½ cup wet sweetener (brown rice syrup or FruitSource) or
   dry sweetener (granular FruitSource or evaporated sugar cane juice)

1 vanilla bean, split lengthwise, or ½ teaspoon vanilla extract

½ cup water

1 tablespoon lemon juice

¼ teaspoon sea salt

¼ cup sliced almonds, lightly toasted

Tofu Chantilly Cream for garnish (see page 112), optional

Single-Crust Pastry (see page 96)

1. To make filling, combine figs, sweetener, vanilla bean (if included), water, lemon juice, and salt in a large (wide) pan. Stir and bring to a boil. Turn heat down and simmer uncovered until fruit is soft and liquid becomes syrupy, 45 to 60 minutes. Stir the compote occasionally taking care not to break fruit.

2. Preheat oven to 350°F. Prepare the pastry with ¼ cup sweetener. Transfer to tart pan, prebake for 10 minutes, and allow to cool.

3. Gently swirl vanilla extract (if included) into filling by tilting pan in a circular motion. Allow it to cool somewhat, about 10 minutes. Remove vanilla bean and sprinkle in most of the almonds before gently spooning filling into the pastry in a single layer. Sprinkle remaining almonds on top. Return to oven until the syrup is firm and edges of pie are golden, about 15 minutes more.

Variation

Fig and Walnut Tart: Omit almonds. Instead, stir ½ cup toasted walnut halves into figs and syrup and transfer to pastry.

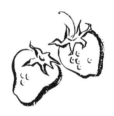

Strawberry-Rhubarb Pie

Makes 10 servings

Rhubarb is one of the only plants to produce fruit almost year-round in backyard gardens here in northern California. Once or twice during the early spring season, I like to harvest the stalks for this tart and tangy treat. This recipe is a variation of the award-winning Strawberry Pie in my other cookbook, Fresh From a Vegetarian Kitchen.

The leaves of the rhubarb plant contain oxalic acid in such quantities that they can be toxic, so make sure all the green leaves are cut off when you use the stalks. Nutritionally speaking, oxalic acid may prevent the absorption of calcium. (Oxalic acid is also prevalent in the other members of this plant family— spinach, Swiss chard, and beet greens—and so they are best served after a brief period of boiling to leach out the acid.)

Single-Crust Pastry with Glaze (see page 96)

Calories: 198

Protein: 2g

Saturated Fat: 0.4g

Fiber: 2g

Carbohydrate: 34g

Fat: 6g

Cholesterol: 0

Sodium: 139mg

Calories from
Carbohydrate: 68%

Calories from Fat: 28%

Calories from Protein: 4%

Filling

2 pints strawberries

2 cups sliced (½ inch) rhubarb

½ teaspoon sea salt

½ cup brown rice malt syrup, or part maple syrup

⅓ cup agar flakes

1. Preheat the oven to 350°F. Prepare the pastry and bake it.

2. To prepare the filling, leaving berries whole, layer the ingredients in a 3-quart pot in the order listed. Bring to a boil over medium-low heat. Cover and cook until the ingredients are submerged in strawberry juice and the agar is completely dissolved, about 15 minutes. Stir several times after the juice starts coming out of the berries. Allow to cool for 15 minutes. Taste to determine balance of sweet and tart flavors.

3. Pour the filling into the pie shell and allow it to cool to gel, about 1 hour refrigerated or 2 hours at cool room temperature.

Bramble Berry Pie

Makes 8 to 10 servings

Calories: 362

Protein: 4g

Saturated Fat: 1g

Fiber: 3g

Carbohydrate: 55g

Fat: 15g

Cholesterol: 0

Sodium: 203mg

Calories from Carbohydrate: 60%

Calories from Fat: 36%

Calories from Protein: 4%

Every July since 1961, the little northern California coastal town of Westhaven holds its Wild Blackberry Festival. During the preceding autumn, the local blackberries—wild brambles called Himalaya berries—are picked and frozen. During the gray winter months, the ladies of Westhaven get together at the Volunteer Fire Hall on weekends and make a total of 600 wild blackberry pies and many jars of jam and jelly. The pies are frozen for the summer festival.

I asked Hazel Moon, a longtime Westhaven resident who recently made the change to a more wholesome lifestyle, about the pies' contents. The crust ingredients are white flour, shortening, sugar, and salt; the filling is made of blackberries, sugar, and flour. This was Hazel's favorite dessert, and despite her commitment to healthful eating, she was tempted to enjoy the festival's pies even if it meant eating a little refined white sugar.

My challenge was obvious. Could I make a pie using more healthful ingredients that even Hazel would enjoy? The nectarlike sweetness of the berries came through with glorious intensity. Hazel loved the pie: *"Why, it's every bit as sweet and tasty as the usual blackberry pie!"*

Blackberries are just one type of bramble—berries that grow on vines with thorns. Blackberries are ready to eat from July through September. Olallieberries, Youngberries, Loganberries, and Nectarberries are all blackberries. Raspberries are also bramble berries and are available through the beginning of November.

Filling

6 cups blackberries (5 or 6 6-ounce baskets, ripe and
   sweet; 3 pints; or 3 1-pound packages frozen berries)
¾ cup brown rice malt syrup or FruitSource syrup for sweet berries,
   or pure maple syrup or honey with tart-sweet berries, or part of each
Zest of half an orange
⅓ cup arrowroot powder
½ teaspoon sea salt

Single- or Double-Crust Pastry or Lattice Pastry with Glaze (see pages 96, 101 or 100)

1. Preheat the oven to 350°F. Oil a 9-inch tart or pie pan.
2. To make the filling, quickly and gently rinse the berries by dropping them into a bowl of cool water. Swish berries, strain, transfer to a towel and pat dry and drain. With a rubber spatula, gently mix berries with other filling ingredients.
3. Prepare the pastry. Lay the bottom crust in the tart or pie pan. Fill and cover with the top pastry or lattice (or just leave the top open).
4. Bake until the berry juices are bubbling or oozing from the top crust, 60 to 75 minutes. If desired, lightly brush the top and rim with glaze. Return the pie to the oven until golden, 10 to 25 minutes more. Serve lukewarm or at room temperature.

Variation

Substitute raspberries for blackberries.

Blueberry Nut Crumb Pie

This generous pie is filled with plump blueberries and covered to overflowing with crunchy nuts in a streusel topping.

Single-Crust Pastry with Glaze (see page 96)

Nut Crumb Topping

1½ cups walnuts or pecans, toasted; ¾ cup finely ground, ¾ cup coarsely chopped

¼ cup whole wheat pastry flour

¼ cup unbleached white flour

Few grains of sea salt

2 tablespoons light walnut oil (or another light vegetable oil)

3 tablespoons brown rice malt syrup or FruitSource syrup

Filling

6 cups blueberries, about 2 pounds, 5 or 6 6-ounce containers or 3 pints, fresh or
    frozen (a 10-ounce bag contains 1¾ to 2 cups)

½ teaspoon sea salt

¾ cup brown rice malt syrup or FruitSource syrup

6 tablespoons arrowroot powder

Water

Zest of 1 lemon

1 tablespoon lemon juice

1. Preheat the oven to 350°F. Prepare and bake the pastry. Line a baking sheet with parchment or brush it lightly with oil.
2. To make topping, mix nuts, flours, and salt. Work in oil, then sweetener. Rub mixture between your palms. Add a little more flour if necessary for a moist, crumbly texture. Transfer to baking sheet and bake until golden, 10 to 15 minutes, stirring a couple of times.
3. Place a third of the berries in a 3-quart saucepan with salt and sweetener. Bring ingredients to a boil. Turn heat down and simmer until berries are tender, about 5 minutes.
4. Dissolve arrowroot powder in enough water to cover. Add to pot along with remaining berries, lemon zest, and juice. Stir to thicken.

Cook until mixture bubbles, berries soften, and color is somewhat clear and shiny, not chalky, for another couple of minutes.

5. Allow berries to cool in pot for 10 minutes, then pour filling into pastry. Allow filling to set up somewhat before adding topping, then allow pie to cool completely before serving.

Fresh Blueberry Pie

Makes 8 to 10 servings

Alex McIntyre is co-creator of this whimsical and delightfully simple pie in which the sauce is simply mixed with fresh berries and the filling is strewn with small pastry hearts and/or stars. See the photo on the cover.

Single-Crust Cutout Pastry with Glaze (see page 98)

Filling

4 cups blueberries

¾ cup brown rice malt syrup with ¾ cup water; or ½ cup pure maple
  syrup or honey with I cup water; or part of each to total I½ cups

I½ tablespoons agar flakes

I teaspoon nutmeg

¼ teaspoon sea salt

I½ tablespoons arrowroot powder

I tablespoon lemon juice

Calories: 240

Protein: 2g

Saturated Fat: 0.4g

Fiber: 2g

Carbohydrate: 45g

Fat: 6g

Cholesterol: 0

Sodium: 35mg

Calories from

Carbohydrate: 73%

Calories from Fat: 23%

Calories from Protein: 3%

I. Preheat the oven to 350°F. Prepare the pastry including sweetener and bake it. Roll out extra dough to make 12 to 16 pastry cutouts—I like small stars from an hors d'oeuvre cutter set for this pie. Bake cutouts separately and glaze both rim of pastry and cutouts in last several minutes of baking. Return to oven until done. Allow to cool.

2. Rinse and drain berries. Place sweetener, water, agar, nutmeg, and salt in a 1-quart saucepan. Stir to submerge agar and bring to a boil over medium heat. Stir occasionally and cook until agar dissolves, 3 to 5 minutes.

3. Dissolve arrowroot in the lemon juice and a little water to cover. Add to pan and whisk as mixture comes to a boil all the way to the center and becomes slightly thicker, clearer, and glossier. Turn off heat.

4. Place berries in a large bowl and pour hot sauce over them. Mix gently with a rubber spatula. Refrigerate filling for 10 minutes, then transfer to pastry shell and return to refrigerator to cool completely. Arrange pastry cutouts randomly over the top. Serve slightly chilled or at room temperature.

Variations

Fresh Raspberry Pie: Substitute raspberries for blueberries. Cut both little star and heart shapes for pastry cutout decoration.

Tri-Berry Pie: Include a mixture of blueberries, raspberries, and blackberries. Cut little hearts for the pastry cutouts.

Peach and Cherry Pie in Pecan Pastry

Makes 10 servings

Calories: 323
Protein: 4g
Saturated Fat: 1g
Fiber: 2g
Carbohydrate: 48g
Fat: 14g
Cholesterol: 0
Sodium: 162mg
Calories from
Carbohydrate: 58%
Calories from Fat: 37%
Calories from Protein: 5%

This pie is easier to make than an all-cherry pie with the pitting it entails, and the flavors and colors combine nicely.

Filling

1½ pounds peaches, about 4 cups thinly sliced

½ pound cherries, about 1½ cups, stemmed and pitted

1 tablespoon lemon juice

¼ cup arrowroot powder or whole wheat pastry flour

½ teaspoon nutmeg

½ teaspoon sea salt

¼ to ½ cup brown rice malt syrup or pure maple syrup (or part of each), or fruit juice concentrate, to taste

Double-Crust Pecan Pastry with Glaze (see page 98)

1. Preheat the oven to 350°F.

2. Combine the filling ingredients.

3. Prepare the pastry. Spoon the filling into the bottom crust. Lay on the top crust. Seal and crimp the edges. Poke holes in the surface with a fork. Press a cookie cutter to mark the center for decoration and for a place to check for doneness. Cover the rim with aluminum foil.

4. Bake until you no longer see the thickener on the fruit, 40 to 50 minutes. This shows the fruit has softened and released its juices. Remove foil and, if desired, brush the glaze on the surface and return the pie to the oven to brown it further, about 5 minutes more. Allow to cool for filling to set.

Ginger-Lime Peach Pie

Filling

1 tablespoon light vegetable oil (canola, almond, or walnut)

3 pounds peaches, about 10 cups sliced

½ cup brown rice malt syrup or pure maple syrup, or half of each

1 tablespoon peeled and grated fresh ginger

½ teaspoon powdered ginger

½ teaspoon sea salt

2 tablespoons arrowroot powder

Juice of 1 lime, about 2 tablespoons

Double-Crust Pastry (see page 101)

1. Preheat the oven to 350°F. Brush a pie pan with oil.

2. To prepare filling, heat oil in a large/wide pot over medium heat. Add peaches and sauté for several minutes. Add sweetener, gingers, and salt and cook until tender, about 10 minutes. Dissolve arrowroot in juice and stir into mixture to form a nice saucy texture upon boiling. Allow mixture to cool somewhat, about ½ hour.

3. Prepare pastry, including baking powder as in the variation on that recipe. Fill, crimp edges, and cover rim with foil. Bake until done, 30 to 40 minutes. Glaze, if desired.

Makes 10 servings

Calories: 344

Protein: 4g

Saturated Fat: 1g

Fiber: 2g

Carbohydrate: 55g

Fat: 13g

Cholesterol: 0

Sodium: 163mg

Calories from Carbohydrate: 62%

Calories from Fat: 33%

Calories from Protein: 4%

Mango-Key Lime Pie with Coconut Crust and Candied Macadamia Nuts

Makes 8 servings

Calories: 373

Protein: 5g

Saturated Fat: 4g

Fiber: 5g

Carbohydrate: 65g

Fat: 13g

Cholesterol: 0

Sodium: 164mg

Calories from
Carbohydrate: 66%

Calories from Fat: 29%

Calories from Protein: 5%

Key limes are smaller and more tart than the more familiar seedless Persian limes. Key limes do have seeds and their skins turn yellow as they ripen. They once flourished in the Florida Keys, but are now grown in the Bahamas, Mexico, and the Caribbean. They may be used in much the same way as regular limes.

A classic Floridian dessert and very popular throughout the Caribbean, key lime pie is usually made with dairy products (canned sweetened condensed milk—a blend of milk and sugar created in 1857—or water thickened with cornstarch for the filling, and whipped cream for the topping), eggs (hence the yellow color), and sugar. The original filling often wasn't baked as it is today; instead, the ingredients were either whipped together and refrigerated until firm, or heated through in a saucepan.

In this delectable adaptation, soy milk is gelled and thickened with agar sea vegetable flakes and arrowroot powder. A choice of sweeteners is given because the light color from FruitSource syrup or brown rice malt syrup allows for a pie with a more authentic light yellow color from the mango purée than does maple syrup, although maple syrup tastes the best even when used in such a small amount.

Coconut Crust

Graham crackers were invented by Sylvester Graham, who preached the virtues of a high-fiber diet in the 1800s, especially a vegetarian diet featuring home-baked whole wheat bread. For this recipe, go to a natural foods store to choose a brand of Graham crackers that contains whole grain flour and other high-quality ingredients.

1 to 1¼ cups graham cracker crumbs, made from 4 to 5 ounces crackers

½ cup shredded coconut

2 tablespoons canola oil

⅓ cup brown rice syrup, FruitSource syrup, or maple syrup

Filling

1½ cups soy milk

2 tablespoons agar flakes

⅛ teaspoon sea salt

1 ripe medium mango, about 1 pound, peeled and pitted

2 tablespoons arrowroot powder

Water

⅓ cup freshly squeezed lime juice, 5 to 7 key limes or 2 to 3 regular limes

½ cup FruitSource syrup or brown rice malt syrup, or part pure maple syrup

Candied Macadamia Nuts

Most often macadamia nuts come roasted and salted. Rinse them in cool water to remove the salt.

16 macadamia nuts, toasted

Brown rice syrup or FruitSource syrup to barely cover

Topping

1 ripe mango, peeled and thinly sliced lengthwise off pit

3 kiwi fruit, peeled, halved lengthwise, and thinly sliced crosswise

1. Preheat the oven to 350°F.

2. To prepare the crust, grind graham crackers with coconut in a food processor. Pulse in the oil and then the sweetener. The consistency should be such that the ingredients hold together when squeezed between your fingers. Add a little more sweetener if necessary. Transfer the mixture to a lightly oiled 10-inch pie pan and press it to cover the bottom and sides. Bake until golden, 10 to 12 minutes. Transfer to a rack to cool. If the crust buckles, gently press it back down after it cools.

3. To prepare the filling, place the soy milk, agar, and salt in a 1-quart saucepan. Stir to submerge the agar. Bring the mixture to a boil over medium heat. Do not cover the pot. Stir occasionally to prevent scorching and watch for foaming upon boiling. Turn the heat low and simmer until the agar dissolves, about 5 minutes.

4. Blend the mango until smooth. Makes 1 cup purée.

5. Dissolve the arrowroot in water to cover and add it to the pot. Whisk until somewhat thickened and smooth. Turn heat off. Whisk in lime juice, sweetener, and mango purée.

6. Transfer filling to pie shell. Refrigerate until set, 45 to 60 minutes. Gels at room temperature in about 1½ hours.

7. To candy the nuts, mix nuts with sweetener and transfer to an oiled pie pan. Bake until dry, 10 to 15 minutes. Allow to cool, then scrape nuts off sheet. Soak sheet in water for ease in cleaning.

8. For topping, peel mango and kiwi with a vegetable peeler. Arrange slices spoke-fashion and slightly overlapping over filling. Place nuts in center of pie, letting a few fall where they may.

Variation

For a simpler topping, omit fruit. Instead, coarsely chop 1 cup candied macadamia or cashew nuts and sprinkle over surface.

HARVEST VEGETABLE PIES

Pumpkin Pie with Autumn Leaves Cutout Pastry

Makes 8 to 10 servings

Calories: 198
Protein: 4g
Saturated Fat: 0.5g
Fiber: 1g
Carbohydrate: 33g
Fat: 6g
Cholesterol: 0
Sodium: 154mg
Calories from
Carbohydrate: 65%
Calories from Fat: 28%
Calories from Protein: 7%

Vegetable custard pies are an historic favorite in North America. Yankees prefer pumpkin or squash pies while Southerners cherish their sweet potato or yam pies.

This very fine pumpkin pie satisfies every time without the usual ingredients: brown or white sugar, honey or molasses, eggs, butter, and cream, half-and-half, or condensed (evaporated) or regular milk. Its reduced fat content compares favorably to the traditional pie containing 260 calories and 60 grams of fat per serving.

I prefer to use freshly baked sweet winter squash for my "pumpkin" pies. The color is richer and the flavor is naturally sweeter than either canned or even fresh sugar pie pumpkin purée. Squash is the main ingredient in canned pumpkin purée.

Baking enhances the sweetness of butternut squash, the variety most widely available. Other favorites are buttercup, sweetmeat, kabocha, delicata, sweet mama, or sweet dumpling squashes, and Hokkaido pumpkin.

To compensate for the great variety in textures of cooked squash from dry to quite moist, when puréeing in a food processor, add water to very dry squash to make it thick, smooth, and creamy.

This no-bake recipe uses soy milk for a custardy filling texture. Both agar sea vegetable flakes (for a gelled consistency) and arrowroot starch (for the creamy smooth consistency) are used to create the great mouth-feel. Rice and almond milks may serve as stand-ins for soy milk, but the pie will not be as rich in flavor or texture. Maple syrup lends the best flavor in the sweetener category.

Since commercial pumpkin pie spice may contain sugar, dextrose, and extractive of spice, look for a more natural combination of cinnamon, ginger, nutmeg, and allspice. Or measure your own as in this recipe.

Filling

1½ cups baked winter squash purée, or a 15-ounce can pumpkin purée

2 tablespoons arrowroot powder

1½ cups soy milk, rice milk, or almond milk

1 teaspoon cinnamon

¼ teaspoon each nutmeg and ginger (or 1 teaspoon freshly grated ginger)

1/16 teaspoon each allspice and cloves

½ teaspoon sea salt

½ cup pure maple syrup or another wet sweetener (all or part brown
   rice malt syrup, FruitSource syrup, or barley malt syrup)

3 tablespoons agar flakes

Single Crust Cutout Pastry with Glaze (see page 98)

Tofu Cream (makes 2⅓ cups)

Fresh tofu has a clean, neutral flavor. It takes on other flavors easily and whips up to a smooth creamy consistency. The light color resembles a traditional crème fraîche, the mildly cultured French cream made by stirring heavy cream with buttermilk or sour cream and letting it stand at warm room temperature for several hours. Medium or soft tofu is too watery to hold up with blending for application with a pastry bag, even when less sweetener is included in the recipe.

1 pound tofu, fresh and firm or medium

½ cup pure maple syrup or part brown rice syrup

1 tablespoon vanilla

Nutmeg for garnish

1. To prepare the squash, place it either whole or halved and cut side down on a baking sheet. (Halving the squash cuts the cooking time in half, but leaving large hard squashes whole makes for a happy cook.) Bake squash at 450°F until quite soft when pierced with a fork or knife, 20 minutes to 1½ hours depending on the size of the squash. Discard skin or shell and seeds. Purée squash. You may need to add a tablespoon of water if squash is quite dry, e.g. kabocha squash. Measure yield; a pound of squash yields a bit less than 1 cup of purée.

2. Turn heat down to 350°. Prepare the pastry and the cutouts. My favorite shape for this pie is 10 autumn leaves. Transfer pastry to pan and cutouts to a parchment-lined baking sheet. Bake, glazing rim and leaves after 8 minutes. Return to oven until done, 5 to 10 minutes more.

3. To make the filling, place the arrowroot powder in a small bowl with enough of the measured liquid (one of the milks) to cover generously. Place the remaining ingredients in a small saucepan and whisk to submerge agar. Bring to a boil, stirring occasionally, and simmer until agar dissolves, about 5 minutes. Whisk arrowroot mixture into hot liquid and return to a simmer to thicken.

4. Whisk the hot liquid with the squash purée and transfer filling to pastry. Filling gels refrigerated or at room temperature. Decorate surface with pastry cutouts.

5. To prepare the tofu cream, blend the ingredients until creamy smooth. This takes about a full minute in a food processor. Spoon a large dollop (a little less than ¼ cup) on top of each serving of pie, or squeeze the cream through a pastry bag with a small tip for a more decorative effect. (Refrigerate the cream if you need to firm up the texture.) Garnish with nutmeg.

Variation

Hobnail Pie: The early American settlers referred to raisins as hobnails. In this pie, the brilliant orange color of the squash is accented by the dark raisins.

Simmer ½ cup raisins in ½ cup water with a pinch of salt for 5 minutes. Drain and mix the raisins with the squash.

Yam Spice Pie

Makes 10 servings

Some people find garnet yams too sweet, but this quality along with their moist texture and rich flavor make them perfect for a pie. Studded with currants and topped with small pastry cutouts, this cute pie is sweetener-free.

Garnet yams have darker skins and flesh than jewel yams. Both are sweet, although the degree of sweetness varies from batch to batch. Sweet potatoes may be yellow or white. The yellow ones are often called yams, but the yam actually belongs to another family.

Calories: 340

Protein: 5g

Saturated Fat: 1g

Fiber: 5g

Carbohydrate: 60g

Fat: 10g

Cholesterol: 0

Sodium: 148mg

Calories from Carbohydrate: 70%

Calories from Fat: 25%

Calories from Protein: 5%

Filling

3 pounds yams, 4 cups purée

Zest of 1 orange

½ cup orange juice

1½ tablespoons agar flakes

½ cup currants

1 teaspoon vanilla

1 teaspoon cinnamon

¼ teaspoon each nutmeg, ginger, allspice, and cloves

½ teaspoon sea salt

½ cup walnuts, toasted and coarsely chopped

Single-Crust Cutout Pastry and Glaze (see page 98)

1. To bake the yams whole for the sweetest-tasting purée, preheat the oven to 450°F. Bake until the yams are easily pierced with a fork, about 1 hour, depending on size. Discard skins.

Or boil yams for a slightly milder sweetness and a shorter cooking time. Peel, then cut yams in halves or quarters lengthwise depending on size. Cut crosswise into 2-inch slices (makes 10 cups). Boil with water to cover in a 4-quart pot until tender, about 15 minutes. Drain the boiled yams and allow them to cool briefly.

2. In a small saucepan, bring to a boil the other filling ingredients, except the walnuts. Simmer covered until agar dissolves, 3 to 5 minutes.

3. Mash or purée the yams while still warm. Mix the purée with the currant-spice mixture and the walnuts.

4. Turn oven to 350°F. Prepare the pastry and 10 small pastry cutouts. Transfer the pastry to an oiled pie pan and prebake it for 5 minutes. Bake the cutouts separately, glazing if desired.

5. Transfer the filling to the pastry and smooth the surface. Bake for 20 minutes, glazing the rim in the last several minutes. Set the cutouts in place and allow the pie to cool somewhat before serving.

Parsnip-Pecan Pie

Makes 10 servings

Calories: 258
Protein: 3g
Saturated Fat: 1g
Fiber: 5g
Carbohydrate: 43g
Fat: 9g
Cholesterol: 0
Sodium: 145mg
Calories from
Carbohydrate: 64%
Calories from Fat: 31%
Calories from Protein: 5%

Single-Crust Pastry (see page 96)

Filling

1 tablespoon light vegetable oil (walnut, canola, etc.)
8 cups thinly sliced parsnips, about 2 pounds
½ teaspoon sea salt
1½ cups water
½ cup raisins
¼ cup pure maple syrup
¼ cup agar flakes
1 teaspoon vanilla
½ teaspoon cinnamon
¼ cup pecans, toasted and finely ground

1. Preheat the oven to 350°F and oil a pie pan. Prepare pastry and bake it.

2. To make filling, heat oil in a pressure cooker. Add parsnips and sprinkle with salt. Stir well, then add the water. Cover and bring to pressure. Cook for 5 minutes. Drain reserving liquid.

3. In a small saucepan, bring raisins to a boil with maple syrup and agar in ⅔ cup of the parsnip cooking broth. Simmer until agar dissolves, about 5 minutes. Drain, reserving liquid.

4. Purée parsnips with vanilla, cinnamon, and the sweet raisin cooking liquid. Stir in raisins and 2 tablespoons pecans. Transfer filling to pie shell. Smooth surface.

5. Sprinkle remaining 2 tablespoons nuts around outer rim of filling. Allow filling to gel before serving, 1 to 1½ hours at cool room temperature.

Pecan Pie

Makes 8 to 10 servings

Calories: 424

Protein: 3g

Saturated Fat: 2g

Fiber: 2g

Carbohydrate: 58g

Fat: 21g

Cholesterol: 0

Sodium: 35mg

Calories from
Carbohydrate: 53%

Calories from Fat: 44%

Calories from Protein: 3%

After the pecans, sorghum syrup is the main ingredient in this pie as it's made in southern kitchens. The other traditional ingredients are white or brown sugar, dark corn syrup or molasses, lard or shortening, butter or margarine, and eggs. This more healthful version sacrifices none of the luscious sticky sweet texture or taste.

For the predominant sweetener in this recipe, the taste of brown rice malt syrup is the best, followed by enzyme-converted brown rice syrup (be sure to follow the directions for simmering the mixture for 5 minutes to deactivate the enzyme ensuring that texture thickens), sorghum syrup, and lastly, barley malt syrup, which is too strong in flavor for use here.

See the photo of the variation.

Single-Crust Pastry with Glaze (see page 96)

Filling

1¼ cups brown rice malt syrup

¼ cup pure maple syrup

1½ cups water

¼ cup agar flakes

½ teaspoon cinnamon

½ teaspoon sea salt

2 tablespoons arrowroot powder

Water

2 cups pecans, toasted

1 teaspoon vanilla

1. Preheat the oven to 350°F. Lightly oil a pie pan.

2. Prepare the pastry and bake until done, 15 to 20 minutes.

3. To make filling, bring the syrups, water, agar, cinnamon, and salt to a boil. Simmer until the agar dissolves completely, about 5 minutes, stirring occasionally. Dissolve arrowroot in cool water to barely cover and add to pot. Whisk until chalky color changes to clear. Let mixture cool somewhat, about 15 minutes, then add pecans and vanilla and transfer to pastry shell. Filling sets up in 1 to 2 hours in the refrigerator, longer at room temperature. For large amounts such as 9 pies, arrange pecans in pie shells, then pour in the liquid part of the filling.

Variation

Five-Nut Tart: Substitute a combination of toasted nuts (hazelnuts, almonds, walnuts, pecans, and pine nuts) for all pecans and decrease the total volume of nuts to 1½ cups. Bake pastry in a tart pan. You may have a little liquid filling left over since tarts are smaller in depth than pies.

Makes 10 to 12 servings

Calories: 259
Protein: 5g
Saturated Fat: 1g
Fiber: 2g
Carbohydrate: 37g
Fat: 12g
Cholesterol: 0
Sodium: 139mg
Calories from
Carbohydrate: 55%
Calories from Fat: 38%
Calories from Protein: 7%

Poppy Seed Strudel

Called kulachi *in Poland and popular in Russia as well, this pastry is traditionally prepared by each family and served to guests during the winter holidays. It may be made up to 2 feet in length—if you can find a suitable baking sheet! Raisins sweeten this strudel so much that no other sweetener is called for.*

Filling (makes 2 cups)

1 cup poppy seeds, about 4 ounces

2 cups raisins

1 cup water

Zest of 1 lemon

½ teaspoon sea salt

1 teaspoon vanilla

Single-Crust Pastry II (see page 100)

1. Preheat the oven to 300°F. The flavor of poppy seeds is heightened when lightly toasted on a dry baking sheet before use, about 10 minutes in a 300-degree oven. Set aside ¼ teaspoon for garnish.

2. To prepare the filling, bring ingredients, except vanilla, to a boil. Turn the heat to medium-low and slow-boil until liquid is absorbed, about 5 minutes. This thoroughly plumps both the seeds and the raisins, preparing them for crushing. Add the vanilla. Purée the mixture in a food processor, a blender, or a hand-powered food mill. Allow the purée to cool completely. Turn oven temperature up to 350°F.

3. Line a baking sheet with parchment or brush with oil. Roll out pastry dough to a thin rectangle. Transfer to baking sheet. Trim edges to fit pan.

4. Spread the filling evenly over the dough to within an inch of the top and side edges. Roll strudel up lengthwise from one long side to the other, ending with seam side down. Score the top in 1½-inch slices for ease in cutting later.

5. Bake until pastry is golden, about 30 minutes. Brush surface of pastry with water and sprinkle with reserved poppy seeds, or brush glaze ingredients including ¼ teaspoon poppy seeds over surface of pastry. Return pastry to the oven for 5 minutes more. Slice to serve.

Crisps & Cobblers

Crisps and cobblers are nostalgic desserts that revive memories of farm kitchens and cold winter nights in the north country. Cobblers, along with pies, were a daily part of the large breakfasts rural families once enjoyed. It's easy to see why: the enticing combination of summer's bounty of bubbling fruit, their wine-sweet juices absorbed into the golden crisp or biscuit dough topping, makes these treats some of the ultimate seasonal desserts.

Crisps and cobblers are variations on deep-dish fruit pies. The difference between them is the topping. A crisp has a crunchy, sweet-textured streusel topping made with flour, sweetener, and fat. (Streusel is the German word for "sprinkling" or "strewing.") Today's natural foods-style crisp recipes call for a crumbly mixture of whole grain flour and oat flakes, sometimes with nuts, which is baked until nicely browned and crisp on top. The idea must have come from the English, who call this combination a fruit crumble or crumble pudding. A crunch is a crisp-type dessert with a crunchy granola topping.

Fresh fruit cobblers might be made with peaches in the South, apples in New England, or raspberries in the Midwest. Although there are many different ways to make this homespun dessert, the time-honored version that is continued here consists of a thick or thin top crust of biscuit dough and no bottom crust.

The name cobbler most likely comes from the look of the finished dessert—the biscuitlike topping, with a texture somewhere between a pie crust and a cake, either rolled out and blanketing the fruit, giving the dish the appearance of cobblestones, or spoon-dropped by large dollops or cobbles. Or perhaps the word refers to the phrase "cobble up," meaning to put something together in a hurry.

Crisps and cobblers are easier to make than pies because they require no crimping around the edges. Cobbler dough is pliable and more forgiving than pie dough, not likely to break or crumble. And unlike pie dough, cobbler dough contains baking powder, which makes it rise to puffy heights. Tender handling of the dough makes the difference between a decent biscuit and one that is sublime.

INGREDIENTS

The toppings in this book call for new versions of the ingredients normally used—white flour, sugar, butter, and also milk, buttermilk or half-and-half, and eggs in the case of cobblers. It's liberating to remember that when the first biscuits were made in pioneer days on the prairie where harsh circumstances often required improvisation—water might stand in for milk, or 'coon fat for butter. Here you'll see that aluminum-free baking powder eliminates the need for eggs. Vegetable oils stand in for dairy fats. And soy milk, nut or rice milk, amazake, or apple juice all work well as the liquid ingredient in cobbler toppings. Soy milk is my personal favorite for the rich flavor and texture it imparts compared with the others. Wheat-, gluten-, fat- and sweetener-free recipes are included as variations on the master recipes in this chapter.

In the apple recipes, either a single variety or a mixture of apples is nice. I usually base mine on Pippins or Granny Smiths with equal or lesser amounts of other kinds. Even Red Delicious, the apple most people consider suitable only as an eating apple, tastes great combined in this way.

As with making cakes, only brown rice malt syrup works well for crisps and cobblers. The filling juices will not thicken and the topping won't be as light when other rice syrups containing enzymes are used. For example, the desired effects from using arrowroot powder and baking powder will be canceled out. Read the ingredients labels and see page 39 for further explanation.

Both crisps and cobblers are normally served hot or warm from the oven with a cloud of whipped cream, heavy cream, crème fraîche, or vanilla ice cream—make that a scoop of nondairy vanilla ice cream.

TECHNIQUES

When apples or pears are featured, I sometimes peel none or just half the fruit so the natural nutrition is more intact. The recipes call for peeled fruit since that completely smooth and even texture is what most people expect. Even underripe fruits soften completely with baking.

For people who would rather not use baking powder, a pie or cookie dough crust may be substituted for a cobbler topping, just as Rebecca Boone (Daniel's wife) did in her day.

For both crisps and cobblers, I find that cooking the filling fully before adding the topping keeps the topping from either burning or from sinking and remaining slightly undercooked in the middle. This is the most reliable method, especially for deep casserole dishes.

COOKWARE

Attractive glass and stoneware baking dishes or individual ramekins are the best choices as metal may react with the fruit. To avoid the use of aluminum foil, cover with an inverted baking dish of the same size.

Old-Fashioned Apple Crisp

Makes 6 to 9 servings

Calories: 287
Protein: 2g
Saturated Fat: 1g
Fiber: 3g
Carbohydrate: 50g
Fat: 10g
Cholesterol: 0
Sodium: 153mg
Calories from
Carbohydrate: 67%
Calories from Fat: 30%
Calories from Protein: 3%

Filling

1 pound each Pippin and Granny Smith apples, or any variety or combination, 2 or 3 of each, 6 to 8 cups peeled and thinly sliced

2 tablespoons arrowroot powder

1 teaspoon cinnamon

½ teaspoon nutmeg

¼ teaspoon cardamom

½ teaspoon sea salt

½ cup brown rice malt syrup or FruitSource syrup or honey

Zest of half a lemon

1 tablespoon lemon juice

1 teaspoon vanilla

Streusel Topping (makes about 1¼ cups)

½ cup whole wheat pastry flour

½ cup unbleached white pastry flour

⅛ teaspoon sea salt

3 tablespoons light vegetable oil (walnut, canola, or safflower)

3 to 4 tablespoons brown rice syrup or FruitSource syrup or honey

½ cup walnuts, toasted and finely chopped (optional)

1. Preheat the oven to 400°F.

2. To make filling, mix apples with dry ingredients. In another bowl, whisk wet ingredients together and stir them into dry ingredients. Transfer mixture to a 2-quart baking dish. Place the baking dish on a larger piece of aluminum foil or on a rimmed baking sheet to avoid possible spillage. Cover dish with foil and bake until fruit is tender and you can see and hear the juices bubbling, 45 to 55 minutes.

3. To make topping, mix dry ingredients. Work in oil, then sweetener. Rub mixture between your palms until texture resembles coarse crumbs. Stir in nuts.

4. Remove cover from apples and sprinkle topping over fruit to cover. Return to oven until top is golden, 10 to 15 minutes more.

Variations

Apple-Berry-Nut Crumble: Himalaya berries are the kind of blackberries that grow wild all over northern California. When fully ripe from July through September, these big berries are oh-so-sweet and succulent. If the berries you find are very ripe and juicy, avoid rinsing them. Instead, simply pick through them and discard any that aren't plump and perfect.

Substitute 1 cup blackberries for that amount of apples and stir berries into filling last. Increase arrowroot powder to 3 tablespoons and sweetener to ¾ cup. Substitute ½ cup hazelnuts—toasted, skins rubbed off and discarded, nuts coarsely chopped—for walnuts in topping.

Apple Cornmeal Crisp: For a slightly sunnier color and a bit of crunch, substitute ¼ cup finely ground cornmeal (not polenta) for that amount of flour.

All the other whole grain flours are great included in small amounts with whole wheat or unbleached pastry flour.

Wheat-Free and Gluten-Free Crisp and Cobbler Toppings: See page 10 for a thorough description of each of the alternative whole grain flours.

Fat-Free Toppings: Omit the oil in the topping, substituting that much more sweetener for crisps or soy milk for cobblers. Or substitute an oil-free granola for a crisp topping.

For example, see the recipes for Pear Crunch with Fat-Free Granola Topping on page 145 or for Peach Cobbler with Fat-Free Topping on page 154.

Sweetener-Free Toppings: Substitute fruit juice or concentrate for sweetener in both the filling and the toppings. In addition to apple juice, cherry juice works nicely with peaches and berries.

Pear and Apple Pecan Crisp

This delectable autumn dessert with a nutty oat topping appeared in the fall 1995 issue of Vegetarian Gourmet *magazine.*

Pippin and Jonathan apples with red crimson or red Bartlett pears is one great combination for use in this recipe (be sure to leave the skins on), but any variations will be sure to please.

Filling

1 pound each pears and apples, 2 to 3 of each, about 6 cups, peeled
  if desired and thinly sliced

1 tablespoon arrowroot powder

½ teaspoon Chinese five-spice powder

¼ teaspoon sea salt

¼ cup pure maple syrup

¼ cup pear or apple juice

Zest of half an orange

Topping

½ cup rolled oats, old-fashioned or quick-cooking

½ cup whole wheat pastry flour

⅛ teaspoon sea salt

3 tablespoons light vegetable oil (canola or walnut)

2 to 3 tablespoons pure maple syrup

½ cup pecans, toasted and finely chopped

1. Preheat the oven to 400°F.

2. Combine the filling ingredients and transfer to a 1½- to 2-quart baking dish or a 9-inch deep-dish pie pan. Set either on a baking sheet to avoid dripping.

3. To prepare the topping, mix the dry ingredients. Work in the oil, then the sweetener. Rub the mixture between your palms. Toss in the nuts. Distribute the mixture over the fruit.

4. Cover the dish and bake until fruit is soft when pierced with a fork and juices are bubbling, about 45 minutes, but check after 30 minutes. Uncover and return the dish to the oven until the topping is golden, about 10 minutes more. Serve hot or warm.

Breakfast Fruit Crisp: For a whimsical effect at breakfast or brunch, substitute dry cereals such as corn flakes, puffed wheat, or Grape Nuts for the rolled oats in the crisp topping.

Pear Crunch with Granola Topping

Makes 9 servings

2 pounds pears (they don't need to be ripe), about 4 to 5 pears,
  or 6 cups peeled and thinly sliced

2 tablespoons whole wheat pastry flour

1 teaspoon nutmeg

½ teaspoon ginger

¼ teaspoon sea salt

⅓ cup FruitSource syrup

Zest and juice of a lime

2 cups store-bought granola with nuts

Calories: 211

Protein: 4g

Saturated Fat: 1g

Fiber: 5g

Carbohydrate: 42g

Fat: 4g

Cholesterol: 0

Sodium: 64mg

Calories from
Carbohydrate: 76%

Calories from Fat: 18%

Calories from Protein: 7%

1. Preheat the oven to 400°F.

2. Mix fruit with flour, nutmeg, ginger, and salt, then stir in sweetener, zest, and juice. Transfer the mixture to a 2-quart baking dish. Bake covered until edges are bubbling and center is softened, about 30 minutes.

3. Sprinkle granola over the surface and return to oven until golden, about 5 minutes more.

Variation

Pear Crunch with Fat-Free Granola Topping: Substitute fat-free granola made without oil or nuts. Ingredients may include: rolled oats (and perhaps rolled rye and barley flakes), fruit concentrate (or water, or brown rice syrup or maple syrup), oat flour, raisins or dried apples, seeds (sunflower or sesame), and vanilla.

Stove-Top Strawberry Crunch

Calories: 285

Protein: 5g

Saturated Fat: 1g

Fiber: 7g

Carbohydrate: 57g

Fat: 6g

Cholesterol: 0

Sodium: 184mg

Calories from

Carbohydrate: 77%

Calories from Fat: 17%

Calories from Protein: 6%

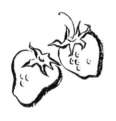

6 cups strawberries, about 2 pounds, stemmed and halved or quartered

½ teaspoon sea salt

½ cup brown rice malt syrup

2 tablespoons orange marmalade

1½ tablespoons agar flakes

2 tablespoons arrowroot powder

¼ cup orange juice or strawberry-apple juice

1½ cups store-bought granola with nuts

1. Layer berries, salt, syrup, marmalade, and agar flakes in a 3-quart saucepan. Cover and bring to a boil over medium-low heat. Liquid will come out of the berries to cover the bottom of the pot in about 5 minutes. Stir, then simmer until berries are soft and juicy and agar has dissolved, about 5 minutes more.

2. In a small bowl, dissolve arrowroot in juice. Add to pot and stir until simmering resumes and texture thickens, about 1 minute. Makes 3 to 4 cups filling.

3. Transfer berries to a 1½- to 2-quart baking dish or 4 dessert bowls. Allow to cool, then sprinkle granola over the top to serve.

Peach Crisp

Filling

2 pounds peaches, 5 to 6 cups, peeled if desired and thinly sliced

2 tablespoons arrowroot powder

½ teaspoon cinnamon

½ teaspoon mace (or more cinnamon)

¼ teaspoon sea salt

½ cup brown rice malt syrup

Zest of a small lemon, chopped

1 tablespoon lemon juice

1 teaspoon almond extract

Topping

¾ cup rolled oats

¼ cup whole wheat pastry flour

¼ cup almonds, toasted and finely chopped

⅛ teaspoon sea salt

3 tablespoons light vegetable oil (canola or almond)

3 tablespoons brown rice syrup

1. Preheat the oven to 400°F. To peel peaches, immerse them in boiling water for 1 to 5 minutes. Remove from water, and when cool enough to handle, peel off and discard skin.

2. To prepare filling, combine fruit with dry ingredients, then stir in wet ingredients. Transfer to a 1½- or 2-quart baking dish or a deep-dish pie plate.

3. To prepare topping, mix dry ingredients. Stir in oil, then sweetener. Rub the mixture between your palms. Distribute mixture over fruit.

4. Cover dish with foil. Bake until fruit is tender when tested in the middle, about 45 minutes. Uncover and return to oven to bake until topping is golden, about 10 minutes more. Serve hot or warm.

Variations

Substitute other stone fruits such as plums, nectarines, or apricots for peaches.

Peach and Berry Crisp: Sprinkle a handful of fresh berries over the peaches before adding the topping.

Calories: 235

Protein: 3g

Saturated Fat: 1g

Fiber: 3g

Carbohydrate: 40g

Fat: 8g

Cholesterol: 0

Sodium: 93mg

Calories from Carbohydrate: 67%

Calories from Fat: 29%

Calories from Protein: 5%

Brandied Plum and Nectarine Crisp

Makes 6 to 9 servings

Calories: 210

Protein: 2g

Saturated Fat: 0

Fiber: 2g

Carbohydrate: 40g

Fat: 6g

Cholesterol: 0

Sodium: 128mg

Calories from
Carbohydrate: 74%

Calories from Fat: 22%

Calories from Protein: 4%

NOTE

To substitute FruitSource syrup for the granular FruitSource, simply substitute the same amount in the filling and in the topping

Filling

1 pound each plums and nectarines, about 5 cups sliced

2 tablespoons arrowroot powder

1 teaspoon cinnamon

½ teaspoon aniseed

¼ teaspoon sea salt

½ cup granular FruitSource

2 tablespoons brandy

½ teaspoon vanilla

Topping

Millet flour contributes a nice sunny color to this topping.

¼ cup millet flour

¼ cup whole wheat pastry flour

½ cup unbleached white pastry flour

2 tablespoons granular FruitSource

¼ teaspoon sea salt

3 tablespoons light vegetable oil

2 tablespoons apple juice

1. Preheat the oven to 400°F.

2. Mix filling ingredients and transfer mixture to a 2-quart baking dish or a 9-inch deep-dish pie plate. Cover and place in oven on a baking sheet to avoid dripping on oven floor. Bake until fruit is tender in the middle and juices are bubbling, 30 to 40 minutes.

3. To prepare topping, mix dry ingredients. Work in oil, then drizzle in sweetener and mix by rubbing mixture between palms. Sprinkle over fruit. Return to oven and bake until topping is golden, 10 to 15 minutes more.

Apple Cobbler

Makes 6 to 9 servings

Calories: 289

Protein: 2g

Saturated Fat: 0

Fiber: 4g

Carbohydrate: 71g

Fat: 1g

Cholesterol: 0

Sodium: 304mg

Calories from
Carbohydrate: 94%

Calories from Fat: 3%

Calories from Protein: 3%

Filling

3 pounds apples (e.g. a combination of Pippin and Jonathan or McIntosh or
    Granny Smith alone), 11 to 12 cups peeled and thinly sliced

⅓ cup arrowroot powder

2 teaspoons cinnamon

1 teaspoon nutmeg

⅛ teaspoon each allspice and cloves

½ teaspoon sea salt

1½ tablespoons lemon juice

¾ cup FruitSource syrup, brown rice malt syrup, or ½ cup pure maple syrup

Rolled or Dropped Biscuit Topping

*With this choice in sweeteners, you'll notice that FruitSource syrup gives a rich
golden color to the crust, more so than either brown rice malt syrup or maple
syrup. All taste great.*

¾ cup whole wheat pastry flour

¾ cup unbleached white pastry flour

2¼ teaspoons aluminum-free baking powder

¼ teaspoon sea salt

¼ cup light vegetable oil, plus some to brush the surface

¼ cup FruitSource, brown rice malt syrup, or pure maple syrup

2 to 3 tablespoons soy milk for rolled biscuit, ½ cup for dropped biscuit

1. Preheat the oven to 400°F. Place a piece of foil or a baking pan under
dish to prevent spillage—with 3 pounds of fruit, this dessert does bubble over a bit.

2. Mix filling ingredients in a large bowl and transfer to a 2-quart baking dish. Cover and bake until fruit is tender all the way to the center,
45 to 60 minutes.

3. To prepare rolled biscuit topping, mix dry ingredients. Whisk together wet ingredients and gradually pour into dry ingredients, stirring
with a wooden spoon until dough sticks together. For the lightest pastry, do not overwork the dough—handle it as little as possible. (Or pulse

mixture just 4 or 5 times in a food processor so as not to overactivate the gluten, which toughens the dough.) Roll the moist dough between sheets of waxed paper to ¼- to ½-inch thickness. (Flour the bottom sheet.)

For dropped biscuit topping, proceed in the same manner, adding the greater volume of soy milk.

4. Transfer rolled dough to cover fruit, and tuck it down around the edges. Make holes in the pastry with the tines of a fork every inch or so for steam to escape.

For dropped biscuit topping, spoon dough over top of fruit, then spread it with the back of the spoon.

5. Return cobbler to oven until golden, 5 to 10 minutes more.

Variations

Harvest Season Cutout Topping: To extend the feeling of autumn, cut shapes with seasonal cookie cutters and place on top of fruit to bake, at least one per serving, e.g. squirrel, acorn, owl, leaf, and pumpkin shapes.

In addition to laying cutouts directly on the fruit, you can roll a thin layer of cobbler topping and lay it on top of fruit, then cut thin shapes and place them on the topping, e.g. stars or hearts.

Apple Lattice Cobbler: It's easy to weave biscuit dough into a lattice top for a cobbler. Roll or pat dough thin enough—⅛ to ¼ inch is perfect—at least as large as the baking dish. Cut the dough into 1½-inch-wide strips with a fluted pastry wheel. The wider you cut the strips, the easier they are to work with.

Lay half the strips across the fruit. There will be 5 or 6 in each direction, depending on baking dish size. Let the extra dough hang over the sides of the dish. To weave in the remaining strips, fold back every other strip to its midway point. Starting at the fold, place a new strip at a 90-degree angle over the unfolded strips. Unfold the folded strips, crossing the new one. Now fold back the strips that alternate with the first ones you folded. Place another new strip parallel to and evenly spaced from the first. Continue in this fashion until you reach the edge of the pie, half of which is now latticed. Repeat the process on the other half. Cut off overhanging dough with a sharp knife in a quick downward motion flush with the edge of the baking dish and tuck in ends.

Cover loosely with foil and bake until apples test done in the middle when pierced with a wooden skewer or a thick knife, for about an hour. Topping will brown even when covered.

Pear and Walnut Cobbler

Makes 9 servings

Filling

3 pounds pears, 6 to 8 pears, 7 cups peeled and thinly sliced

2 tablespoons arrowroot powder

I teaspoon Chinese five-spice powder, or I teaspoon each cinnamon and ginger

¼ teaspoon sea salt

¾ cup brown rice malt syrup or pure maple syrup

Zest of an orange or lemon, or half of each

Topping

½ cup whole wheat pastry flour

½ cup unbleached white pastry flour

I½ teaspoons aluminum-free baking powder

⅛ teaspoon sea salt

3 tablespoons light vegetable oil (canola or walnut)

⅓ cup brown rice malt syrup or pure maple syrup

¼ cup soy milk or part orange juice

½ cup walnuts, toasted and chopped

Calories: 360

Protein: 3g

Saturated Fat: Ig

Fiber: 10g

Carbohydrate: 67g

Fat: 10g

Cholesterol: 0

Sodium: 171mg

Calories from
Carbohydrate: 72%

Calories from Fat: 25%

Calories from Protein: 3%

I. Preheat the oven to 400°F.

2. Mix filling ingredients and transfer to a standard 8-inch square baking dish or any casserole of 2-quart capacity. Bake covered until fruit is tender and juicy, 40 to 60 minutes depending on firmness of pears.

3. Mix the dry ingredients for the topping. Whisk the wet ingredients together, then stir them into the dry ingredients. Stir in the nuts. Spoon the dough over the pears, spreading it as evenly as possible with the back of a spoon. Return dish to oven and bake until the top is nicely browned, about 15 minutes more.

Warm Pear and Cranberry Cobbler with Gingered Tofu Cream: For the filling, add 1 cup fresh or frozen cranberries, 1 tablespoon more arrowroot powder, and ¼ cup more sweetener.

To make 1 cup Gingered Tofu Cream, in a food processor purée until creamy smooth: 1 cup fresh tofu (½ pound), ¼ cup pure maple syrup, 1½ teaspoons vanilla, 1½ teaspoons peeled and grated fresh ginger. Add a little water only if necessary to blend, depending on texture of tofu.

Serve cobbler warm with a dollop of tofu cream atop individual servings.

Nectarine Cobbler with Sweet Biscuit Cutout Topping

Makes 6 to 9 servings

Filling

2 pounds nectarines, 6 or 7 cups sliced

3 tablespoons arrowroot powder

½ teaspoon cinnamon

¼ teaspoon mace

¼ teaspoon sea salt

¼ cup brown rice malt syrup

¼ cup pure maple syrup

Zest of lime

1 tablespoon lime juice

½ teaspoon almond extract

Calories: 303

Protein: 3g

Saturated Fat: 1g

Fiber: 2g

Carbohydrate: 55g

Fat: 9g

Cholesterol: 0

Sodium: 273mg

Calories from
Carbohydrate: 70%

Calories from Fat: 26%

Calories from Protein: 4%

Topping

1 cup whole wheat pastry flour

1 cup unbleached white pastry flour

1 tablespoon aluminum-free baking powder

¼ teaspoon sea salt

⅓ cup light vegetable oil (canola, walnut, almond, or safflower)

⅓ to ½ cup pure maple syrup or part brown rice malt syrup

⅓ to ½ cup soy milk, nut or rice milk, amazake, or
  apple juice, less with more sweetener

1. Preheat the oven to 400°F.

2. Mix filling ingredients in a large mixing bowl and transfer to a 2-quart baking dish. Cover and bake until fruit is bubbling and soft in the middle, 30 to 45 minutes.

3. To prepare topping, mix dry ingredients in a large bowl. Whisk wet ingredients in a small bowl and add to dry. Dough should be soft but pliable.

4. Roll dough out ¾ inch thick between sheets of waxed paper. Flour the bottom sheet. Cut nine shapes with a 3-inch-wide, heart-shaped cookie cutter.

5. Remove cover and place cutouts on top of fruit so they barely touch each other. Arrange in rows of three if using a square baking dish. If using an oval dish, place 5 shapes in a row down the middle and 2 on either side. Return to oven until biscuits are beginning to turn golden, about 15 minutes.

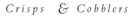

Peach Cobbler with Fat-Free Topping

Makes 9 servings

Calories: 210

Protein: 3g

Saturated Fat: 0

Fiber: 3g

Carbohydrate: 50g

Fat: 1g

Cholesterol: 0

Sodium: 176mg

Calories from
Carbohydrate: 92%

Calories from Fat: 3%

Calories from Protein: 6%

Filling

3 pounds peaches, 6 large, or 7 cups, peeled if desired, sliced

¼ cup fruit-sweetened marmalade

1 tablespoon lemon juice

¼ cup granular FruitSource

3 tablespoons arrowroot powder

¼ teaspoon sea salt

Topping

½ cup whole wheat pastry flour

½ cup unbleached white flour

½ cup granular FruitSource

1½ teaspoons aluminum-free baking powder

⅛ teaspoon sea salt

½ cup soy milk

1 teaspoon vanilla

2 tablespoons oatmeal

1 teaspoon nutmeg

1. Preheat the oven to 400°F. To peel peaches, bring a pot of water to a boil. Add peaches, and when boiling resumes, turn off heat and transfer peaches to a cutting board. When barely cool enough to handle, peel off and discard skins.

2. In a large bowl, mix filling ingredients. Transfer to a 2-quart baking dish. Place a piece of foil or a baking pan under dish to prevent spillage. Cover and bake until fruit is bubbling, about 40 minutes.

3. In a medium-large bowl, mix dry ingredients for topping. Stir in soy milk and vanilla. Transfer heaping tablespoons of dough to top of fruit, spreading with back of spoon to cover surface. Sprinkle oatmeal and nutmeg on top. Return to oven and bake until golden, 15 minutes more.

Cherry-Berry-Peach Cobbler with Almond Dropped Biscuit Topping

Makes 9 servings

Calories: 232

Protein: 3g

Saturated Fat: 1g

Fiber: 2g

Carbohydrate: 43

Fat: 6g

Cholesterol: 0

Sodium: 175mg

Calories from
Carbohydrate: 72%

Calories from Fat: 23%

Calories from Protein: 5%

Filling

8 to 10 ounces fresh or frozen cherries, about 1⅓ cups pitted

1 pint strawberries, halved or quartered

1 pound peaches, 2 large, or 2¾ cups diced

¼ cup fruit-sweetened peach jam, marmalade, or strawberry jam

½ teaspoon almond extract

¼ cup granular FruitSource

2 tablespoons arrowroot powder

1 teaspoon nutmeg

¼ teaspoon sea salt

Topping

½ cup whole wheat pastry flour

½ cup unbleached white flour

½ cup granular FruitSource

1½ teaspoons aluminum-free baking powder

⅛ teaspoon sea salt

3 tablespoons light vegetable oil (canola or almond)

⅓ cup soy milk, nut or rice milk, amazake, or apple juice

½ teaspoon almond extract

2 tablespoons sliced almonds

1. Preheat the oven to 400°F.

2. In a large bowl, mix filling ingredients. Transfer to a 2-quart baking dish. Place a piece of foil or a baking pan under dish to prevent spillage. Cover and bake until fruit is bubbling, about 40 minutes.

3. In a medium-large bowl, mix dry ingredients for topping. Work in oil, then liquid. Transfer dough by heaping tablespoons to top of fruit to make 9 dropped biscuit shapes. Sprinkle almonds on top of dough shapes. Return to oven and bake until golden, 15 minutes more.

Makes 9 servings

Calories: 202

Protein: 3g

Saturated Fat: 1g

Fiber: 2g

Carbohydrate: 30g

Fat: 9g

Cholesterol: 0

Sodium: 240mg

Calories from

Carbohydrate: 57%

Calories from Fat: 38%

Calories from Protein: 5%

Blueberry Cobbler

This seasonal delicacy is perfect for afternoon tea or as the finale to a summertime dinner party with friends. The sweetener looks like brown sugar and so lends its color to the crust.

Filling

4 cups blueberries

⅓ cup dehydrated organic sugar cane juice

1½ tablespoons arrowroot powder

¼ teaspoon sea salt

1 tablespoon lemon juice

Topping

¾ cup whole wheat pastry flour

¾ cup unbleached white pastry flour

⅓ cup dehydrated organic sugar cane juice

2¼ teaspoons aluminum-free baking powder

¼ teaspoon sea salt

⅓ cup canola oil

⅔ cup soy milk

1. Preheat the oven to 400°F. An easy way to sort through and destem the blueberries is to spread them on a white plate, one layer thick, in batches. Pass sweetener through a strainer if it appears at all lumpy.

2. In a medium-large bowl, mix filling ingredients and transfer to any casserole of 1½- or 2-quart capacity or a deep-dish pie plate.

3. Cover and place in oven on a baking sheet to avoid dripping on oven floor. Bake until berries are bubbling and done in the center as well as the edges, 30 minutes.

4. In a medium-size bowl, mix dry ingredients for topping, then work in oil. Stir in soy milk just to blend.

5. Remove cover from berries. Spoon the dough over the berries, spreading it as evenly as possible with the back of spoon. Return cobbler to oven and bake until browned on top, about 15 minutes more.

Blackberry Cobbler

Filling

4 cups blackberries

½ to ⅔ cup granular FruitSource, depending on sweetness of berries

2 tablespoons arrowroot powder

¼ teaspoon sea salt

Zest of an orange

Topping

This topping has a pleasing sunny color from the orange juice.

½ cup whole wheat pastry flour

½ cup unbleached white pastry flour

½ cup granular FruitSource

1½ teaspoons aluminum-free baking powder

⅛ teaspoon sea salt

¼ cup canola oil

¼ cup soy milk

¼ cup orange juice

Calories: 227

Protein: 2g

Saturated Fat: 1g

Fiber: 4g

Carbohydrate: 41g

Fat: 7g

Cholesterol: 0

Sodium: 176mg

Calories from
Carbohydrate: 71%

Calories from Fat: 25%

Calories from Protein: 4%

1. Preheat the oven to 400°F. Avoid rinsing very soft blackberries. Instead, just pick them over, discarding any that are less than desirable. **2.** In a large bowl, mix filling ingredients. Taste to determine sweetness. Transfer to a casserole of 1½- or 2-quart capacity or a deep-dish pie plate. Cover and bake until fruit is soft and bubbly, about 30 minutes. **3.** Just before filling is done, mix dry ingredients for topping. Mix wet ingredients and stir into dry ingredients just to blend. Spoon the dough over the berries, spreading it as evenly as possible with the back of a spoon. Return cobbler to oven until browned, about 15 minutes more.

Cakes, Tea Breads, & Muffins

Making your own cakes from scratch shows friends and family that time spent with them is special. The cakes in this book are quick and easy to assemble with tender and moist results. Although they contain no eggs or dairy products, these vegan cakes make elegant edibles.

Cakes don't have to be junk food to be delicious. Cakes often contain more sugar than flour. The original early American pound cake recipes contain 1 pound each of sugar and butter with 8 large eggs (1 pound) to 4½ cups flour. Commercially available muffins and scones may contain more fat and calories than the doughnut or Danish they are meant to replace.

The cakes in this book are made with wholesome ingredients like whole grain flours with their balanced nutrition supplied in the fiber, B-vitamins, and minerals. For the lightness it imparts, unbleached white pastry flour, organically grown when available, replaces the bleached, chemicalized, and enriched variety for up to half the volume of flour in many of the recipes.

Natural sweeteners, vegetable oils, soy milk and nut milk, and aluminum-free baking powder replace white sugar, hydrogenated vegetable shortening, dairy products such as butter, whole milk, and eggs, and regular baking powder. And with homemade cakes you are sure to avoid additives such as propylene glycol monoesters (used to increase texture and blendability) and artificial colors in conventional baking mixes.

For people on special diets, fat-free as well as wheat- and gluten-free variations on the Basic Vanilla Cake recipe are included.

HOW DOES CAKE RISE?

Cake batters are a combination of protein and starch in the grain and a leavening agent. As a cake begins to heat, the proteins firm up, squeezing out liquid. In turn, the liquid is absorbed by the batter's starch component.

Starch has the ability to absorb many times its own volume in liquid, and this ability increases with temperature. So, as the cake bakes, the protein and starch work together to keep the cake's moisture at a constant equilibrium. At the same time that the protein is firming up and the starch is swelling, the leavener is reacting with oven heat to produce carbon dioxide gas, which gets trapped in the layers of starch and protein, causing the cake to rise.

The cakes in this chapter are all leavened with aluminum-free baking powder. Those quick bread batters made with 1½ cups flour measure 2 inches deep in the pan before baking and 2½ inches afterward. Bundt cake batters made with 3 cups flour measure 2 to 2½ inches deep in the pan and rise to 3½ inches.

INGREDIENTS AND TECHNIQUE

When designing your own cake recipes, keep in mind that the proportion of liquid and dry ingredients should be about the same. The resulting batter should be pourable for a cake or slightly thicker for muffins. If batter is too thick or too thin, make corrections as early as possible during mixing, adding a bit more flour or liquid.

These recipes are less time-consuming than usual because with vegetable oil there's no need to cream the butter or shortening for an even-textured velvety crumb, or for the traditional butter cream, the sugar and shortening icing. Instead, try the frostings based on a fruit glaze, cocoa, or tofu.

I prefer wet over dry sweeteners because their natural humectancy makes for moist cakes without adding much fat. Applesauce (in vanilla cakes) and prune purée (in chocolate cakes) are suitable substitutes for oil as well.

Pure maple syrup is always a reliable and dependable sweetener for making light cakes with a tender crumb. And, to my taste, maple syrup has the most exquisite flavor of all the sweeteners.

Brown rice malt syrup is by far the most healthful of all the sweeteners. In cakes, it makes for a slighter moister crumb with a mild sweetness, nice when fruits are included to enhance the sweet taste, or you may decide to combine the rice syrup with pure maple syrup (see the Basic Vanilla Cake recipe).

Be sure to use brands of brown rice malt syrup without "natural cereal enzymes" listed as an ingredient on the label (see page 20). Or, before use, bring the enzyme-treated rice syrup to a boil, then turn heat down very low to simmer for 5 minutes to neutralize the enzymes; 3 minutes isn't long enough. Watch to avoid foaming over upon boiling. Boil just what you need or the rice syrup will thicken into a taffy consistency with storage, even at room temperature. Whisk the hot rice syrup into the liquid ingredients before mixing the batter.

Brown rice malt syrup, barley malt syrup, and FruitSource syrup (brown rice syrup and grape juice concentrate) work well in single layer cakes, cakes with 1½ cups flour per layer. However, for single layer cakes based on 2 cups flour (Basic Vanilla Cake 2) and for Bundt cakes (based on 3 cups flour), FruitSource makes a cake that is too moist to be acceptable even though the cake looks and tests done when it first comes out of the oven. Both brown rice malt syrup and barley malt syrup work well in Bundt cakes.

A company spokesperson suggested the recipe may need more protein. (In contrast to the recipes in this book, the FruitSource company's recipes call for eggs, a protein source, and high amounts of sweetener and fat [butter and margarine] even though the product is marketed as a "fat replacer.") I followed his recommendation to blend the liquid ingredients together in the food processor, substituting 4 ounces (½ cup) tofu for ½ cup of the soy milk, both vegetarian sources of protein. The cake looked all right with just 25 to 30 minutes of baking, but with cooling, the texture was still too heavy and moist even though the outside was excessively browning.

Sorghum syrup is very nice in cakes, contributing to a beautiful yellow-gold color and sweet malt flavor.

When designing these cake recipes, I tried pure maple syrup and brown rice malt syrup with all the available liquids—soy milk, homemade and commercial almond milks, rice and other grain milks, light amazake, and apple juice. Soy milk and the rice milk-soy milk blend made by Eden Foods work the best consistently. Homemade almond milk and apple juice work, but the commercial almond milk and the rice and other grain milks are usually sweetened by converting the grains starches to sugars by the addition of laboratory-extracted enzymes, which counteracts leavening, thereby creating a mushy texture, just like the enzyme-treated rice syrups do.

The Eden Foods rice milk blend tastes sweet because the soy milk is combined with amazake, a traditional naturally cultured rice porridge made of koji fermented organic brown rice.

STORAGE

Although they are always best served the same day they're baked, cakes can be made a couple of days ahead. Cool completely. Cover with cake dome or store in an airtight container at room temperature overnight, or for up to two days in the refrigerator. Or wrap cake tightly in plastic wrap to prevent drying out and store in the refrigerator for up to a week, or overwrap in aluminum foil and freeze for up to a month.

Serve cake at room temperature. To use frozen cakes soon, remove plastic wrap and rewrap in foil before partially defrosting in a 300-degree oven for 20 minutes. Remove foil and continue to heat until loaf is fully defrosted, another 10 to 15 minutes.

APPLIANCES AND COOKWARE

It's easier to frost a cake when you use a cake decorating turntable. The side of the cake you want to work on comes to you, instead of your having to reach around. Use a cake spatula to spread the frosting evenly and piping bags fitted with a variety of decorating tips for simple decorating.

Stainless steel pans allow for more even heating. They last a long time and they don't react with acid ingredients. The recipes in this chapter call for pans with the standard 9-inch diameter that are 1½ inches deep. My concession to Teflon-lined pans is the Bundt pan for a deep cake that releases easily every time.

Wooden skewers, toothpicks, or a straw from a new broom are natural materials that make great cake testers, better I think than the stainless one designed for the purpose, which is too smooth to pick up the wet cake flour particles.

Basic Vanilla Cake

Makes 10 to 16 servings; two thin 9-inch layers (¾- to 1-inch thick), three 7½-inch heart-shaped layers, one 8-inch square cake, one 9 x 13 x 2-inch cake, one 9-inch springform cake, one Bundt cake, or 1 dozen cupcakes

Calories: 203
Protein: 3g
Saturated Fat: 1g
Fiber: 0.1g
Carbohydrate: 32g
Fat: 7g
Cholesterol: 0
Sodium: 79mg
Calories from Carbohydrate: 62%
Calories from Fat: 33%
Calories from Protein: 5%

To the delight of the health-conscious baker, the amounts of fat, sweetener, and salt in this basic cake recipe are less than you'll find in other recipes. The cake is a beautiful blonde color, light in texture, and sumptuous—without the addition of eggs, refined sugar, dairy products such as butter or milk, or margarine. Although soy milk makes for the best texture—that is, slightly richer—all the liquids work nicely in the recipe.

This basic cake recipe is almost foolproof. It assembles quickly and is so versatile it can be changed to suit the season and the ingredients you have on hand. You'll notice that all the recipes in this chapter are tight or broad interpretations of this basic recipe, historically known as Plain Cake and All-Occasion Cake. The ingredients are varied by substituting other oils, sweeteners, nuts, seeds, or fruits, and seasonings such as sweet spices and extracts. Making use of a variety of baking pans—springform, tubes such as plain or Bundt, heart shapes, or bread pans—also helps to create dramatically different effects with the same basic ingredients. See the photo.

Cake

1½ cups whole wheat pastry flour

1½ cups unbleached white flour

1½ tablespoons aluminum-free baking powder

½ teaspoon sea salt

½ cup light vegetable oil (almond, canola, sesame, walnut, or high oleic safflower and sunflower oils)

1 cup pure maple syrup; or brown rice malt syrup or barley malt syrup (for both layer and Bundt cake); boiled brown rice syrup (in layer cake only, not Bundt cake) alone or with ¼ cup maple syrup; or FruitSource syrup (in layer cake only, not Bundt cake); or sorghum syrup (in layer cake)

1½ cups plain soy milk or soy milk-rice milk blend; or 1¼ cups almond milk (homemade or commercial), rice milk, light amazake, or apple juice (use soy milk only with FruitSource syrup)

1 tablespoon vanilla

Toppings (see variations)

1. Preheat the oven to 350°F. If appropriate depending on the pan(s), line the bottom with baking parchment (or waxed paper if parchment isn't available) and brush the sides with oil. Line muffin tins with papers.

2. To prepare cake, in a large bowl mix the dry ingredients well, sifting them only if desired. In a medium bowl, whisk the wet ingredients together. Add wet ingredients to dry. Whisk until batter is smooth with no lumps remaining, but not so much that you overdevelop the gluten, thereby toughening the texture. For this purpose, I like a whisk with large spaces between the wires. Makes 5 cups batter. Pour batter into pan(s).

3. Bake until cake tests done in the middle when pierced with a wooden skewer, toothpick, broomstraw, cake tester, or knife. The cake will look golden on top, spring back when touched, and pull away from the sides of the pan, 20 minutes for muffins, 25 to 30 minutes for standard cake pans, or 30 to 45 minutes for the larger pans, 30 minutes for a Bundt cake sweetened with brown rice malt syrup, 35 to 40 minutes for a cake sweetened with barley malt syrup.

4. Transfer pan(s) to a wire rack and allow cake to cool in pans for 10 to 15 minutes, less for single layers, more for Bundt shape. Serve warm or transfer cake to a wire rack to cool completely before serving or before frosting to avoid cake absorbing topping.

5. Slice with a serrated knife.

Variations and Serving Suggestions:

Fat-Free Basic Vanilla Cake: It's the cellulose in applesauce that holds in moisture and makes it suitable as a fat replacement. Substitute an equal volume of applesauce for oil. The texture is a bit spongier but quite nice. However, I find that adding any more applesauce than ½ cup makes the texture too moist.

Linen Cake: Linen is made from flax seeds. Follow the Basic Vanilla Cake recipe, reducing baking powder to 2½ teaspoons and substituting ½ cup Flax Slurry for that volume of soy milk.

Flax Slurry: Grind ¼ cup flax seeds in the small container of a blender until completely pulverized—this will take a couple of minutes. (Or better yet, purchase ground flax seeds in the refrigerator section of well-stocked natural foods stores.) Then blend flax powder with ¾ cup

water to attain a slurry with the frothy consistency of whipped eggs, for about a minute. Makes ¾ cup.

Add ¼ cup of the mixture to the wet ingredients in place of each egg called for in recipes. Use the slurry within a few days. Keep flax powder in the refrigerator to preserve freshness.

Geranium-Scented Vanilla Cake: Rose- and then lemon-scented geranium leaves are my favorites for infusing cakes with a very exotic fragrance and flavor. Pick the smaller/younger leaves and lay on bottom of cake pan, on top of parchment, with at least 2 inches of space between the leaves. You may choose to peel leaves off before serving.

Orange Blossom- and Rose Water-Scented Basic Cake: Substitute 1 teaspoon orange blossom (also orange flower) water or 2 teaspoons rose water for vanilla.

Liquor-Scented Basic Cake: Substitute 2 tablespoons rum, brandy, or Cognac for vanilla.

Vanilla Cake with Tofu Cream and Fresh Berries: Slice layers thin and place 3 slices on individual serving plates with the tips pointing toward the center. Spoon tofu cream (see page 133) over the center portion and sprinkle fresh berries over it and the cake. Garnish plates with mint sprigs.

Vanilla Cake with Season's Fruit Sauce: Spread jam between layers of cake, or prepare the cake as a Bundt cake. Either way, make sauce (see page 168) for a glorious presentation. Garnish.

Sliced strawberries carry on the heart-shaped theme should you choose to use those pans. They add drama placed on chocolate or carob icing (see page 186).

Brandied Peaches (see page 65) and the other fresh fruit compotes such as Strawberries in Vinegar (see page 65) serve as great toppings for this basic cake.

Blueberry (Balsamic) Sauce: Bring to a boil in a 2-quart saucepan 2 cups fresh or thawed, frozen blueberries (a 1-pound bag contains 2¾ cups), ½ cup maple sugar or dry FruitSource, 2 tablespoons lemon juice or balsamic vinegar, and ¾ cup water. Stir, turn heat down, and cook until berries soften, about 3 minutes. (Dry FruitSource lumps initially, but dissolves as liquid heats.) Dissolve 2 teaspoons arrowroot powder in ¼ cup water and stir into berries until bubbling resumes, color turns from chalky to clear, and mixture thickens, in a minute or two. Serve warm or at room temperature. Makes a little more than 2 cups.

Rose Petal Honey: In a small saucepan over low heat, cook 1 cup unsprayed rose petals, preferably a fragrant old-fashioned variety, with 1 cup honey. Stir occasionally over a 15- to 20-minute period. Makes ⅔ cup. Drizzle both honey and petals over nondairy ice cream served with cake. To soften texture, reheat honey briefly.

Basic Vanilla Cake 2

This recipe makes 5½ cups batter for slightly higher layers, 1 to 1½ inches.

2 cups whole wheat pastry flour

2 cups unbleached white flour

2 tablespoons aluminum-free baking powder

½ teaspoon sea salt

⅔ cup light vegetable oil (almond, canola, sesame, walnut, or high oleic safflower and sunflower oils)

1⅓ cups pure maple syrup or brown rice malt syrup; or 1 cup brown rice malt syrup with ⅓ cup maple syrup

2 cups plain soy milk, or 1⅔ cups almond milk, rice milk, light amazake, or apple juice

1 tablespoon vanilla

1. Proceed according to Basic Vanilla Cake recipe on page 162.
2. Bake for 30 minutes.

Makes 12 to 16 servings, or two 9-inch layers

Calories: 258

Protein: 4g

Saturated Fat: 1g

Fiber: 0.03g

Carbohydrate: 41g

Fat: 10g

Cholesterol: 0

Sodium: 248 mg

Calories from
Carbohydrate: 61%

Calories from Fat: 33%

Calories from Protein: 5%

Wheat-Free Basic Vanilla Cake

**Makes 12 to 16 servings,
or two 9-inch layers**

Calories: 247
Protein: 3g
Saturated Fat: 1g
Fiber: 5g
Carbohydrate: 41g
Fat: 8g
Cholesterol: 0
Sodium: 139mg
Calories from
Carbohydrate: 66%
Calories from Fat: 30%
Calories from Protein: 4%

This cake featuring three grains has great texture and taste with a sunny yellow color. The sweetness derived from brown rice malt syrup is so mild, you may choose to combine it with maple syrup.

2 cups barley flour

½ cup brown rice flour

½ cup millet flour

1½ tablespoons aluminum-free baking powder

½ teaspoon sea salt

½ cup light vegetable oil (almond, canola, sesame, walnut, or high oleic safflower
and sunflower oils)

1 cup pure maple syrup, FruitSource syrup, sorghum syrup, brown rice malt syrup,
or barley malt syrup; or ¾ cup brown rice malt syrup or barley malt syrup with
¼ cup pure maple syrup

1½ cups soy milk

1 tablespoon vanilla

Follow directions for Basic Vanilla Cake on page 162. Bake for 25 minutes. Allow to cool in pans for at least 15 minutes before transferring to a rack.

Variations

Other great wheat-free combinations:

1. For a true Barley Cake, include 3 cups barley flour and barley malt syrup for the sweetener.

2. For a cake with a subtle chestnut flavor, a combination of 2¼ cups barley flour with ¾ cup chestnut flour is delicious.

3. Combine 1 cup each oat flour, buckwheat flour, and quinoa flour. This cake has a fine-textured crumb and is speckled throughout from the buckwheat.

Wheat-alternative Basic Vanilla Cake: Substitute spelt flour (all whole grain spelt or half white spelt flour) or kamut flour for regular wheat flour for a light and spongy cake that many wheat-sensitive people tolerate well. Baked goods made with these flours are also called "wheat alternative."

Gluten-Free Basic Vanilla Cakes: Gluten-free grains and starches include quinoa, brown rice, millet, buckwheat, chestnut, teff, and amaranth flours and arrowroot powder.

Brown Rice Cake: Brown rice flour makes a good cake on its own. For two layers, decrease liquids to ⅔ cup pure maple syrup and 1⅓ cups soy milk. Cake cracks on surface but has a nice taste and texture.

Buckwheat Cake: Buckwheat Cake is really light and fluffy. Include 2¾ cups buckwheat flour with ¼ cup arrowroot powder and proceed as above. Buckwheat flour has the color of a light chocolate and so would be nice with a little of that frosting and some toasted almonds or hazelnuts.

Quinoa Cake: Another workable combination is 2¾ cups quinoa flour with ¼ cup arrowroot powder. The batter is a bit thinner than usual, but it bakes up fine to a beautiful color and a tender crumb. However, the flavor is a bit strong for some people's taste (see page 14).

NOTES

Combined rice and millet flours make a cake that is crumbly (from the millet) even when made with some arrowroot powder and less liquid. Use millet flour as support for others such as buckwheat or quinoa. Chestnut flour does not hold up on its own as the base, but is nice in combination. More than ½ cup arrowroot powder makes a cake that is too spongy.

Season's Fruit Sauce

Calories: 56
Protein: 1g
Saturated Fat: 0
Fiber: 1g
Carbohydrate: 14g
Fat: 0.3g
Cholesterol: 0
Sodium: 3mg
Calories from
Carbohydrate: 92%
Calories from Fat: 4%
Calories from Protein: 4%

This sauce is very popular served over cake because of its generous presentation and the dazzling colors of the luscious fresh fruit. Any of the liquid sweeteners work well here.

3 cups apple juice

⅓ cup FruitSource syrup, pure maple syrup, or brown rice syrup

¼ cup arrowroot powder

Zest of half an orange and/or half a lemon or lime

Pinch of nutmeg

2½ cups fruit (peaches or apricots; strawberries, raspberries, or blueberries; cherries; red and green grapes; or apples or pears; orange or tangerine segments; alone or mixed), sliced when appropriate

1. To prepare sauce, mix all ingredients except fruit in a 2-quart saucepan. Bring to a boil, whisking occasionally. When mixture thickens and clears, in a minute or so, turn heat off.

2. Add fruit. Refrigerate for at least 15 minutes before serving. Or remove sauce from refrigerator an hour before serving and whisk again or gently heat (do not boil) if sauce has thickened too much. Pour ¼ to ⅓ cup sauce over each portion of cake.

Variations

Strawberry Sauce: Feature strawberries, left whole if small, halved or quartered if large.

Minted Berry Sauce or Summer Berry Sauce: Include a combination of strawberries, quartered, blueberries, and raspberries or blackberries, along with 2 large mint sprigs or 1 mint tea bag. Crush fresh mint by squeezing it between your fingers to release flavor. Take care not to rip tea bag (if included) when stirring. Remove mint before adding fruit. Fold in very ripe raspberries or blackberries just before serving.

Rose Geranium-Scented Berry Sauce: Include a rose geranium leaf in the preceding variation in place of mint.

Hazelnut Vanilla Cake with Chocolate Sauce on a Bed of Strawberry Coulis with Chocolate Candy Garnish

Makes 12 to 16 servings, or 1 Bundt cake

Calories: 366

Protein: 5g

Saturated Fat: 2g

Fiber: 3g

Carbohydrate: 54g

Fat: 17g

Cholesterol: 0

Sodium: 244mg

Calories from Carbohydrate: 56%

Calories from Fat: 39%

Calories from Protein: 5g

Cake

1½ cups whole wheat pastry flour

1½ cups unbleached white flour

1 cup hazelnuts, toasted and skinned, nuts finely ground

1½ tablespoons aluminum-free baking powder

½ teaspoon sea salt

½ cup light vegetable oil

1 cup pure maple syrup

1½ cups plain soy milk

2 tablespoons vanilla

1 cup Chocolate Sauce I (see Chocolate Cake recipe on page 185)

Strawberry Coulis   **(makes about 2½ cups)**

1½ pints strawberries, about 4 cups, hulled

½ cup pure maple syrup, FruitSource syrup, or brown rice syrup

Zest of ¼ orange or lemon

Garnishes

½ cup hazelnuts, toasted and skinned, nuts chopped

Rose geranium or mint leaves

Chocolate Candy (see Biscotti recipe on page 216)

1. Preheat the oven to 350°F. Brush Bundt pan with oil.

2. To prepare cake, mix the dry ingredients well in a large bowl. In a medium bowl, whisk the wet ingredients together. Add wet ingredients to dry and whisk gently until smooth with no lumps remaining. Pour batter into pan.

3. Bake until cake tests done in the middle, looks golden on top, springs back when touched, and pulls away from the sides of the pan, 45 minutes.

4. Allow cake to cool in pan for 15 minutes. Transfer cake to a wire rack to cool completely.

5. Pour warm chocolate sauce over cake and immediately sprinkle hazelnuts on top to facilitate their sticking to the surface.

6. To make strawberry coulis, purée ingredients until smooth. Pass through a strainer and refrigerate until serving. Sauce may be refrigerated for up to a week.

7. To serve, place a little less than ¼ cup strawberry coulis on plate. Slice cake with a serrated knife and transfer to plate. Garnish.

Variations:

Hazelnut Vanilla Cake with Summer Berry Sauce: This is a very beautiful and generous dessert. A crowd pleaser.

Omit chocolate sauce and coulis. Instead, prepare Minted Berry Sauce on page 168 and pour it over individual servings of cake.

Hazelnut Vanilla Cake with Blackberry Coulis: In a food processor, purée six 6-ounce baskets of blackberries with 1 cup brown rice syrup or another liquid sweetener. Strain. Taste and add more sweetener as needed depending on tartness of berries. Makes 3 to 4½ cups. Sauce may be refrigerated for 5 days or so.

To serve, place ¼ to ⅓ cup coulis on plate. Top with a slice of cake. Spoon a dollop of tofu cream (see page 133) on top of cake and sprinkle with toasted and ground hazelnuts. For extra drama, strew whole blackberries around cake on top of coulis and garnish with yellow and brown/deep red/or black-hued pansies, gold or yellow chrysanthemums, and/or a sprig of mint.

(Blood) Orange Hazelnut Cake: This irresistible cake is subtly perfumed with orange. Include blood orange when available.

Add the zest of an orange and substitute ½ cup orange juice for that amount of soy milk.

Light and Luscious Lemon Cake

**Makes 12 to 16
servings, two 9-inch
layers or one
Bundt cake**

A moist, light cake with a delicately sweet and refreshingly zesty flavor.

I often make this cake in a fluted 10-inch Bundt pan (12-cup capacity). First made in 1949, the Bundt design is based on a mold that found its way to America in the belongings of an immigrant family early in the century.

1½ cups whole wheat pastry flour

1½ cups unbleached white flour

1½ tablespoons aluminum-free baking powder

½ teaspoon sea salt

A little less than ¼ teaspoon turmeric

½ cup light vegetable oil (walnut or canola oil)

1 cup pure maple syrup

1½ cups plain soy milk

Zest of a lemon

⅓ cup lemon juice

1 tablespoon vanilla

Calories: 341

Protein: 7g

Saturated Fat: 1g

Fiber: 1g

Carbohydrate: 57g

Fat: 10g

Cholesterol: 0

Sodium: 229mg

Calories from

Carbohydrate: 57g

Calories from Fat: 26%

Calories from Protein: 8%

Lemon Cream **(makes 3¼ cups)**

1½ pounds tofu, fresh, soft, or medium

⅔ cup pure maple syrup

1½ tablespoons vanilla

½ cup lemon juice

Pinch of sea salt

Lemon Sauce **(makes 1½ cups)**

When you look closely at the colors of rice milk (white), almond milk (off-white), and soy milk (tan or beige), you see that rice milk gives you the best background for light-colored sauces. Any rice sweetener works well here.

1½ cups rice milk

6 tablespoons brown rice syrup or FruitSource syrup (brown rice syrup and grape juice concentrate)

2½ tablespoons arrowroot powder

A little less than 1/16 teaspoon turmeric

3 tablespoons lemon juice

Sweet, fragrant and so juicy, yet hardy and almost constantly in bloom, Meyer lemons are the new favorite citrus from California to Boston and New York. Even the mention of them on an upscale restaurant menu can help sell a dish. Named for the researcher who found the variety in a Beijing courtyard, the thin-skinned lemons were brought to California in 1908 by Frank N. Meyer, an internationally renowned "agricultural explorer" working for a predecessor agency of the U.S. Department of Agriculture. Unable to say whether it was a combination of lemon and orange or lime, turn-of-the-century botanists gave up and named it after Meyer. Alice Waters popularized the Meyer lemon at her restaurant, Chez Panisse. Quoted in a recent article in the *San Francisco Chronicle*, Waters says, "Back in the 1970s, when we were getting started, we never ordered Meyers. We just collected them in the backyards of Berkeley. When we were foraging, we found them mixed in with the nasturtiums and plum blossoms."

Lemon balm or mint leaves

Edible (chemical-free) yellow flowers such as calendulas, pansies, rose petals, or small whole roses

1. Preheat the oven to 350°F. Lightly oil the sides of two 9-inch cake pans and line the bottom with parchment. Or brush or spray a Bundt pan with oil.

2. In a large bowl, mix dry ingredients well. In a medium bowl, whisk wet ingredients. Add wet mixture to dry and whisk until flour is fully moistened.

3. Pour batter into prepared pan(s) and smooth surface. Bake until cake tests clean, 25 to 30 minutes for layers, 40 to 45 minutes for Bundt cake.

4. To make lemon cream, purée ingredients until creamy smooth. Refrigerate until an hour before serving.

5. To make sauce, whisk first four ingredients in a 1-quart saucepan and bring to a boil. Simmer for a few seconds. Turn off heat and whisk in lemon juice. Refrigerate for 10 to 15 minutes to thicken.

6. Transfer cake pan(s) to a wire rack for 10 minutes, then remove from pans to cool completely.

7. To serve layer cake, spread ¼ cup lemon cream on a dessert plate. Place slices with the pointed ends facing each other, overlapping a bit. Drizzle sauce across slices. For Bundt cake, simply place a slice of cake on cream and pour the lemon sauce over the top. Either way, garnish to serve.

8. Cake and sauces may be frozen. Whip tofu cream after it thaws.

Variations

Lemon-Poppy Seed Cake: Add ¼ cup poppy seeds, toasted for 8 minutes at 300°F.

Lemon-Walnut Bread or Tea Cake: Oil the sides and line the bottom of a 9 x 5 x 3-inch bread pan with parchment. Halve the ingredients in the master recipe. Fold in 1 cup walnuts, toasted and chopped. Pour batter into pan and bake until it tests done, 40 to 45 minutes. Great on its own or with an apricot spread. Makes 8 to 10 servings.

Wheat-Free Lemon Cake: Either spelt (whole grain spelt flour or part white spelt flour) or kamut flours fill in nicely for pastry flour here.

Meyer Lemon Cake: Substitute Meyer lemon juice and zest for a flavor that is milder, not as tart and slightly sweeter than regular lemons.

Almond-Orange Cake

Makes 8 servings, or one layer

Calories: 496

Protein: 13g

Saturated Fat: 3g

Fiber: 4g

Carbohydrate: 60g

Fat: 25g

Cholesterol: 0

Sodium: 211mg

Calories from

Carbohydrate: 47%

Calories from Fat: 25g

Calories from Protein: 10%

This scrumptious little cake is modeled on several sampled in Italy. It is simply topped with a marmalade-based glaze and served with a dollop of tofu-almond cream. See the photo.

Cake

¾ cup whole wheat pastry flour

¾ cup unbleached white flour

2¼ teaspoons aluminum-free baking powder

¼ teaspoon sea salt

½ cup almonds, toasted and finely ground (2 tablespoons set aside for garnish)

½ teaspoon Chinese five-spice powder or nutmeg

¼ cup light almond oil or canola oil

½ cup pure maple syrup

¾ cup soy milk

Zest of half an orange

2 tablespoons orange juice

½ teaspoon vanilla

¼ teaspoon almond extract

Tofu-Almond Cream   (makes 2 cups)

1 pound fresh tofu

½ cup pure maple syrup

2 tablespoons almond butter

2 teaspoons vanilla

⅛ teaspoon almond extract

Few grains of sea salt

Orange Glaze (makes ⅔ cup)

½ cup fruit-juice sweetened marmalade (half a 10-ounce jar)

2 tablespoons water

2 teaspoons arrowroot powder

1. Preheat the oven to 350°F. Line the bottom of a 9-inch cake pan with parchment. Brush the sides with oil.

2. To prepare cake, mix dry ingredients in a large bowl. In a medium bowl, whisk wet ingredients together and add to dry. Whisk until batter is almost smooth. Pour batter into pan.

3. Bake until cake tests done in the middle, 25 to 30 minutes. Allow cake to cool in pan for at least 10 minutes, then transfer to a wire rack to cool completely.

4. To make cream, purée ingredients until creamy smooth. Refrigerate.

5. To make glaze, in a small saucepan whisk ingredients together. Bring to a boil, whisking occasionally. Transfer to a shallow bowl and refrigerate for 5 to 10 minutes for texture to firm, then spread over top of cake. Sprinkle reserved ground almonds over glaze.

6. Place a spoonful of cream at the side of each serving of cake. Or refrigerate cream in order to pipe it through a pastry bag fitted with a large star tip. Cream based on firm tofu sets up better than medium or soft tofu.

Variation

For an even quicker topping, omit water and arrowroot powder and simply spread jam over cake.

Apple Streusel Crunch Cake with Orange-Cashew Cream

Makes 8 servings

Calories: 326

Protein: 4g

Saturated Fat: 1g

Fiber: 1g

Carbohydrate: 46g

Fat: 12g

Cholesterol: 0

Sodium: 214mg

Calories from
Carbohydrate: 55%

Calories from Fat: 40%

Calories from Protein: 5%

This recipe is a quick-bread version of a traditional German yeast-raised coffeecake. Great served any time of day.

Streusel Topping

¼ cup whole wheat pastry flour

¼ cup unbleached white flour

¼ cup walnuts, toasted and finely chopped

½ teaspoon nutmeg

¼ teaspoon cinnamon

⅛ teaspoon cardamom

Pinch of sea salt

1½ tablespoons light vegetable oil (walnut or canola oil)

1 tablespoon pure maple syrup

Cake

¾ cup whole wheat pastry flour

¾ cup unbleached white flour

2¼ teaspoons aluminum-free baking powder

¼ teaspoon sea salt

¼ cup light vegetable oil

½ cup pure maple syrup or brown rice malt syrup

½ cup apple juice

¼ cup soy milk

1½ teaspoons vanilla

2 small Granny Smith or Golden Delicious apples, peeled, cored, and thinly sliced

1. Preheat the oven to 350°F. Oil the bottom and sides of a cake or pie pan or an 8- or 9-inch springform pan. (No paper lining for the pan is called for here because a cake with a streusel topping cannot be easily removed and therefore must be cut in the pan.)

2. Prepare streusel topping. Mix dry ingredients, then work in oil and sweetener. Texture should be moist.

3. Prepare cake batter by mixing dry ingredients in one bowl and whisking wet ingredients together in another bowl.

4. Stir wet ingredients into dry with a whisk with widely spaced wires. Transfer batter to pan. Arrange apple slices core side down in an overlapping circle around the outside of the batter like spokes of a wheel, then press them down into batter so just tops are showing. Distribute topping evenly over apples.

5. Bake until cake tests done in the middle, 40 to 45 minutes. Transfer to a rack to cool.

6. Serve warm or at room temperature, as is, or atop a spoonful of nut cream (e.g. Orange Cashew Cream on page 244) or with a scoop of vanilla-flavored nondairy frozen dessert.

Makes 8 servings

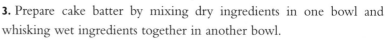

Apple Upside-Down Cake

Moist and fruity and sweetly spiced, upside-down cakes call for fruit that is firm but ripe. Unlike bananas and berries, apples hold up well with baking.

Cake

¾ cup whole wheat pastry flour

½ cup unbleached white flour

¼ cup fine cornmeal or corn flour

2¼ teaspoons aluminum-free baking powder

¼ teaspoon sea salt

¼ cup light vegetable oil (walnut or canola oil)

½ cup pure maple syrup

⅔ cup apple juice

1½ teaspoons vanilla

Topping

1 tablespoon light vegetable oil

2 tablespoons pure maple syrup or FruitSource syrup

1 pound apples (2 or 3), peeled and thinly sliced

1 teaspoon each cinnamon and nutmeg

½ cup walnuts, toasted and chopped

Calories: 313

Protein: 4g

Saturated Fat: 1g

Fiber: 2g

Carbohydrate: 46g

Fat: 14g

Cholesterol: 0

Sodium: 204mg

Calories from Carbohydrate: 56%

Calories from Fat: 39%

Calories from Protein: 5%

I. Preheat the oven to 350°F. Place a baking parchment circle or square in the bottom of a cake pan, a deep-dish pie pan, or an 8-inch square baking dish to ensure that all the fruit will be released from the pan. Oil the sides.

2. To prepare the cake batter, mix the dry ingredients. In a separate bowl, whisk wet ingredients together and mix into dry.

3. Spread the oil and sweetener evenly over the paper lining in the pan. Toss fruit with spices and arrange a single layer of fruit close together or overlapping in a spiral or concentric circles. Or layer fruit slices in 3 rows to cover the bottom of the square pan. Sprinkle with walnuts and pour batter evenly over fruit.

4. Bake until cake tests done in the middle and apples are tender, about 40 minutes.

5. Cool the cake in the pan set on a wire rack for about 10 minutes. Invert the cake onto a serving plate and leave it there for about 2 minutes. Lift off the pan and peel off the paper.

Variations

Pear-Pecan Upside-Down Cake: Substitute pears for apples and pecans for walnuts. Add ½ teaspoon Chinese five-spice powder along with other spices.

Peppered Plum Upside-Down Cake: Substitute 1 pound halved and sliced plums for apples and substitute hazelnuts for walnuts. Arrange fruit skin side down on pan. For topping seasonings, substitute 1 teaspoon cinnamon with ½ teaspoon each cloves, allspice, and black pepper.

Rhubarb Upside-Down Cake

Makes 8 servings

1 tablespoon light vegetable oil

¼ cup brown rice syrup

1 cup rhubarb, 1 or 2 stalks, or about 6 ounces cut into ¼-inch slices

1½ cups whole wheat pastry flour

2¼ teaspoons aluminum-free baking powder

½ teaspoon cinnamon

¼ teaspoon each ginger, nutmeg, and cloves

¼ teaspoon sea salt

¼ cup vegetable oil (canola, walnut)

½ cup brown rice malt syrup or FruitSource syrup

⅔ cup soy milk

1½ teaspoons vanilla

1. Preheat the oven to 350°F.

2. Oil the sides of a 9-inch cake or pie pan and line the bottom with parchment for added ease in unmolding the cake. Drizzle in oil and sweetener, then arrange fruit to cover bottom of pan.

3. To make cake, mix dry ingredients well. In a separate bowl, whisk wet ingredients and add to dry. Stir well. Pour evenly over fruit mixture.

4. Bake until center tests done, about 40 minutes. Allow to cool for 10 minutes before inverting cake onto cooling rack or plate to serve.

Plum Kuchen with Cinnamon Sugar

Makes 9 servings

Kuchen is the German word for cake. Ripe or not, the plums in this dish soften nicely with baking, imparting either a sweet or tart flavor to the dessert. FruitSource does not work as a sweetener here.

1 cup whole wheat pastry flour

1 cup unbleached white flour

1 tablespoon aluminum-free baking powder

1½ teaspoons cinnamon

¼ teaspoon sea salt

⅓ cup canola oil

⅔ cup brown rice malt syrup or part honey or pure maple syrup

½ cup soy milk

1 teaspoon vanilla

4 cups plums, 1 pound, halved and cut into ½-inch slices

2 teaspoons Cinnamon Sugar (recipe follows)

Almond Cream (see page 242), optional

Cinnamon Sugar

I experimented with four dry sweeteners for a cake topping. Organic sugar crystals are light and shiny. FruitSource is quite pleasing as long as it is finely distributed (too much of it bubbles). Sucanat (dehydrated sugar cane juice) is dark. Maple granules didn't melt where there was any more than a dusting.

2 teaspoons dry FruitSource or organic sugar crystals

¼ teaspoon cinnamon

1. Preheat the oven to 350°F. Brush an 8 x 12 x 2-inch pan (2-quart capacity) with oil.

2. In a medium-large mixing bowl, mix dry ingredients. In a medium bowl, whisk together wet ingredients and add to dry. Stir well but with minimal strokes.

3. Transfer batter to pan. Spread it out and smooth the surface with a rubber spatula. Arrange plums in 3 rows overlapping lengthwise. Press plums into the batter so their skins are showing.

4. Bake for 15 minutes. Mix ingredients for cinnamon sugar and dust the surface. Bake until cake tests done, 8 to 15 minutes more.

5. If desired, pour a couple of tablespoons of almond cream over or to the side of each serving.

Variation

Old-Fashioned Holiday Fruit Kuchen: Include 2 peeled, cored, and thinly sliced apples, 16 lightly toasted walnut or pecan halves, 4 each halved dried figs and pitted prunes, ½ cup large raisins (or ¼ cup each golden and large raisins), ¼ cup fruit juice-sweetened dried cranberries or 8 sliced glazed kumquats (see page 230). Artfully arrange fruit on top of cake.

Calories: 289

Protein: 3g

Saturated Fat: 1g

Fiber: 1g

Carbohydrate: 49g

Fat: 9g

Cholesterol: 0

Sodium: 219mg

Calories from

Carbohydrate: 75%

Calories from Fat: 29%

Calories from Protein: 5%

Gingerbread

Calories: 330

Protein: 5g

Saturated Fat: 1g

Fiber: 1g

Carbohydrate: 53g

Fat: 10g

Cholesterol: 0

Sodium: 226mg

Calories from
Carbohydrate: 66%

Calories from Fat: 28%

Calories from Protein: 6%

According to Food of the Western World *by Theodora FitzGibbon, gingerbread originated in England and Ireland. The earliest form was a solid block made of honey, flour, ginger, and spices, which was baked and then decorated to resemble a piece of tooled leather. It made a popular edible sweet present.*

In this quick bread recipe, the sweeteners, along with an unexpected pungent jolt from the fresh ginger, contribute to the color and flavor. Like the Gingerbread Cookies on page 212, the spices are based on the gingerbread of Mary Ball Washington (the mother of the President). Because barley malt syrup is just mildly sweet and too thick to stand on its own as the sweetener, I've combined it with maple syrup and some currants. Note that while molasses is included as an alternate sweetener, Barbados molasses is sweeter than blackstrap.

Gingerbread is wonderful served with applesauce, apple butter, or apple cider jelly. Or barley malt syrup heated to warm with a drizzle of lemon juice and oil serves as a healthier version of a dark sugar syrup made of equal parts butter, molasses, and brown sugar. Or try a dollop of rum or Cognac cream.

1 cup whole wheat pastry flour

1 cup unbleached white flour

1 tablespoon aluminum-free baking powder

1¼ teaspoons powdered ginger

½ teaspoon each cinnamon and nutmeg

⅛ teaspoon each cloves, allspice, and mace

¼ teaspoon sea salt

1 tablespoon peeled and grated fresh ginger

⅓ cup canola oil

½ cup pure maple syrup

¼ cup barley malt syrup or molasses

Zest of half an orange

⅔ cup soy milk

1 teaspoon vanilla

¼ cup currants (optional)

Cognac or Rum Cream (optional), see page 75

1. Preheat the oven to 350°F. Oil an 8-inch square baking dish.

2. In a large bowl, mix the dry ingredients. In a medium bowl, whisk the wet ingredients together, reserving currants. Whisk wet ingredients into dry and transfer batter to pan. Sprinkle currants over the surface and gently smooth them in with a rubber spatula.

3. Bake until a toothpick inserted in the center comes out clean and color is quite golden, 35 to 40 minutes. Allow cake to cool completely before serving, at least 2 hours.

4. If desired, serve a heaping tablespoon of Cognac or rum cream underneath, across the midsection, or on the side of individual slices of cake.

Carrot Cake

Makes 9 servings

Vegetables—carrots, yams, sweet potato, pumpkin, and winter and summer squashes—were often used to lend sweetness to eighteenth-century cakes and puddings just as they are today.

A cheap and cheerful vegetable, carrots are full of beta carotene and vitamin A and are credited with cancer-fighting abilities. Researchers at the U.S. Department of Agriculture say that eating just two carrots a day can reduce cholesterol levels by as much as 20 percent.

A combination of maple syrup, barley malt, a little carrot juice, and golden raisins sweeten this new version of an old-time favorite. In particular, barley malt— a malted grain sweetener with more complex sugars than maple syrup, honey, or fruit concentrate—substitutes very nicely for the chemically refined simple sugars in molasses and brown sugar.

Calories: 274

Protein: 3g

Saturated Fat: 1g

Fiber: 0.5g

Carbohydrate: 41g

Fat: 11g

Cholesterol: 0

Sodium: 220mg

Calories from
Carbohydrate: 60%

Calories from Fat: 35%

Calories from Protein: 5%

Cake

1 cup whole wheat pastry flour

1 cup unbleached white flour

1 tablespoon aluminum-free baking powder

1½ teaspoons cinnamon

1 teaspoon powdered ginger

¼ teaspoon sea salt

⅓ cup light vegetable oil (e.g. walnut or canola oil)

½ cup pure maple syrup

¼ cup barley malt syrup

¼ cup carrot juice

¼ cup soy milk

1½ teaspoons vanilla

1 cup carrot, 1 large carrot, grated large

⅓ cup walnuts or pecans, toasted and finely chopped

⅓ cup golden raisins (sultanas)

Carrot or Orange Cream (Optional) **(makes 2 cups)**

These undersauces are nice alternatives to the icing based on cream cheese sometimes mixed with confectioners' sugar, butter, orange juice concentrate, and grated orange rind.

1 pound tofu, fresh

½ cup pure maple syrup and ¼ cup carrot juice (for Carrot cream), or

1⅓ cups fruit-sweetened orange fruit spread or marmalade (for Orange cream)

1 tablespoon vanilla

1. Preheat the oven to 350°F. Lightly oil an 8-inch square baking dish.
2. In a large bowl, mix dry ingredients well. In a medium bowl, whisk wet ingredients and carrot. Add wet mixture to dry and whisk until flour is fully moistened. Reserve half the nuts and raisins to sprinkle on top. Fold remaining nuts and raisins into batter.
3. Transfer batter to prepared pan. Sprinkle reserved nuts and raisins on top and gently smooth surface with a rubber spatula so they are barely visible.
4. Bake until cake tests clean and is quite golden, about 35 minutes. Transfer cake to a wire rack to cool for at least 2 hours before serving.
5. To prepare either carrot or orange cream, purée ingredients until creamy smooth. Refrigerate, then serve a dollop under each serving of cake.

Fig Cake with Cashew-Almond Cream

Makes 12 to 16 servings, or 1 Bundt cake

This pretty blonde cake is studded with plump jewel-like nuggets of fig.

Cake and Garnish

1½ cups almond milk

2 cups combined dried black figs and blonde calamyrna figs, about 10 ounces, ends trimmed and figs cut into small pieces

1½ cups whole wheat pastry flour

1½ cups unbleached white flour

1½ tablespoons aluminum-free baking powder

½ teaspoon sea salt

½ cup light almond oil or canola oil

⅔ cup brown rice malt syrup

Zest of an orange

⅔ cup orange juice

Zest of half a lemon

1 tablespoon lemon juice

1 teaspoon vanilla extract

½ teaspoon almond extract

2¼ cups Cashew-Almond Cream for garnish (see page 244)

Calories: 376

Protein: 6g

Saturated Fat: 2g

Fiber: 4g

Carbohydrate: 51g

Fat: 18g

Cholesterol: 0

Sodium: 75mg

Calories from Carbohydrate: 52%

Calories from Fat: 42%

Calories from Protein: 6%

1. Preheat the oven to 350°F. In a small saucepan, heat almond milk to warm and pour over figs in a bowl to soak for 10 minutes. Oil a Bundt pan.

2. In a large bowl, mix dry ingredients.

3. Measure liquid remaining from soaking figs and, if need be, add more almond milk to equal 1 cup. In a medium bowl, whisk wet ingredients together including almond milk, then whisk into dry ingredients. Fold figs into batter.

4. Transfer batter to pan and bake until done, 45 to 50 minutes.

5. Allow cake to cool in pan for 15 minutes before turning out on a rack to cool completely. Serve individual slices with a little less than ¼ cup Cashew-Almond Cream poured on the plate or on top of the cake.

Coco-Orange-Date Cake

Makes 12 to 16 servings, or 1 Bundt cake

Calories: 427
Protein: 7g
Saturated Fat: 9g
Fiber: 2g
Carbohydrate: 59g
Fat: 19g
Cholesterol: 0
Sodium: 272mg
Calories from Carbohydrate: 55%
Calories from Fat: 39%
Calories from Protein: 6%

This recipe calls for date sugar, the dry sweetener made from pitted, dehydrated and pulverized dates. An equal volume of brown rice malt syrup is included to mellow out the effect of the simple sugars in date sugar. The cake tastes sweet with a mild date flavor.

Light coconut milk has the texture of cream. I use Thai Kitchen brand. If you can find only full-strength coconut milk, dilute 3 parts milk with 1 part water.

Cake

8 medjool dates, ¼ pound, halved lengthwise and pitted

½ cup unsweetened shredded coconut, lightly toasted (4 minutes at 300°F)

1½ cups whole wheat pastry flour

1½ cups unbleached white flour

½ cup date sugar

1 tablespoon aluminum-free baking powder

1½ teaspoons baking soda

1 teaspoon cardamom

½ teaspoon sea salt

½ cup canola oil

½ cup brown rice malt syrup

1½ cups pure light coconut milk

Zest of an orange

1 cup orange juice

2 teaspoons vanilla

Coconut Cream (makes 3½ cups)

1½ pounds tofu, about 3 cups, fresh, soft to medium

⅔ cup brown rice syrup

¼ cup pure maple syrup (optional)

2 tablespoons lime juice

1 tablespoon vanilla

¼ teaspoon sea salt

½ cup light coconut milk

½ cup shredded coconut, plain or lightly toasted, for garnish

10-ounce jar fruit-sweetened orange marmalade, ¾ cup, for garnish

¼ cup water

1. Preheat the oven to 350°F. Oil a Bundt pan or another ring mold with indentations in its design. Place dates in the scalloped indentations. Sprinkle bottom of pan with 2 tablespoons of shredded coconut.

2. In a large bowl, mix dry ingredients, including remaining coconut. In a medium bowl, whisk wet ingredients together and add to dry. Stir to moisten completely. Transfer batter to pan, taking care not to disrupt the positioning of the dates.

3. Bake until cake tests done, 45 to 50 minutes. After 15 minutes, remove cake from pan and transfer to a wire rack to cool.

4. To prepare coconut cream, purée tofu with sweetener(s), lime juice, vanilla, and salt. Add coconut milk gradually until creamy smooth.

5. Place ¼ to ⅓ cup portions of cream on dessert plates with a slice of cake perched on top. Sprinkle a little coconut around the cake on the cream and plate. Whisk marmalade with water to thin it and drizzle it over top of individual servings of cake.

Chocolate Cake with Chocolate Sauce and Raspberry Coulis

Makes 12 to 16 servings, 1 or 2 layers or a Bundt cake

Chocolate and vanilla cakes are the most popular variations in America today. The following recipes make cakes that are sumptuous and rich yet exceptionally light.

See chocolate and carob information on pages 52 to 54. Using cocoa powder instead of chocolate chips or bars cuts down on fat. Look for 97 percent caffeine-free and fat-free cocoa powder (WonderFree brand). An 8-ounce can contains 3 cups.

Cake

1 cup whole wheat pastry flour

1 cup unbleached white flour

1 cup cocoa powder, sifted

2 teaspoons aluminum-free baking powder

1 teaspoon baking soda

½ teaspoon salt

½ cup light vegetable oil (e.g. walnut or canola)

1 cup pure maple syrup

1 cup soy milk

Zest of an orange

½ cup orange juice

1 tablespoon vanilla

Filling *(for layer cake only)*

10-ounce jar fruit-sweetened raspberry jam

Raspberry Coulis **(makes ¾ to 1 cup)**

Coulis (pronounced koo-lee) means "drip" in French. Actually a thick purée of fruit (or vegetables or even slowly stewed meat juices), a coulis is used as a flavorful and decorative undersauce (spooned directly onto the serving plate) for entrées or desserts. For special effect, use two different coulis of compatible flavors and colors. Or fill a plastic bottle with a pointed nozzle with plain tofu cream and paint a design on the coulis before adding the slice of cake.

Try any very ripe fruit such as apricots, plums, or peaches, peeled. As for berries, 2 cups raspberries or blueberries yield a little more than ¾ cup purée. The same volume of blackberries yields ⅔ cup.

1½ cups raspberries, about 6 ounces, or 10-ounce bag frozen
  berries (1 cup 2 tablespoons)

¼ to ⅓ cup brown rice syrup, more with frozen berries

½ teaspoon vanilla

Chocolate Sauce or Icing 1 **(makes about 2 cups)**

1½ cups pure maple syrup

3 tablespoons light vegetable oil (optional)

2 cups cocoa powder, sifted

1 teaspoon vanilla

1. Preheat the oven to 350°F. Oil the sides and cut parchment or waxed paper to fit the bottom of 2 cake tins or a 9-inch springform pan, or oil a Bundt pan.

2. To prepare cake, mix dry ingredients in a large bowl. In a medium bowl, mix wet ingredients and add to dry. Whisk gently to form a smooth batter. Pour batter into pan(s).

3. Bake until cake tests done, 25 to 30 minutes for layers, 50 to 60 minutes for springform cake, or 40 to 45 minutes for Bundt cake.

4. Transfer pan(s) to a cooling rack for at least 15 minutes. Remove cake from pan(s) and allow to cool completely.

5. To make raspberry coulis, purée berries in a food processor or food mill. Strain through a fine strainer to remove seeds. Whisk in sweetener and vanilla and chill.

6. To make chocolate sauce or icing, in a 2-quart saucepan heat together sweetener and oil. (The oil adds a slightly more luscious quality, but may be omitted for a sweeter and less bittersweet taste.) Whisk in cocoa powder. Simmer for several minutes, less for sauce, more for icing. Turn heat off and stir in vanilla.

7. Pour 1 cup warm sauce over Bundt cake, or refrigerate icing until spreadable for layer or springform cake, up to an hour in a shallow bowl.

For layers, spread jam in center and frost top and sides with chocolate icing. Keep cake cool.

8. Spoon coulis onto individual plates and place a slice of cake on top to serve.

Variations

Chocolate Hazelnut Cake with Raspberry Coulis: Include 1 cup hazelnuts, toasted, skins rubbed off and discarded, nuts finely ground. Add three quarters to batter and sprinkle remainder over chocolate sauce.

Carob Cake: Substitute carob powder, lightly toasted and sifted, for cocoa powder in cake and sauce/icing. Toasting the carob in a dry skillet revives its flavor by bringing out the natural oils.

Chocolate or Carob Swirl Cake: Marbling lends an exciting twist to cake making. Prepare batters for one half recipe each of Basic Vanilla Cake (see page 162) and Chocolate or Carob Cake.

For standard cake tins, pour dark batter over plain batter in cake tin. Run a thin-bladed knife through the batter in a broad zigzag or daisy petal pattern.

For springform or Bundt pan, spoon the light and dark batters alternately to form 4 layers, then swirl.

Calories: 309

Protein: 4g

Saturated Fat: 2g

Fiber: 4g

Carbohydrate: 55g

Fat: 11g

Cholesterol: 0

Sodium: 216mg

Calories from

Carbohydrate: 66%

Calories from Fat: 29%

Calories from Protein: 5%

NOTES

Doubling the volume of orange juice makes for a fudgelike consistency in the cake. Allow to cool in pan for 20 minutes before transferring to rack. Substituting brown rice, barley malt, or FruitSource syrups for maple syrup in the icing makes a taffy consistency, tasty but impossible to spread.

Fat-Free Chocolate Cake: Prune purée is perfect here because both the flavor and color are harmonious and unobtrusive when combined with chocolate.

Substitute prune purée (see page 236) for oil in cake. Cake bakes about 5 minutes sooner than normal.

Nutted Chocolate Frosting: For a spreadable and pipable frosting, work ½ cup almond, hazelnut, or cashew butter into chilled frosting in food processor.

Chocolate-Pecan Bourbon Bundt Cake

Makes 12 to 16 servings

Calories: 320

Protein: 4g

Saturated Fat: 2g

Fiber: 4g

Carbohydrate: 45g

Fat: 16g

Cholesterol: 0

Sodium: 270mg

Calories from
Carbohydrate: 53%

Calories from Fat: 42%

Calories from Protein: 5%

See the photo.

Cake

1 cup pecans, toasted and finely ground

1 cup whole wheat pastry flour

1 cup unbleached white flour

1 cup cocoa powder, sifted

2 teaspoons aluminum-free baking powder

1 teaspoon baking soda

½ teaspoon sea salt

½ cup light vegetable oil (walnut or canola)

1 cup pure maple syrup, or a small part barley malt syrup or brown rice malt syrup

1 cup soy milk

⅓ cup bourbon

Zest of an orange

½ cup orange juice

1 tablespoon vanilla

1¼ cups Chocolate Sauce (see preceding recipe)

1. Preheat the oven to 350°F. Brush a Bundt pan with oil. Set aside 2 tablespoons ground pecans for topping.

2. To prepare cake, mix dry ingredients in a large bowl. In a medium bowl, whisk wet ingredients and add to dry. Whisk gently until smooth and pour batter into pan.

3. Bake until cake tests done, 40 to 45 minutes.

4. Transfer pan to a cooling rack for at least 20 minutes. Remove cake from pan and allow to cool.

5. Prepare and pour warm chocolate sauce over Bundt cake so it drips down the sides. Immediately sprinkle reserved nuts on top and, if needed (e.g. they are slipping off), lightly pat them in place.

Almond Mocha Cake with Mocha Mousse Frosting

Makes 16 servings

Calories: 484

Protein: 10g

Saturated Fat: 3g

Fiber: 6g

Carbohydrate: 76g

Fat: 34g

Cholesterol: 0

Sodium: 197mg

Calories from

Carbohydrate: 47%

Calories from Fat: 47%

Calories from Protein: 6%

Rich, moist, and luscious.

Cake *(Prepare Chocolate Cake on page 185 adding these ingredients.)*

1 cup almonds, toasted and finely ground

⅓ cup instant grain coffee or instant coffee, sifted

¾ cup almond milk in place of 1 cup soy milk

1 teaspoon almond extract

Mocha Mousse Frosting **(makes 4¼ cups)**

½ cup apple juice or water

2 cups pure maple syrup

¼ cup agar flakes

2 cups cocoa or carob powder

⅓ cup instant grain coffee or instant coffee

1½ teaspoons vanilla

1½ teaspoons almond extract

1½ pounds tofu, fresh and soft or medium

¼ cup almond butter

¾ cup malt-sweetened chocolate or carob chips, whole, chopped, or ground for garnish

⅓ cup sliced almonds, lightly toasted for garnish

1. Preheat the oven to 350°F. Line two cake pans with parchment and oil the sides.

2. Prepare cake batter and transfer to cake tins.

3. Bake until cake tests done, 40 to 50 minutes. Allow layers to cool in pans for 20 minutes before transferring to a rack to cool completely before frosting.

4. Frost cake no longer than 8 hours before serving to avoid frosting cracking on the sides. To prepare frosting, in a 2-quart saucepan whisk together and heat to boiling water, syrup, and agar. Simmer until agar dissolves, about 5 minutes. Whisk in chocolate or carob and instant grain or regular coffee and cook for a minute more. Turn off heat and stir in extracts.

5. Purée with tofu and almond butter until smooth. Refrigerate for frosting to set up, at least an hour. Frosting may be made ahead and refrigerated for several days. Frosting may be blended again if desired.

6. Line the bottom of a cake stand or serving plate with two sheets of waxed paper that meet in the center of the plate. Generously frost layers and transfer to cake stand or plate. Garnish top of cake by strewing it with a mixture of the chocolate chips and sliced almonds. With the help of a spatula, gently lift cake and pull out waxed paper for a clean appearance.

Polenta Cake

The polenta found in natural foods stores has a coarse grind like grits, too rough for use in cake. Instead, look for fine polenta in gourmet food stores or Italian delis or use cornmeal as for cornbread.

⅔ cup fine polenta or cornmeal

⅔ cup whole wheat pastry flour

¾ cup unbleached white flour

1 tablespoon aluminum-free baking powder

2 teaspoons anise or fennel seeds

¼ teaspoon sea salt

⅓ cup canola oil

⅓ cup pure maple syrup or brown rice malt syrup

⅔ cup soy milk

Zest and juice of a large orange, about ½ cup

1 teaspoon vanilla

½ cup golden raisins (sultanas)

¼ cup pine nuts, lightly toasted

Calories: 279

Protein: 6g

Saturated Fat: 1g

Fiber: 2g

Carbohydrate: 47g

Fat: 14g

Cholesterol: 0

Sodium: 260mg

Calories from

Carbohydrate: 58%

Calories from Fat: 37%

Calories from Protein: 7%

NOTE

FruitSource syrup does not work in this recipe.

1. Preheat the oven to 350°F. Oil a 9-inch springform pan.

2. Combine dry ingredients in a large bowl. Whisk wet ingredients in a smaller bowl. Add to dry ingredients and whisk until fully moistened. Fold in raisins and nuts. Transfer to springform pan.

3. Bake until center tests clean, 30 to 35 minutes.

4. Transfer pan to a cooling rack. Allow to sit for 10 minutes before removing sides. To avoid splitting cake, allow it to sit for at least 10 minutes more before removing bottom.

5. If desired, place melon ball scoops of vanilla nondairy ice cream on or next to cake and garnish with edible yellow or orange flowers, e.g. calendula.

Variation

Marzipan Polenta Cake: Omit pine nuts. Make Marzipan on page 245. Roll ¼ cup marzipan into little balls and sprinkle them over the top of the batter in the pan. Lightly smooth surface with a rubber spatula to submerge marzipan.

Chestnut Cake

Calories: 331

Protein: 8g

Saturated Fat: 1g

Fiber: 2g

Carbohydrate: 55g

Fat: 13g

Cholesterol: 0

Sodium: 213mg

Calories from

Carbohydrate: 60%

Calories from Fat: 32%

Calories from Protein: 8%

The old-world Italian sweet bread or cake called Pisticcini is an earthy confection made exclusively from chestnut flour. No wheat flour, leavening, or sweetener is included. The recipe that follows is lighter and mildly sweet, a trendier version of the original. Its exotic flavor is just perfect with afternoon tea, cappuccino, or cereal grain coffee.

Until about the mid-1930s, American chestnuts were known as "the grain that grows on a tree" because they are nutritionally more like grains than they are like nuts. While they are high in complex carbohydrates like grains, they are very low in fat, only 1 percent to 3 percent compared with about 50 percent for most nuts. Chestnuts are low in calories too, about 300 calories per cup. The protein in chestnuts has a good balance of amino acids.

They were an American culinary staple until the great chestnut blight, when a bark fungus introduced by chestnut trees imported from China wiped out the American chestnut and almost put an end to chestnut use in this country. While researchers continue to develop a blight-resistant American variety, Gold Mine Natural Foods mail-order catalog is a source for organic steam-peeled and dried chestnuts and organic chestnut flour from Italy (see Resources).

Chestnut flour imparts a rich, nutty sweet taste and adds moisture to baked goods. It also serves as a gluten-free alternative to wheat-based cakes when used to replace up to 25 percent of the wheat flour called for in a recipe, along with barley flour as seen in the variation on this recipe.

This cake recipe is delicious with a choice of two toppings.

1½ cups chestnut flour

¾ cup whole wheat pastry flour

¾ cup unbleached white flour

1½ tablespoons aluminum-free baking powder

½ teaspoon sea salt

¼ cup extra virgin olive oil

¼ cup light vegetable oil (e.g. canola)

1 cup FruitSource syrup or brown rice malt syrup

1½ cups soy milk

Zest and juice of an orange

1 tablespoon fresh rosemary, chopped, or ½ teaspoon dried, minced

¼ cup pine nuts, lightly toasted

¼ cup golden raisins (sultanas)

Chestnut Purée (makes 2 cups)

1½ cups or ½ pound peeled and dried chestnuts

Water to barely cover (for pressure cooking) or 6 cups water (for boiling)

Topping 1: Chestnut Cream (makes about 2⅓ cups)

Tofu Cream (see page 133)

½ cup chestnut purée

Topping 2: Orange Cream (see page 182)

Garnishes

Tiny sprigs fresh rosemary, lightly-toasted pine nuts, and golden raisins

1. Preheat the oven to 350°F. Line the bottom of two 9-inch cake pans with parchment and oil the sides.

2. In a large bowl, mix dry ingredients. In a medium bowl, whisk together wet ingredients, then stir into dry with whisk until evenly moistened. Fold in pine nuts and raisins.

3. Transfer batter to cake pans and bake until cake tests done and is golden, about 30 minutes.

4. To prepare chestnut purée, cook chestnuts with water until soft (pressure cook for ½ hour or boil for 1 hour). Drain and purée chestnuts while they are still warm. The chestnut flavor concentrates with time, e.g. several hours or overnight.

5. To make the chestnut cream, purée ingredients until smooth. Or prepare the orange cream. Refrigerate for a firmer texture for piping through a pastry bag.

6. Transfer cake pans to a wire rack for 10 minutes before turning cake out.

7. When completely cool, serve cake plain or with a dollop of your choice of topping. Or for easily achieved beauty, with a large star tip pipe either cream to cover the top of the cake. Decorate the top of each star with your choice of garnish.

Wheat-Free Chestnut Cake: For a cake with a more subtle chestnut flavor, include just ¾ cup chestnut flour and substitute barley flour for the remaining chestnut flour and for the wheat flours called for in the original recipe, 2¼ cups total. This is a really delicious combination.

Almond Torte with Fruit Topping (Italian Torta di Frutta)

Makes 12 servings

Calories: 431
Protein: 10g
Saturated Fat: 2g
Fiber: 6g
Carbohydrate: 47g
Fat: 25g
Cholesterol: 0
Sodium: 59mg
Calories from
Carbohydrate: 42%
Calories from Fat: 50%
Calories from Protein: 10%

A torte is most often a flourless cake based on ground nuts or bread crumbs instead of flour, and bound together and leavened with whole eggs or egg whites. A rather simple cake to make, lending itself to all kinds of variations, a torte may be baked in any size pan from 6 to 10 inches in width, and it may be presented plain, iced, or piled high with fruit. Or a torte may also contain butter, and a small amount of flour, bread crumbs or potato starch, and possibly a liqueur, or rum or brandy. According to author Marcella Hazan in Essentials of Classic Italian Cooking, *the almond is by far the most favored nut in Italian cakes (particularly in Venice), producing a firm, but fairly light cake. One of the most famous tortes to come from Austria is the Linzertorte, made in a tart shell with a nut dough, a raspberry jam filling, and a lattice top.*

In this torte, flour is included as a major ingredient with a lesser but substantial quantity of ground nuts, e.g. half the volume of flour. Baking powder replaces eggs. The oil content has been kept quite low because of the higher volume of nuts.

The concentrated nature of this nut cake makes a modest slice amply satisfying. Topped with a luscious nut cream layer and fresh fruits in a sweet apricot or raspberry glaze, prepare for this beautiful jewel of a confection to be received with rapture.

Cake

½ cup almonds, lightly toasted
½ cup whole wheat pastry flour
½ cup unbleached white flour

2 teaspoons aluminum-free baking powder

¼ teaspoon sea salt

2 tablespoons light almond or canola oil

½ cup brown rice malt syrup

½ cup soy milk

I teaspoon vanilla extract

I teaspoon almond extract

Almond Paste and Cream (see page 243; include blanched almonds; almonds with
skins are difficult to squeeze through a pastry bag)

Fresh Fruit

¾ pound or 2 cups seedless green, red, and/or black grapes combined (tiny red
Champagne grapes are nice when available)

½ pint red raspberries or strawberries, left whole, halved, or sliced

A few blackberries

Jam Glaze (see page 119)

1. Preheat the oven to 350°F. Brush a 9-inch cake pan with oil or line
with parchment.

2. To prepare the torte, grind almonds to a powdery consistency in a
food processor.

3. Mix dry ingredients in a medium-size bowl. Whisk wet ingredients
in another bowl. Add to dry ingredients and mix. Transfer to prepared
pan.

4. Bake until cake is golden and tests clean in the middle when pierced
with a toothpick or broom straw, 20 to 25 minutes. Allow to cool on
a wire rack for 10 minutes in pan before removing cake from pan.

5. Prepare about half each of the nut paste and cream. Spread ¾ cup
cream on top of cooled torte.

6. Rinse fruit, drain, and pat dry. Leaving room for a small border, artfully and generously arrange fruit on top of nut cream layer setting
blackberries on top last for accent. Brush the surface of the fruit with
glaze(s) and pour some of remaining glaze to fill in spaces between
pieces of fruit. With a pastry bag, pipe nut paste around the edge of the
cake for a border.

Other nice fruit combinations include: Whole cherries with their stems intact, or raspberries and kiwi fruit, peeled and sliced. See the New Classic Tart recipe on page 118 for other ideas.

Easy Raspberry- or Apricot-Almond Torte: Quick and easy, omit the nut cream, paste, and fruit layers. Include ¼ cup raspberry or apricot jam and ⅓ cup sliced almonds, lightly toasted. Spread the jam over the cake and top with sliced almonds.

TEA BREADS

Cakes or breads based on fruits or vegetables and nuts are lovely served at festive breakfasts or brunches, afternoon teas, or for dessert after dinner. Try these delicious, healthful variations—free of butter, eggs, and inordinate amounts of fat and refined sugar.

For the best results, bake quick breads at least a day in advance of serving. This way the flavors are intensified and the texture is set, making it easier to slice breads thin.

Zucchini-Walnut Bread

Makes 8 to 10 servings

Calories: 196
Protein: 3g
Saturated Fat: 1g
Fiber: 0.5g
Carbohydrate: 26g
Fat: 10g
Cholesterol: 0
Sodium: 206mg
Calories from Carbohydrate: 52%
Calories from Fat: 43%
Calories from Protein: 6%

Summer squashes are soft-skinned, watery vegetables that are best added raw and grated to a batter. Along with carrots, and as opposed to hard-fleshed winter squashes, summer squashes are wet enough to cook through during the baking process. The results are deliciously moist with a subtle hint of the vegetable's flavor.

It is widely held that zucchini was first bred in Italy. However, according to archaeological finds, squash was cultivated in Mexico, Central America, and in the Andes as far back as 3,000 B.C. Spanish explorers carried the seeds to North America and throughout Europe.

This recipe is inspired by one from the Culinary Institute of America that appeared in our local paper.

¾ cup whole wheat pastry flour
¾ cup unbleached white flour

2 teaspoons aluminum-free baking powder

¼ teaspoon baking soda

¼ teaspoon sea salt

½ teaspoon each ginger and cinnamon

¼ cup light walnut or canola oil

½ cup pure maple syrup or brown rice malt syrup, or part of each

¼ cup soy milk

¼ cup apple juice

Zest of half a lemon

I teaspoon vanilla

I cup green and/or yellow zucchini, about 4 ounces, grated large or
medium (not small)

½ cup walnuts, toasted and chopped

Lemon-Maple Glaze (makes 3 tablespoons)

¼ cup pure maple syrup

2 tablespoons lemon juice

I. Preheat the oven to 350°F. Line the bottom of a standard loaf pan (9 x 5 x 3-inch) with parchment and oil the sides. Set aside a tablespoon of grated zucchini to garnish surface of bread.

2. Mix dry ingredients in a large bowl. Whisk wet ingredients in a medium bowl and add to dry. Stir just enough to incorporate all ingredients, then fold in squash and nuts.

3. Transfer mixture to loaf pan. Distribute remaining zucchini over surface. Bake until cake tests done and is quite golden, about 45 minutes.

4. Allow loaf to sit for 10 minutes in the pan, then turn loaf out to cool completely on a wire rack.

5. To make glaze, bring ingredients to a boil in a small saucepan, then turn heat to low and simmer for about 5 minutes. Whisk occasionally. Brush surface of cake with glaze, if desired.

Variation

Zucchini-Carrot-Nut Bread: Substitute grated carrots for half the volume of zucchini.

Pumpkin-Nut Bread

Makes 8 to 12 servings

Calories: 175

Protein: 2g

Saturated Fat: 1g

Fiber: 1g

Carbohydrate: 26g

Fat: 8g

Cholesterol: 0

Sodium: 130mg

Calories from

Carbohydrate: 57%

Calories from Fat: 38%

Calories from Protein: 5%

Winter squashes include butternut, acorn, buttercup, Hubbard, delicata, sweet-meat, kabocha, and sugar pumpkin among others. These vegetables are hard-skinned and dense-fleshed, so they don't have enough moisture to cook through if added raw to a batter. They must first be cooked, then puréed. Vegetables prepared in this way serve as part of the liquid in the recipe's formula just as bananas do in banana bread. The results are wonderfully moist and colorful. This quick bread is great served as is, glazed, or with apple butter.

¾ cup whole wheat pastry flour

¾ cup unbleached white flour

2¼ teaspoons aluminum-free baking powder

½ teaspoon each cinnamon and nutmeg with ¼ teaspoon cloves; or

  1½ teaspoons pumpkin pie spice

¼ teaspoon sea salt

¾ cup sweet winter squash purée

¼ cup light walnut or canola oil

½ cup pure maple syrup, or ½ cup barley malt syrup with ¼ cup pure maple syrup

½ cup walnuts, toasted and chopped

¼ cup raisins

2 tablespoons golden raisins

Orange Glaze (optional), see page 199

1. Preheat the oven to 350°F. Line the bottom of a standard 9 x 5 x 3-inch loaf pan with parchment and brush the sides with oil.

2. In a large bowl, mix dry ingredients. In a small bowl, whisk wet ingredients together, then stir into dry until well moistened. Fold in nuts and raisins.

3. Transfer this thick batter to pan and smooth surface. Bake until bread tests done, is golden brown, and pulls away from the sides of the pan, about 45 minutes.

4. Set pan on a rack to cool for 10 minutes, then turn loaf out to cool completely.

Variations

Pumpkin-Nut Muffins: Transfer batter to lined or oiled muffin tins. Bake until golden on top, about 20 minutes. Makes 6.

Sweet Potato Streusel Muffins: Substitute sweet potato purée for squash. To make topping, combine ¼ cup each dry sweetener (dry FruitSource, maple granules, or evaporated sugar cane juice) and pastry flour with ¼ teaspoon each cinnamon, nutmeg, and cloves and 1½ to 2 tablespoons oil (start with less). Rub mixture between palms until it resembles crumbs. Add more oil if necessary. Sprinkle evenly over muffins before baking.

Cranberry-Nut Bread

Makes 8 to 10 servings

Cranberries are the native American fruit of the late fall and early winter season. See the Resource section to find a listing for fruit juice-sweetened dried cranberries.

¾ cup whole wheat pastry flour

¾ cup unbleached white flour

2 teaspoons aluminum-free baking powder

¼ teaspoon baking soda

¼ teaspoon sea salt

¼ cup light vegetable oil

½ cup pure maple syrup

Zest and juice of half an orange, about ¼ cup

¼ cup soy milk

1 cup cranberries, sliced in half, or ½ cup fruit juice-sweetened dried cranberries

½ cup hazelnuts, toasted, skinned, and coarsely chopped

Calories: 242

Protein: 3g

Saturated Fat: 1g

Fiber: 1g

Carbohydrate: 38g

Fat: 10g

Cholesterol: 0

Sodium: 223mg

Calories from

Carbohydrate: 61%

Calories from Fat: 34%

Calories from Protein: 4%

Orange Glaze **(makes 3 tablespoons)**

¼ cup orange juice

¼ cup dry or liquid FruitSource, pure maple syrup, or brown rice syrup

1. Preheat the oven to 350°F. Line the bottom of a 9 x 5 x 3-inch loaf pan with parchment and oil the sides.

2. In a medium bowl, mix the dry ingredients. In a smaller bowl, whisk together the wet ingredients. Add to dry ingredients and whisk until combined. Fold in cranberries and nuts. Transfer the batter to the pan.

3. Bake until cake tests done, is quite golden, and pulls away from the sides of the pan, 40 to 45 minutes.

4. To make glaze, bring ingredients to a boil in a small saucepan, then turn heat to low and simmer until a light syrup forms, 5 to 8 minutes. Whisk occasionally. Only the enzyme-treated brown rice syrup burns if cooked for more than 5 minutes.

5. Allow cake to cool in the pan for 10 minutes, then transfer to a wire rack. Brush with glaze and allow to cool completely before serving.

Variation

Date-Nut Bread: Substitute chopped date pieces for dried cranberries.

Makes 8 servings

Banana Bread

This aromatic sweet bread is a favorite, delicious served with jam or apple butter.

Calories: 246
Protein: 3g
Saturated Fat: 1g
Fiber: 1g
Carbohydrate: 32g
Fat: 12g
Cholesterol: 0
Sodium: 163mg
Calories from
Carbohydrate: 51%
Calories from Fat: 44%
Calories from Protein: 5%

1½ cups whole wheat pastry flour

1½ teaspoons aluminum-free baking powder

¼ teaspoon sea salt

½ cup walnuts, toasted and coarsely chopped

1 cup ripe bananas, 2 or 3 bananas, mashed

¼ cup light vegetable oil (e.g. canola)

¼ cup brown rice malt syrup

2 tablespoons pure maple syrup

1½ teaspoons vanilla

¼ teaspoon citrus zest (lemon, lime, or orange)

2 tablespoons to ⅔ cup soy milk

1. Preheat the oven to 350°F.

2. In a medium bowl, mix dry ingredients and stir in nuts.

3. In another bowl, whisk wet ingredients together starting with the smaller volume of soy milk. (In a warm environment such as the Bahamas, batter froths from the combined factors of a warm outside temperature, very soft bananas, and soft syrup, thereby requiring a lot less soy milk than in a cold kitchen.)

4. Add wet ingredients to dry to form a somewhat thick batter. Add more soy milk as needed.

5. Line the bottom of a 9 x 5 x 3-inch loaf pan with parchment and oil the sides. Transfer batter to pan. Bake until quite golden, 45 to 60 minutes. Turn onto a rack to cool.

Variations

Banana-Nut Muffins and Mini-Muffins: Bake until golden, about 20 minutes. Makes 8 to 12 regular size and 2 dozen mini-muffins.

Fruit-Filled Mini-Muffins: Spoon batter into mini-muffin cups halfway. Place ½ teaspoon jam in the middle and cover jam with the remaining batter.

Bahamian Banana-Yam Bread: Yams are a staple in the Bahamas. Substitute ½ cup cooked and mashed sweet yam for the same amount of banana. You may need to add a little more soy milk if yam is dryer in texture than banana.

Coconut and Macadamia Nut Banana Bread: Add ½ cup unsweetened shredded coconut, lightly toasted. Substitute lightly toasted macadamia nuts for walnuts. If needed, rinse salt off roasted and salted nuts.

Sweetener-Free Banana Bread: Omit sweeteners, substituting that much more soy milk. With very ripe bananas, it's quite delicious.

Blueberry Muffins

Calories: 194

Protein: 2g

Saturated Fat: 0.4g

Fiber: 0.5g

Carbohydrate: 33g

Fat: 6g

Cholesterol: 0

Sodium: 196mg

Calories from

Carbohydrate: 66%

Calories from Fat: 29%

Calories from Protein: 5%

A classic American treat, these whole grain muffins are tender, fragrant, moist, and sweet. Perfect for a special breakfast, dessert, or snack.

Blueberries are native to North America. A relative of the huckleberry, the wild blueberry is still found in many parts of the country and is smaller and more tart than the commercial variety. Indians presented the Pilgrims in Plymouth, Massachusetts, with wicker baskets filled with dried blueberries. Nowadays they're the second most popular berry after the strawberry.

Low-bush or "wild" blueberries are raised commercially in Maine, New Hampshire, and parts of eastern Canada. High-bush or "cultivated" blueberries are grown in New Jersey, North Carolina, Michigan, Oregon, Washington, Arkansas, Georgia, and Florida.

Muffins sweetened with fresh fruit and a sweetener are great served on their own or with a fruit spread.

Homemade Cider Syrup (makes 2 cups)

1 gallon apple cider

Muffins

2 cups whole wheat pastry flour or part unbleached white flour

1 tablespoon aluminum-free baking powder

1 teaspoon nutmeg or mace

Zest of an orange

¼ teaspoon sea salt

¼ cup canola oil

½ cup brown rice malt syrup, sorghum syrup, Homemade Cider Syrup,
  or pure maple syrup for a sweeter taste

⅔ cup soy milk, or part orange or apple juice

1 teaspoon vanilla

1 cup blueberries

Cinnamon Sugar for topping (see page 179)

1. To prepare cider syrup ahead of time, bring cider to a boil, then slow-boil uncovered until reduced in volume to 2 cups, about 2 hours in a 6-quart pot. Keeps for months stored in the refrigerator.

2. To make muffins, preheat the oven to 350°F.

3. Mix dry ingredients. Whisk wet ingredients together and add to dry. Combine ingredients with minimal strokes so as not to activate gluten. Gently fold in most of the berries, reserving a few to sprinkle on top.

4. Transfer batter to paper muffin cups (I use the large 2½-inch size) or oiled muffin pans. Fill to near the brim.

5. Bake until golden brown, 20 to 30 minutes. Let cool for 5 minutes, then transfer muffins to a wire rack to cool completely.

Variations

Raspberry-Nut Muffins: Substitute 1½ cups raspberries for blueberries. Add ½ cup walnuts, toasted and chopped. Sprinkle the top with a little more nutmeg.

Strawberry-Hazelnut Muffins: Substitute strawberries, chopped small, for blueberries. Include ½ cup hazelnuts, toasted, skinned, and chopped.

Very Berry Muffins: Include an assortment of berries such as raspberries, blackberries, and blueberries.

Very Low-Fat Bran Muffins: Thanks to Rachel Matesz for this creative variation on the blueberry muffin recipe. Bran, the outermost layers of whole grains—wheat bran, oat bran, and rice bran—is known for its soluble fiber that helps lower cholesterol. In a diet that contains whole grains on a regular basis, e.g. brown rice and whole grain breads and pastas, bran muffins are an unnecessary but fun variation on the muffin theme.

Substitute ½ cup bran for that amount of flour. Substitute cinnamon for nutmeg. To reduce fat even further, substitute applesauce for half (2 tablespoons) of the oil. Include ½ cup raisins, reserving a few to sprinkle on top of each muffin.

Granola Muffins: Substitute cinnamon for nutmeg and lemon zest for orange zest. Fold in ½ to 1 cup granola, with raisins in place of blueberries.

Amaranth Muffins: Substitute ¼ cup amaranth flour for that amount of pastry flour. For a wheat-free variation, substitute barley flour alone or with oat, brown rice, or millet flours for the pastry flour. Increase soy milk—up to double the amount called for—to form a thick but pourable batter. Fold in toasted nuts and raisins if desired.

Cookies

Cookies are pleasing, quick treats for the child in all of us. When they are homemade, these all-American comfort foods make the kitchen fragrant with sweet spices and toasting nuts. Great served alone, cookies also make wonderful textural counterpoints to simple soft desserts like puddings and gels, or desserts based on fresh or dried fruits such as sorbets and compotes. And cookies make fine presents at holiday time.

Historically speaking, the word "cookie" appears after the introduction of baking powder. Until then, leavening agents included eggs, yeast, pearl ash, and saleratus or baking soda. Many New England seaport towns in the early nineteenth century had bake-houses, or bakeries as we call them today. They baked hard biscuits and crackers for the sailing ships stocking provisions for their voyages. A typical recipe of the time was high in sugar and fat. Cookie recipes that appear in today's popular magazines and newspapers usually aren't any healthier than the Colonial ones, often containing equal volumes of flour, fat, and sugar.

Nowadays, adults and children alike rely more and more on packaged baked goods, including cookies, for their snacks and instead of whole meals. An infinitely better idea, it would seem, is first to learn and then to teach the children in our lives how to make a few great-tasting, healthful and easy-to-prepare cookie recipes. By doing so, our children experience their connection with the larger environment (plants from the earth—grains, fruits, nuts, and seeds) and will see themselves as knowledgeable and self-sufficient people capable of transforming natural foods into satisfying snacks.

INGREDIENTS

Liquid, in contrast to fat, makes for a cakier cookie. The liquid adds steam as the cookies bake, making them puff. On the other hand, cookies made without liquid are quite crisp and crunchy—and also higher in fat and sugar, even natural sugar. Fat gets hotter than the water in the dough and drives out the moisture. Fat also makes the dough softer so it melts when hot, making cookies spread.

In contrast to cakes, any brand of brown rice syrup and FruitSource (a brand of sweetener containing brown rice syrup and grape juice concentrate) works well in cookie making. The enzyme added to produce most brands of rice syrup does not affect the leavening power of baking powder or baking soda in this case. I believe this is because such a small amount of both baking powder or soda and liquid is called for in making cookie doughs. (See page 21 for more information on FruitSource.) These sweeteners combine especially well with dried fruits such as raisins to increase the sweetness quotient.

TECHNIQUE

This chapter is organized by technique from rolled to dropped cookies and on to bars. Wheat-free cookie recipes are sprinkled throughout; see the variations.

As with pastries, for rolled cookies a slightly wet dough is easier to work with than a dry one. You can always work in a little more flour if the dough is too wet, but it's next to impossible to add more liquid once the dough is pulled together, unless you drizzle it in before the dough is shaped into a ball. Doing so afterward can toughen the texture of the dough by overdeveloping the gluten in the flour. If you think a dough is too wet, let it sit for a couple of minutes for the flour to absorb the liquid ingredients before working in more flour.

The use of liquid sweeteners and vegetable oils eliminates the need to chill cookie doughs before use. Liquid sweeteners harden with refrigeration, making the dough difficult to roll out without crumbling or cracking. Oil doesn't become solid with refrigeration as do the hard fats used in regular recipes.

Rolled cookie doughs double as pie pastries. The most important things to focus on are getting the texture right—soft, smooth, and pliable, but not wet and sticky—and not overworking the dough. For flaky dough with consistent color, roll out dough between sheets of waxed paper, sprinkling flour or arrowroot powder over the bottom sheet only, not on top of the dough, which can mar the look. Grind leftover cookies into crumbs to use for toppings for puddings or fruit compotes or to use in pressed crusts for cream or pudding pies.

You'll know ahead of time that you will like the outcome if you make it a habit to taste the batter or dough for sweetness and spice.

Stored in the appropriate container, baked cookies will keep for several days. Metal containers with looser lids are good for cookies that must remain crisp. Sturdy plastic containers with tight-fitting lids are good for softer cookies (and cakes) that should retain their moisture.

To refresh (crispen) day-old cookies, return them to a 350-degree oven for 10 minutes.

To freeze baked cookies, cook cookies completely. Place in airtight containers or resealable plastic freezer bags. Thaw covered at room temperature.

FORMULAS

While designing and experimenting with these recipes I noticed how much fat and sweetener it takes to make a great-tasting cookie without sacrificing one's health in the process. Use these recipes to create more of your own. Or gauge other recipes by using these as a basis of comparison, for example, how much sweetener and oil per cup of flour do others use?

In these recipes, the ratio of dry to wet volumes vary from 2 parts dry ingredients (flours) to a little more than two thirds to 1 part wet ingredients (oil, sweeteners, and perhaps liquid such as fruit juice concentrate or water) for rolled cookie cutter cookies, to 2 parts dry to 1 part wet for thumbprint or hand-shaped cookies, to 2 parts dry and 1 to 2 parts wet ingredients for dropped cookies.

I use around ¼ cup (from 2 tablespoons to ⅓ cup) sweetener per cup of flour and 2½ tablespoons (actually from 2 to 4 tablespoons) oil per cup of flour. To use less sweetener or less fat, include fruit juice concentrate, fruit juice, or water to texture desired. The recipes that are highest in fat in this book are the Linzertorte, Peanut Butter, and Chocolate Chip Cookies, each with ¼ cup oil per cup of flour plus ½ cup nuts, nut butter, or chocolate chips per cup flour.

Other cookie recipe formulas I generally follow are: ⅛ teaspoon sea salt per cup flour, ½ teaspoon baking powder or baking soda per cup flour, and around 1 teaspoon each of the sweet spices or vanilla per cup flour.

COOKWARE AND SUPPLIES

Ice cream scoops have a spring action that saves time while ensuring consistent size and shape, and easy cleanup. Stainless steel scoops are best and the right weight will feel good in your hand. Try a small scoop measuring 2 tablespoons or larger ones measuring ¼ to ⅓ cup.

As for shapes, cookie cutters offer the most variety and fun.

Use a flat baking sheet or the bottom of a reversed baking pan so the heat circulates evenly over the cookies. A pan with high sides deflects the heat.

Baking parchment is a real help in making cookies because it prevents the bottoms from browning too much and from sticking to the pan. Parchment eliminates the use of oil, which tends to darken and burn over time, making the pan unfit for use. A sheet of parchment may be used twice.

WHEAT-FREE COOKIES

For cookies that are free of wheat flour, feature other grains such as spelt flours (whole and white) or barley and oat flours with their white color and powdery, light and dry qualities. Spelt and barley flours are the nicest grains to use on their own. A combination of a cup each of oat and barley flours make for cookies that are dry and smooth in texture. Brown rice and/or millet flours are nice additions to this basic combination.

Millet, brown rice, and corn flours (or cornmeal) offer slightly sandy textures that add a bit of chewy crunch. Millet is especially nice for the sunny yellow color it imparts. Chestnut flour lends a distinctively pleasing sweet aroma and taste. Arrowroot powder makes for a very smooth, crisp-tender cookie. Rye, buckwheat, teff, and quinoa are less suitable grains because of their strong flavors, but are nice used in small amounts for variety.

ROLLED (OR COOKIE CUTTER) COOKIES

For cookies with a personality year-round, find appropriate cookie cutters such as hearts for Valentine's Day; flowers, butterflies, and ducks in springtime; fish in the summer; pumpkins, leaves, acorns, and squirrels in the autumn; cats and owls at Halloween; or stars, trees, bells, angels, gingerbread men, or Hanukkah cutouts during the winter holiday season.

Vanilla Cookies

Calories: 59

Protein: 0.4g

Saturated Fat: 0

Fiber: 0.1g

Carbohydrate: 8g

Fat: 2g

Cholesterol: 0

Sodium: 28mg

Calories from
Carbohydrate: 60%

Calories from Fat: 37%

Calories from Protein: 3%

Arrowroot powder makes these cookies perfectly crisp.

¾ cup whole wheat pastry flour or spelt flour

¼ cup arrowroot powder or oat flour

½ teaspoon aluminum-free baking powder

⅛ teaspoon sea salt

3 tablespoons canola oil

¼ cup FruitSource syrup or another liquid sweetener

I tablespoon vanilla

I. Preheat the oven to 350°F. Line a baking sheet with parchment or brush it with oil.

2. Mix dry ingredients. In another bowl, whisk wet ingredients together and add to dry. Stir well and form a smooth ball of dough. Roll dough out quite thin (up to ⅛ inch) between sheets of waxed paper (dust the bottom sheet liberally with arrowroot powder or flour).

3. Cut 3-inch rounds with scalloped cookie cutters and transfer to baking sheet. Bake until golden around the edges and underside, 8 to 12 minutes. Transfer baking sheet to a cooling rack.

Variations

Cardamom Cookies: Cardamom adds a very attractive exotic taste to these cookies. Include ½ teaspoon each cardamom and cinnamon. Decrease vanilla to ½ teaspoon.

Fruit-Filled Cardamom Cookies: With tiny hors d'oeuvre cutters, cut a small round scallop shape or a crescent moon shape out of the center of half the larger round scallop shapes. After baking, fill cookies with colorful jam as in the Heart Tart recipe on page 210.

Sesame Cookies: These cookies are densely covered with crunchy sesame seeds.

Decrease vanilla to ½ teaspoon. Roll out dough, then sprinkle top of dough with ¼ cup toasted sesame seeds. Return waxed paper to dough and roll/press seeds into dough. Cut with seasonal cookie cutters and bake.

Rum Spice Cookies: Reduce vanilla to ½ teaspoon. Add 1 teaspoon cinnamon, ½ teaspoon nutmeg, ¼ teaspoon allspice, and ⅛ teaspoon each ginger and cloves to dry ingredients. Add 1 tablespoon rum to wet ingredients. Work in a bit more flour or arrowroot powder as needed to make a smooth dough. Roll out dough ¼ inch thick and cut into star shapes. Makes 8 to 12.

To decorate, press a fruit juice-sweetened dried cranberry in the center of each cookie if desired. Or, after baking cookies, dip top of stars in a shallow bowl of chocolate sauce (see page 186). Invert onto plate and refrigerate for 10 minutes to set topping.

Bake until golden around the edges, 12 to 15 minutes.

Orange-Date Rugelach: To prepare filling, pit and chop ¼ pound or about 8 dates. Transfer to a small pan with zest and juice of an orange, ½ teaspoon nutmeg, and a few grains of salt. Bring to a boil, then turn heat down and cook until tender, about 5 minutes. Turn off heat and whisk in 1 teaspoon vanilla or orange flower water. Transfer and spread out in a small bowl. Refrigerate while you prepare pastry.

Omit vanilla in pastry. Add more flour as needed to roll dough in a thin circle. With a rubber spatula, spread filling over pastry. Sprinkle a heaping tablespoon of lightly toasted pine nuts over purée. Cut into 12 wedges and roll each up from the outer edge inward.

Bake for 15 minutes. Remove from oven and brush a little Fruit-Source syrup over the top of each cookie. Return to oven and bake 5 minutes more. Makes 12.

Pine Nut Crescent Cookies: Reduce vanilla to ½ teaspoon. Spread ¼ cup lightly toasted pine nuts on counter. Roll dough into a log and cut into 12 portions. Roll each section of dough into a small log and press on nuts. Bend into crescent shapes. Bake for 10 minutes. Brush with diluted sweetener, taking care not to dislodge nuts. Return to oven until golden, about 5 minutes more.

Wheat-Free Vanilla Cookies: Substitute spelt or barley flour for wheat flour.

Heart Tarts

Calories: 205

Protein: 2g

Saturated Fat: 1g

Fiber: 1g

Carbohydrate: 32g

Fat: 8g

Cholesterol: 0

Sodium: 62mg

Calories from

Carbohydrate: 60%

Calories from Fat: 35%

Calories from Protein: 5%

These cookies are fun to serve on Valentine's Day. They are adaptable to any season or occasion by varying the cookie cutters and filling. Less oil is called for in this recipe than in some others because the nuts add a rich quality of their own. See the photo.

½ cup almonds, toasted and finely ground

1 cup whole wheat pastry flour

½ teaspoon aluminum-free baking powder

⅛ teaspoon sea salt

2 tablespoons vegetable oil (light almond or canola)

3 tablespoons brown rice syrup, FruitSource, or barley malt

2 tablespoons pure maple syrup

½ teaspoon vanilla

½ teaspoon almond extract

Up to ½ cup fruit-sweetened raspberry or apricot jam or

    orange marmalade (half a 10-ounce jar)

1. Preheat the oven to 350°F. Line a baking sheet with parchment or lightly brush it with oil.

2. Mix dry ingredients. Whisk wet ingredients together and stir into dry. If necessary, add a little more flour to form a smooth dough.

3. Roll out dough thin (⅛ inch thick or less) between sheets of waxed paper. (Sprinkle flour over the bottom sheet only to avoid marring the surface.) Cut out 3-inch heart shapes as close to each other as possible and transfer to baking sheet. With a small hors d'oeuvre cutter, cut a smaller heart out of the middle of half the cookie shapes.

4. Bake until cookies are lightly toasted on the bottom or around the edges, 7 to 12 minutes, depending on thickness. Cookies become crisp and crunchy as they cool and so shouldn't be cooked a minute too long.

5. When cool, sandwich 2 teaspoons jam between the layers so the pretty color of the jam shows through the top.

Variations

Hazelnut Heart Tarts: Substitute hazelnuts for almonds or omit nuts altogether and include the following filling, if desired. Omit almond extract.

Sweet Hazelnut Filling: This spread tastes like wonderfully rich European chocolate-caramel candies. Mix 3 tablespoons barley malt with 1 tablespoon hazelnut butter and ¼ teaspoon vanilla. (Note: If nut butter has separated, use the thick part, not the oily part.) Refrigerate. Makes about ¼ cup.

Fill cookies just before serving, or keep filled cookies in a cool place to retain firm filling texture.

Almond-Anise Cookies: Add 2 teaspoons anise seeds, ground. Roll dough out ⅛ to ¼ inch thick. Transfer cutouts to baking sheet and garnish each cookie with an almond. Makes 1 dozen.

Ginger Cookies: Omit almonds. Add 1 teaspoon powdered ginger with dry ingredients or 2 teaspoons peeled and finely grated fresh ginger with wet ingredients. Or add half of each. Garnish tops with a single raisin placed in the center of each cookie. Makes 1 dozen.

Big Birthday Cookie: For an extra special birthday cookie, shape the whole mound of dough into a ball and roll out to form a big cookie—½-inch thick by 9 inches in diameter. Set raisins in place to make a happy face.

Wheat-Free Almond Cookies: Substitute a combination of oat and barley flours for whole-wheat pastry flour. Sprinkle in more flour as needed.

Gingerbread Cookies

Calories: 164

Protein: 1g

Saturated Fat: 0g

Fiber: 0.2g

Carbohydrate: 27g

Fat: 6g

Cholesterol: 0

Sodium: 135mg

Calories from

Carbohydrate: 63%

Calories from Fat: 33%

Calories from Protein: 3%

Children are partial to gingerbread men because they're so much fun to decorate and they double as edible Christmas tree ornaments. (Poke a hole in the top for stringing with ribbon or yarn.)

These cookies are a vast improvement on Ginger Snaps, those store-bought childhood staples containing enriched flour, sugar, vegetable shortening, molasses, corn syrup, corn flour, ginger, leavening, salt, caramel color, and a preservative.

The flavorings in this recipe are based on Mary Ball Washington's (mother of the president) gingerbread. Famous in its time, it contained 18 ingredients, including 3 kinds of sweetener (light molasses, dark brown sugar, and honey), butter, sherry, eggs, baking soda, milk, and cream of tartar. (Mace is a spice extracted from the fibrous coating of nutmeg.) Instant grain "coffee" powder and the sweeteners create the authentic color. See the photo.

3 cups whole wheat pastry flour

1 tablespoon aluminum-free baking powder

4 teaspoons powdered ginger, or 2 tablespoons peeled and
   grated small fresh ginger, or half of each

1½ teaspoons cinnamon

½ teaspoon nutmeg

½ teaspoon cloves

¼ teaspoon mace

½ teaspoon sea salt

½ cup light vegetable oil (canola, walnut, etc.)

¾ cup pure maple syrup or part barley malt syrup

⅓ cup instant grain "coffee" powder

¼ cup currants or fruit-sweetened dried cranberries for decoration

1. Preheat the oven to 400°F. Line two baking sheets with parchment or brush with oil.

2. Mix dry ingredients. Include fresh ginger with wet ingredients, and to release color and flavor of grain "coffee," whisk it with wet ingredients. (Note: Finely ground instant grain "coffee" dissolves easily in room temperature liquid, but for grain "coffee" granules, heat the wet ingredients together and let sit until "coffee" granules have dissolved.) Add wet mixture to dry. Mix well and shape dough into a cohesive ball.

3. Roll out dough ¼ inch thick between sheets of waxed paper. To maintain uniformly dark color for gingerbread dough, flour only the bottom sheet. Cut out shapes with cookie cutters. (I have 3 sizes ranging from 2 to 10 inches in height. It's fun to cut out the bigger ones and then cut out little ones from the remaining small pieces of dough.) Transfer to baking sheets and then press currants or dried cranberries in place for eyes, nose, mouth, and 3 buttons.

4. Bake cookies until golden on the bottom, 10 to 12 minutes.

Variations

For more innocent cookies—less rich and sweet—substitute less oil (⅓ cup) and substitute up to 1 cup barley malt for maple syrup. Add more flour as needed.

Gingerbread Cutout Cookies: Include currants or cranberries in the dough and roll out ¼- to ½-inch thick. Cut with cookie cutters— 3-inch hearts or stars are nice. Yield is 2 to 3 dozen cookies.

Multigrain Shortbread

In sixteenth-century Europe, making these attractive treats evolved into an art form that was especially popular during the holiday season. The designs on today's shortbread molds are inspired by antique American butter molds and plaques. For more variety, springerle plaques or cookie stamps made of ceramic are available with traditional European motifs—angels, Santas, grape clusters, winter scenes, even a Hanukkah mold with menorah and dreidl designs. When not in use, the molds make great kitchen decorations.

While shortbread is usually made with 2 parts white flour to 1 part butter and ½ to 1 part white sugar, this new recipe, inspired by my friend Monique Brief, is far more healthful than the Scottish original. Brown rice flour contributes a slightly sandy-smooth texture. See the photo.

1 cup whole wheat pastry flour

1 cup unbleached white flour

Makes about a dozen 3-inch cookies

Calories: 214

Protein: 2g

Saturated Fat: 1g

Fiber: 0.3g

Carbohydrate: 31g

Fat: 9g

Cholesterol: 0

Sodium: 128mg

Calories from Carbohydrate: 57%

Calories from Fat: 39%

Calories from Protein: 4%

1 cup brown rice flour; or ½ cup each brown rice flour and millet flour; or

  ½ cup brown rice flour with 2 tablespoons each amaranth and teff flours

1 teaspoon aluminum-free baking powder

½ teaspoon sea salt

½ cup light vegetable oil

⅓ cup each brown rice malt syrup and pure maple syrup or ⅔ cup pure maple syrup

2 teaspoons vanilla

1. Preheat the oven to 350°F. Brush a shortbread mold with oil (or an 8-inch square baking dish or a 9-inch pie pan).

2. In a medium bowl, mix dry ingredients. In a smaller bowl, whisk together wet ingredients. Add wet ingredients to dry and stir to form dough. Add more pastry flour as necessary to form a smooth dough. Transfer to a floured sheet of waxed paper. Place another sheet on top of dough and roll dough out to a circle that is the size of the mold, about ½-inch thick. Lift off top sheet of waxed paper and invert dough into mold. Firmly press dough into mold and smooth edges. (Prick the pastry with a fork. If not using a shortbread mold that is scored on the bottom, cut the dough into 12 or 16 squares or wedges.)

3. Bake until edges are golden, about 30 minutes. Allow to cool for at least ½ hour before unmolding. Place a serving plate or small cutting board on top of shortbread mold and turn both over to effortlessly release shortbread.

Variations

Lavender Shortbread: For a unique way to enjoy the flavor and fragrance of lavender ("the springtime aphrodisiac" according to a horticultural friend), add 2 tablespoons fresh lavender flowers, stripped from stem and finely chopped, or 1 tablespoon dry flowers, to dry ingredients. If desired, also include 1 tablespoon minced mint leaves.

Multigrain Shortbread Cookies: Roll the dough ½ inch thick between sheets of waxed paper. Cut into desired shapes with cookie cutters and transfer to a baking sheet you have lined with parchment or lightly oiled. Poke holes in the surface with a fork and, if desired, sprinkle dehydrated cane juice or organic sugar crystals over the top.

    Bake until the edges and bottoms are barely golden, 15 to 20 minutes. Cookies harden somewhat as they cool.

Hazelnut Shortbread Cookies: Add ½ cup hazelnuts, toasted, skinned, and chopped or finely ground. The nut meal from making hazelnut milk (called Toasted Hazelnut Sprinkles, see page 242), works nicely too.

Pecan Sandies: Substitute pecan meal for hazelnuts in the preceding variation. Roll out the dough ¼-inch thick and cut it into 3-inch circles or in wavy-edged squares with a pastry wheel. Place one whole pecan in the center of each cookie. Check cookies after 10 minutes of baking.

Almond Tea Cookies: Substitute almond meal (toasted and ground almonds) or Toasted Almond Sprinkles (see page 242) for the nuts in the hazelnut recipe variation.

Millet-Nut Crunchies

Thanks to Barbara Taylor for inspiration on this shortbread-like recipe.

⅓ cup millet

1½ cups millet flour

1½ cups whole wheat pastry flour

1 teaspoon aluminum-free baking powder (optional)

½ teaspoon sea salt

¾ cup pecans, toasted and chopped

¾ cup raisins

⅓ cup light vegetable oil

⅓ cup brown rice syrup

½ cup apple juice concentrate

Makes 9

Calories: 426

Protein: 7g

Saturated Fat: 1g

Fiber: 4g

Carbohydrate: 70g

Fat: 16g

Cholesterol: 0

Sodium: 57mg

Calories from

Carbohydrate: 62%

Calories from Fat: 32%

Calories from Protein: 6%

1. Preheat the oven to 350°F. Soak millet in water to cover for 15 or 20 minutes. Brush an 8-inch square baking dish with oil.
2. Mix the dry ingredients. Drain millet and, in another bowl, whisk millet with wet ingredients and stir into dry to form dough. Transfer mixture to baking dish. Press with moistened fingers and smooth edges with a rubber spatula.

3. Bake until quite golden around edges, about 30 minutes. Cut into squares while still warm.

4. For variety, drizzle top with chocolate sauce (see page 186) by pressing squeeze bottle back and forth across entire surface. Allow to cool in refrigerator for about 10 minutes.

Biscotti

Makes 1½ to 2 dozen

Calories: 147
Protein: 2g
Saturated Fat: 1g
Fiber: 1g
Carbohydrate: 18g
Fat: 8g
Cholesterol: 0
Sodium: 101mg
Calories from
Carbohydrate: 49%
Calories from Fat: 46%
Calories from Protein: 5%

Biscotti are the mildly sweet, crisp, and crunchy biscuits formerly served only in Italian coffee and pastry shops. Now America's hottest cookies, biscotti are often studded with almonds or hazelnuts (and less often with walnuts or pine nuts) or flavored with anise. Piled into clear glass jars and perched on countertops, they beckon to be savored with espresso, cappuccino, tea, wine, or even soup as is done in Tuscany.

The word biscotti means "twice-cooked." A simple dough is formed into a loaf, baked, and then sliced. The pieces are laid out to be baked a second time.

The origin of biscotti goes back to fifth-century Greece where a cinnamon and sesame version was created. Italian biscotti were first baked in thirteenth-century Tuscany. From there they were carried to many parts of the Continent such as Germany, where they were transformed into an almond bread called mandlebrodt. In Sweden they are made with half rye flour and orange juice. In Morocco the cookies are scented with rose water or orange flower water.

This recipe, which appeared in Natural Health *magazine, makes perfect edible gifts any time of the year. See the photo.*

3 cups whole wheat pastry flour (or part barley flour or unbleached white flour)

2 tablespoons anise seed, ground (optional)

1 tablespoon aluminum-free baking powder

½ teaspoon sea salt

1 cup almonds, toasted

½ cup canola oil

⅔ cup pure maple syrup or part brown rice syrup or FruitSource syrup

1 teaspoon vanilla

1 teaspoon almond extract

Chocolate Sauce 2 and Candy (makes 1¼ cups)

2 cups malt-sweetened chocolate chips

⅓ to ½ cup pure maple syrup

2 tablespoons light vegetable oil

1. Preheat the oven to 350°F. Line two baking sheets with parchment or brush with oil.

2. Mix dry ingredients. In a separate bowl, whisk wet ingredients together and add to dry. Add more flour if necessary. Form into 2 logs, each 2 to 2½ inches in diameter. Transfer to one baking sheet.

3. Bake until firm and golden around the edges, about 30 minutes. Remove from oven and allow to cool completely, 30 minutes or so.

4. With a very sharp knife, cut loaves into ¾-inch thick diagonal slices. (It's natural for some cookies to crack with baking or cutting.) Transfer slices to both baking sheets, placing them an inch apart. Bake for 15 minutes more. Allow to cool before storing in an airtight container.

5. To make chocolate sauce, melt chips by bringing water to a boil in a double boiler or regular pot. Place oil (and sweetener if desired), then chips, in top portion of double boiler or in a bowl that can be suspended above the water. Turn heat off and cover pot for melting to occur, 5 to 10 minutes. Stir a couple of times to dissolve chips. (Oil dilutes the texture of the chips, making the sauce dippable rather than just spreadable. Melting chips in a saucepan directly over even very low heat causes chocolate to burn before melting.)

6. Dip one side of each cookie in chocolate and allow to cool to harden, several minutes in the refrigerator. Chocolate remains hard at room temperature.

7. To make chocolate candy, transfer melted chocolate to candy molds and refrigerate for 30 minutes or freeze for just 15 minutes.

Variations

Ginger-Almond-Raisin Biscotti: Substitute ½ cup raisins for half the almonds. Add 1 tablespoon powdered ginger, ½ teaspoon cloves, ½ teaspoon cinnamon.

Greek Biscotti (Paximatha): Substitute ½ cup toasted sesame seeds for all of the almonds. Omit almond extract and add 1 teaspoon cinnamon.

Orange-Ginger Oatmeal Crunch Cookies

Makes 1 dozen

Calories: 316

Protein: 5g

Saturated Fat: 1g

Fiber: 2g

Carbohydrate: 38g

Fat: 16g

Cholesterol: 0

Sodium: 92mg

Calories from
Carbohydrate: 48%

Calories from Fat: 46%

Calories from Protein: 6%

The special flavors and the texture of this glorified version of the plain old-fashioned favorite make it a crowd pleaser.

This recipe appeared in Delicious! *magazine, October 1996. See the photo.*

1½ cups oatmeal

¾ cup whole wheat pastry flour

¾ cup unbleached white flour

1 teaspoon aluminum-free baking powder

½ teaspoon sea salt

¾ cup currants

1 cup walnuts, toasted and coarsely chopped

½ cup canola or light walnut oil

½ cup barley malt or brown rice syrup

Zest of an orange

½ cup orange juice

1 tablespoon peeled and finely grated fresh ginger

1 teaspoon vanilla

1. Preheat the oven to 350°F. Line two baking sheets with parchment or brush with oil.

2. In a medium-large bowl, mix dry ingredients. In a smaller bowl, whisk together wet ingredients. Stir into dry. Makes 3 cups batter.

3. Transfer heaping tablespoons of dough to baking sheet, leaving at least an inch of space between cookies. If uniformity is important, use a ¼- or ⅓-cup scoop. Flatten cookies with the back of fork to make 3- or 4-inch round shapes ½-inch thick. Dip scoop and/or fork in water to keep it from sticking.

4. Bake cookies until edges and undersides are quite golden, 25 to 30 minutes.

For the very crunchy texture many people prefer, omit the orange juice. Substitute the same volume, ½ cup, of oil and sweetener (e.g. 2 tablespoons more oil with 6 tablespoons more sweetener). Check cookies after 20 minutes.

Lemon Tahini Crunch Cookies

Makes 10 to 12

Lemon juice and zest add sparkle to this cookie made richer with sesame tahini.

1½ cups oatmeal

¾ cup whole wheat pastry flour

¾ cup unbleached white flour

½ cup sesame seeds, toasted

1 teaspoon aluminum-free baking powder

½ teaspoon sea salt

½ cup light vegetable oil

¼ cup sesame tahini

¾ cup FruitSource syrup or brown rice syrup

Zest of half a lemon

2 tablespoons lemon juice

1 teaspoon vanilla

Calories: 297

Protein: 5g

Saturated Fat: 2g

Fiber: 2g

Carbohydrate: 36g

Fat: 16g

Cholesterol: 0

Sodium: 98mg

Calories from Carbohydrate: 47%

Calories from Fat: 46%

Calories from Protein: 7%

1. Preheat the oven to 350°F. Line two baking sheets with parchment or brush with oil.

2. In a medium-large bowl, mix dry ingredients. In a smaller bowl, whisk together wet ingredients. Stir into dry.

3. Transfer heaping tablespoons of dough to baking sheet, leaving 2 inches of space between cookies. If uniformity is important, use a ¼- or ⅓-cup scoop. Cookies will spread, but you may choose to flatten batter with the back of a fork to make 3- or 4-inch round shapes ½-inch thick. Dip scoop and/or fork in water to keep it from sticking.

4. Bake cookies until edges are golden, 15 to 20 minutes.

5. For variety, decorate cookies by drizzling chocolate sauce (see page 186) back and forth across cookie surfaces through a plastic squeeze bottle.

Linzertorte Cookies

Calories: 145

Protein: 2g

Saturated Fat: 1g

Fiber: 2g

Carbohydrate: 12g

Fat: 10g

Cholesterol: 0

Sodium: 43mg

Calories from
Carbohydrate: 31%

Calories from Fat: 62%

Calories from Protein: 6%

Also called gems, jewels, or thumbprint cookies, these cookies are based on the linzertorte, the classic Viennese pastry from Linz, Austria, that consists of a cookie-like nut crust covered with a layer of raspberry jam and topped with more cookie crust in a lattice design. Mary Estella, author of the Natural Foods Cookbook, *was the first to please the public with her scrumptious, more health-ful version. Since then, her recipe or variations of it have appeared (often with-out credit) in many vegetarian, vegan, macrobiotic, and allergy-free books and magazines and in cooking class menus.*

1 cup nuts, toasted and coarsely to finely ground (almonds, hazelnuts, walnuts,
  pecans, or cashews), or part shredded coconut, plain or lightly toasted and
  ground with nuts

1 cup oatmeal, plain or finely ground

1 cup whole wheat pastry flour or unbleached white flour

½ teaspoon aluminum-free baking powder (optional)

½ teaspoon cinnamon

¼ teaspoon sea salt

½ cup light vegetable oil

½ cup pure maple syrup, brown rice syrup, or FruitSource syrup

1 teaspoon minced lemon or orange zest

½ teaspoon vanilla or almond extract

¼ cup fruit-sweetened jam (raspberry, apricot, peach, or blueberry jam
  or orange marmalade)

1. Preheat the oven to 350°F. Line two baking sheets with parchment or brush with oil. You may choose to grind the nuts and oatmeal to-gether.

2. Mix dry ingredients. In a separate bowl, whisk wet ingredients to-gether and add to dry. Stir to form a wet dough. Add a little more flour if needed to form balls of dough. Roll into 1½- or 2-inch balls (2 ta-blespoons and ¼ cup dough respectively). Transfer to baking sheet and press thumb in middle. Fill indentations with jam.

3. Bake until golden, 15 to 20 minutes, less with FruitSource syrup for the sweetener.

Variations

Wheat-Free Linzertorte Cookies: Substitute barley flour for wheat flour.

I'm grateful to allergy-free cooking teacher, Dara Thompson, for her good suggestions. A combination of millet and sifted chestnut flours is quite nice here (and offers a satisfying crunch) as is a combination of barley flour, chestnut flour, and a small amount of teff or arrowroot flours. Chestnut flour lends a distinctively pleasing sweet aroma and taste. Both chestnut and especially teff make a darker cookie than the original, but they're good.

Chocolate Chip Cookies

Thanks to Beth Scott for adapting the classic cookie recipe for this healthier treat.

Makes 2 to 3 dozen small or 9 large cookies

1 cup whole wheat pastry flour

1 cup unbleached white flour

1 cup malt-sweetened chocolate chips

½ cup walnuts, toasted and chopped (optional)

1 teaspoon aluminum-free baking powder

½ teaspoon baking soda

¼ teaspoon sea salt

½ cup light vegetable oil

¼ cup brown rice syrup

¼ cup pure maple syrup

½ cup water

1 teaspoon vanilla

Calories: 93

Protein: 1g

Saturated Fat: 1g

Fiber: 0.4g

Carbohydrate: 11g

Fat: 5g

Cholesterol: 0

Sodium: 28mg

Calories from Carbohydrate: 47%

Calories from Fat: 50%

Calories from Protein: 3%

1. Preheat the oven to 350°F. Line two baking sheets with parchment or lightly brush with oil.

2. In a large bowl, mix dry ingredients. In a medium bowl, whisk wet ingredients and stir into dry.

3. For medium-small cookies, transfer heaping teaspoons of dough (from flatware, not measuring spoon) onto baking sheet. For big cookies, use a ⅓-cup ice cream scoop. Leave an inch or two of space between cookies.

4. Bake for 12 to 15 minutes for small cookies, 15 to 20 minutes for large cookies.

Variation

Orange-Pecan Double Chocolate Chip Cookies: Substitute ½ cup cocoa powder for that amount of flour. Substitute pecans for walnuts. Include the zest of half an orange, chopped, and orange juice in place of water.

Peanut Butter Cookies

Makes 2 dozen small or 8 big cookies

See the photo including these cookies.

Calories: 130
Protein: 2g
Saturated Fat: 1g
Fiber: 0.4g
Carbohydrate: 15g
Fat: 7g
Cholesterol: 0
Sodium: 55mg
Calories from Carbohydrate: 45%
Calories from Fat: 49%
Calories from Protein: 6%

¾ to 1 cup whole wheat pastry flour
¾ to 1 cup unbleached white flour
1½ to 2 teaspoons aluminum-free baking powder
¼ teaspoon sea salt
½ cup light vegetable oil
½ cup peanut butter, crunchy or smooth
½ cup FruitSource syrup
1 teaspoon vanilla

1. Preheat the oven to 350°F. Line two baking sheets with parchment or brush with oil.

2. Mix dry ingredients, adding lesser amounts of flours and baking powder for small drop cookies and more for bigger cookies that hold their shapes. Whisk wet ingredients together and add to dry to form a smooth batter or dough.

3. Transfer wetter dough (less flour) to baking sheets by heaping teaspoons or, for perfect shapes, roll that amount in your palms to make balls and flatten somewhat. For firmer dough (more flour), measure in

¼- or ⅓-cup portions with ice cream scoop or measuring cup and shape into balls. Either way, press tops with a fork in classic crisscross design.
4. Bake until bottoms are golden, 12 to 15 minutes.

Variations

Peanut Butter Fudge Cookies: Substitute cocoa powder for ½ cup flour and add ½ cup chocolate chips.

Peanut Butter and Jelly Cookies: Make indentation in center of cookies and fill with 1 teaspoon portions of jelly.

Heavenly Macaroons

Thanks to my friend and fellow natural health educator/consultant and cooking teacher Lenore Yalisove Baum for these creative treats.

2½ cups unsweetened shredded coconut

⅓ cup whole wheat pastry flour

¼ teaspoon sea salt

¼ cup brown rice syrup

¼ cup pure maple syrup

1 teaspoon almond extract

⅓ to ½ cup water

1. Preheat the oven to 350°F. Line a baking sheet with parchment or brush with oil.
2. Mix dry ingredients. In another bowl, whisk wet ingredients together, then add to dry and mix well. With moistened fingers, squeeze 1½-inch balls of "dough."
3. Transfer to baking sheet and bake until golden, about 20 minutes.

Variation

Add ¾ cup malt-sweetened chocolate chips.

Makes 1½ dozen

Calories: 105

Protein: 1g

Saturated Fat: 6g

Fiber: 2g

Carbohydrate: 11g

Fat: 7g

Cholesterol: 0

Sodium: 35mg

Calories from
Carbohydrate: 39%

Calories from Fat: 58%

Calories from Protein: 3%

Lemon Coconut Cornmeal Cookies

Makes 1½ dozen

Calories: 171

Protein: 1g

Saturated Fat: 3g

Fiber: 1g

Carbohydrate: 22g

Fat: 9g

Cholesterol: 0

Sodium: 93mg

Calories from
Carbohydrate: 51%

Calories from Fat: 47%

Calories from Protein: 3%

1½ cups whole wheat pastry flour or part unbleached white flour

1 cup unsweetened shredded coconut

½ cup cornmeal

1 teaspoon aluminum-free baking powder

1 teaspoon nutmeg

½ teaspoon sea salt

½ cup light vegetable oil

1 cup FruitSource syrup or brown rice syrup

Zest and juice of a lemon

1 teaspoon vanilla

1. Preheat the oven to 350°F. Line two baking sheets with parchment or brush with oil. Set aside ¼ cup coconut for decorating cookies.

2. In a medium-large bowl, mix dry ingredients. In a smaller bowl, whisk together wet ingredients. Stir into dry.

3. Transfer tablespoons of dough to baking sheet, leaving an inch of space between cookies. Sprinkle remaining coconut over the surface of cookies.

4. Bake cookies until edges are golden, about 15 minutes.

Puddings

Ranging from homespun comfort foods to gourmet confections, puddings satisfy primal yearnings for simple treats and are soothing remedies for stress. Puddings evolved historically according to what ingredients were on hand. Starchy foods—flour, rice, and tapioca pearls, arrowroot powder and agar flakes—serve as the main ingredients or the thickening agents and form the medium for presenting the sweet tastes of seasonal fruits, gentle sweeteners, and aromatic seasonings. Puddings may be cooked on top of the stove or baked, and may be served warm or chilled.

Fresh fruit puddings and gels contain almost no fat, just the clean and clear flavors of gorgeous fresh fruits and their juices. Light, luscious, and healthy, these naturally sweet desserts require little or no further sweetening. Easily put together, the preparation time is about 15 minutes.

The recipes in this chapter progress from a plain fruit juice gel thickened with mineral-rich agar sea vegetable flakes (instead of gelatin) to gels that are all or partially puréed for a creamy consistency, to puddings textured with a combination of agar flakes and arrowroot powder for a satiny smooth texture. Dairy-free puddings and custards, based on homemade almond milk, coconut milk, or soy milk, compare nicely with the ones composed of milk, half-and-half, or cream, or whipping cream mixed with cream cheese, sugar, egg yolks, flour, butter, and vanilla, all whisked and cooked together. See the sections on Thickening Agents and on Dairy and Its Alternatives for more information on these ingredients.

Basic Fruit Gel

Calories: 56
Protein: 0.2g
Saturated Fat: 0
Fiber: 0.2g
Carbohydrate: 14g
Fat: 0.1g
Cholesterol: 0
Sodium: 64mg
Calories from
Carbohydrate: 97%
Calories from Fat: 2%
Calories from Protein: 1%

See the photo for a visual reference to the Peach and Berry variation of this recipe.

1 quart apple juice or apple cider or a combination of juices
⅓ cup agar flakes
¼ teaspoon sea salt

Optional ingredients

Fresh fruit
Flavoring agents—1 teaspoon vanilla, lemon juice or zest, or
 ginger juice, freshly grated and squeezed
Garnishes—mint or lemon balm sprigs

1. Place ingredients in a 2-quart saucepan and stir to submerge agar. Bring to a boil (watch for foaming over upon boiling), then simmer until agar dissolves, 3 to 5 minutes. Stir in optional flavoring agents.
2. Place optional fruit in an 8-inch square glass baking dish of 2-quart capacity and pour hot or warm juice over fruit. With soft berries such as raspberries, allow to cool for 20 minutes. Transfer to refrigerator to gel for 1 to 1½ hours, or about 2 hours at cool room temperature. Serve garnished, if desired.

Variations

Very Berry Gel-O: Include 2 cups mixed berries.

Peach and Berry Gel with Fresh Peach Coulis: Include 1 or 2 cups sliced peaches combined with raspberries, blueberries, strawberries, or blackberries.

To make coulis, purée until very smooth 3 large pitted peaches (1½ pounds) with the zest of a small lime. To serve, mound 2 to 3 tablespoons coulis in the center of dessert plates. Cut gel in squares and place on top of coulis to spread it out. Garnish.

Mandarin Orange Gel: Mandarin oranges are very popular in China during the winter months. People shared them with us everywhere we went on our travels there. They told us they were the seed stock for California mandarins.

Include 2 whole star anise and 1 mandarin orange—2 teaspoons minced zest and seeded orange segments. After agar dissolves, remove anise with a flat strainer. Add orange sections and cook for another minute.

NOTE

When gel has reached soft gel stage, after about ½ hour, orange sections may be moved so that one appears in each serving of gel.

Basic Fruit Pudding

Makes 4 servings, or about 3½ cups

1 quart apple juice or cider

¼ cup arrowroot powder, tapioca flour, or kuzu root starch

¼ cup agar flakes

¼ cup brown rice syrup, FruitSource syrup, or pure maple syrup (optional)

¼ teaspoon sea salt

1 teaspoon vanilla (optional)

1 teaspoon lemon or orange zest (optional)

Calories: 226

Protein: 0.5g

Saturated Fat: 0.2g

Fiber: 1g

Carbohydrate: 54g

Fat: 1g

Cholesterol: 0

Sodium: 146mg

Calories from Carbohydrate: 96%

Calories from Fat: 4%

Calories from Protein: 1%

1. To make pudding, in a small bowl pour ½ cup juice over arrowroot or another thickener. Do not stir.

2. In a 2-quart saucepan, bring remaining juice to a boil with agar, sweetener, and salt. Stir occasionally. Simmer until agar completely dissolves.

3. Stir arrowroot and add to pot. Stir until simmering resumes and mixture turns from chalky to shiny, in about a minute. Add optional ingredients and transfer to an 8-inch square baking dish. Or allow pudding to cool somewhat, then transfer to individual bowls to set up.

Variation

Apricot Pudding with Almond Cream: The combination of apricot and apple juices makes for a sweeter, more mellow taste than from apricot juice alone with its definite tang. Select brands of apricot nectar sold in natural foods stores to avoid the highly refined corn sweetener and the citric and ascorbic acids that are added to apricot nectars sold in regular supermarkets.

Include 1 quart apple-apricot juice or 2 cups each apricot juice/ nectar and apple juice. Do include optional ingredients. Garnish with 1 cup Almond Cream (see page 242), ½ cup Toasted Almond Sprinkles (see page 242) or sliced almonds, lightly toasted, and 3 or 4 thin slices apricot.

Strawberry Terrine

Makes 9 servings

Calories: 166

Protein: 1g

Saturated Fat: 0

Fiber: 3g

Carbohydrate: 38g

Fat: 1g

Cholesterol: 0

Sodium: 62mg

Calories from
Carbohydrate: 93%

Calories from Fat: 5%

Calories from Protein: 2%

Capture the essence of the spring, summer, and fall seasons with fresh fruit terrines, no-bake desserts featuring whole or sliced ripe fruit suspended in a pale gold gelatin made with sweetened apple juice or cider and sweet wine. As more organic wines come into the marketplace, other dessert wines may be included here such as honey fruit wines (e.g. organic blackberry or cherry wine), port, or sherry.

Gel

3½ cups filtered apple juice or apple cider

¼ cup brown rice malt syrup or FruitSource syrup, or part pure maple syrup

⅓ cup agar flakes

¼ teaspoon sea salt

Zest of ¼ orange

¼ cup sweet wine such as orange muscat or mirin (Japanese sweet rice cooking wine)

1 pint whole small to medium-size strawberries, about 2⅔ cups, hulled

Mint or lemon balm sprigs for garnish

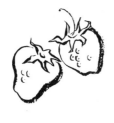

Strawberry Coulis   (see page 169)

1. Place juice, sweetener, agar, salt, and zest in a 2-quart saucepan. Stir to submerge agar, then bring to a boil. Turn heat down and simmer until agar dissolves, 3 to 4 minutes. Turn off heat and stir in wine and berries. Transfer to an 8-inch square glass baking dish of 2-quart capacity. Refrigerate until set, about 1 hour.

2. To serve mound 2 to 3 tablespoons coulis in the center of dessert plates. Cut gel into square servings and place on top of coulis to spread it out. Garnish.

Summer Fruit Terrine with Raspberry Coulis: Include this generous mélange of seasonal fruits: 5 cups strawberries, blueberries, green grapes, and small balls of melon. See recipe for Raspberry Coulis on page 186.

Sweet Hearts with Hazelnut Cream

Makes 5 servings

The combination of apple cider and hazelnut (filbert) butter makes an incredibly delicious pudding with great mouth-feel. It serves as the backdrop for the heart-shaped gel that rests on top and offers a delightful contrast in flavor and texture.

This cute dessert is also nice served on Valentine's Day for children or adults, made with a red juice.

1 quart red fruit juice (one containing part raspberry, strawberry, cherry, or
   cranberry) or apple cider

⅓ cup agar flakes

¼ teaspoon sea salt

1 teaspoon vanilla

2 tablespoons hazelnut butter

2 tablespoons pure maple syrup

2 strawberries, sliced for garnish (optional, in season)

1 tablespoon hazelnuts, finely ground for garnish

Strawberry leaves, scented geranium, or sprigs of mint or lemon balm for garnish

Calories: 169

Protein: 1g

Saturated Fat: 0

Fiber: 1g

Carbohydrates: 32g

Fat: 5g

Cholesterol: 0

Sodium: 116mg

Calories from
Carbohydrate: 72%

Calories from Fat: 25%

Calories from Protein: 3%

1. In a 2-quart saucepan, bring juice to a boil with agar and salt, watching for foaming over upon boiling. Allow to simmer until agar completely dissolves, 3 to 5 minutes. Add the vanilla. Pour into a standard 8-inch square glass baking dish and refrigerate.

2. Cut gel into simple shapes with medium-large, heart-shaped cutters that measure about 3 inches across. (Cutter must measure 1 inch deep to go through gel and be removed easily, or make gel thinner by putting

it in a larger dish to gel.) With a small spatula, transfer cutouts to a cutting board or another flat surface.

2. Purée odd pieces of gel with hazelnut butter and maple syrup in a food processor or blender. Divide purée equally among dessert plates and gently place a cutout on top of each portion of hazelnut cream. Garnish to serve. (Sliced strawberries carry out the heart theme.)

Chinese New Year Citrus Gel with Glazed Kumquats

Makes 9 servings

Calories: 167
Protein: 1g
Saturated Fat: 0
Fiber: 1g
Carbohydrates: 40g
Fat: 1g
Cholesterol: 0
Sodium: 130mg
Calories from
Carbohydrate: 93%
Calories from Fat: 4%
Calories from Protein: 2%

Kumquats have a sweet, aromatic, edible rind and a tart, almost sour pulp. They are a close relative of the citrus fruit family. Native to China, where their resistance to cold enables them to be grown farther north than citrus fruits, kumquats also grow well in the San Francisco Bay area.

This dessert is great served at Chinese New Year celebrations. Thanks to Patrick and Sandra Tam for their help in designing the recipe.

Glazed Kumquats

½ pound kumquats
½ cup brown rice syrup
½ cup water

Gel

2 cups water
½ cup brown rice malt syrup
½ cup agar flakes
½ teaspoon sea salt
1⅓ cups orange juice
⅔ cup grapefruit juice
1 tablespoon lemon juice
Mint sprigs or scented geranium leaves for garnish

1. Rinse kumquats, remove stems, and cut a very small x at the other end. Bring to a boil in water to cover and simmer covered for 3 minutes. Drain off and discard this bitter water.

2. To glaze kumquats, bring rice syrup and water to a boil. Add kumquats and simmer gently for 10 minutes. Drain and set aside.

3. To prepare gel, bring water, sweetener, agar, and salt to a boil. Simmer until agar completely dissolves. Turn off heat. Add citrus juices now to retain their bright colors and flavors. Pour liquid into an 8-inch square glass baking dish or another 2-quart container. Add kumquats, reserving 9 for garnish.

4. To serve, garnish with a thinly sliced kumquat and an aromatic green leaf.

Light Lemon Pudding

Mary O'Leary and Karen Bandy created this refreshingly tart pudding, which they serve with vanilla cookies (see page 208).

¼ cup arrowroot powder

3½ cups apple juice

¼ cup agar flakes

½ teaspoon sea salt

½ teaspoon lemon zest

½ cup lemon juice

2 tablespoons pure maple syrup

2 tablespoons brown rice syrup

I teaspoon vanilla

½ cup combined coconut and nuts (e.g. almonds), toasted and
   nuts ground for garnish

**Makes 5 servings,
or 3½ cups**

Calories: 219

Protein: 3g

Saturated Fat: Ig

Fiber: 2g

Carbohydrates: 37g

Fat: 8g

Cholesterol: 0

Sodium: 2mg

Calories from
Carbohydrate: 64%

Calories from Fat: 31%

Calories from Protein: 5%

I. Place thickener (arrowroot or kuzu) with enough of the apple juice to cover in a small bowl and set aside.

2. Combine remaining apple juice with agar and salt in a 2-quart saucepan. Bring to a boil, then simmer until agar dissolves, 3 to 5 minutes. Add lemon zest and juice, sweeteners, and vanilla to pot. Stir to dissolve thickener. Add it to pot and stir until simmering resumes and texture thickens, in about 1 minute. Transfer mixture to a 2-quart baking dish to cool. Serve garnished.

Pear Trifle

A friend of mine decided that this dessert got its name because it's so good it gets eaten very quickly, and it seems like all you get is a trifle. Actually, trifle is a popular British dessert consisting of sponge cake spread with jam, soaked in wine, sprinkled with crushed macaroons, and topped with custard and whipped cream. This simple variation is inspired by one served in a London restaurant.

2 tablespoons arrowroot powder

2 cups pear juice

2 tablespoons agar flakes

⅛ teaspoon sea salt

1 ripe pear, quartered, cored, and thinly sliced

4 ginger or lemon cookies

½ to ¾ cup Cashew Cream

2 to 3 tablespoons strawberry jam

Mint sprigs for garnish (optional)

Cashew Cream (makes 1 cup)

½ cup cashew nuts

⅓ to ½ cup pear juice

1. To make pudding, place thickener in a small bowl with enough of the juice to cover. Bring remaining juice to a boil with agar and salt. Stir, then simmer gently until agar is dissolved. Stir thickener mixture and add to pot. Stir until simmering resumes. Stir in pear. Allow to cool for 20 minutes.

2. Arrange cookies on bottom of 4 glass dessert bowls and top with warm pear pudding. Refrigerate.

3. To make cashew cream, in the small container of a blender, blend nuts with juice (starting with smaller amount) until smooth and thick. Spoon on top of gel to form a thin layer and place a small dollop of jam on top to serve. Garnish, if desired.

Vanilla Custard

Whereas pudding is defined in Webster's Dictionary as "a dessert of a soft, spongy or thick creamy consistency," custard is defined as "a sweetened mixture of milk and eggs cooked until it is set." This new version of the popular early English dessert tastes surprisingly like the original.

I quart soy milk

½ cup pure maple syrup or ¾ cup FruitSource syrup

¼ to ⅓ cup agar flakes (start with less)

¼ teaspoon sea salt

I teaspoon vanilla

½ teaspoon nutmeg

Garnishes (optional): nuts, toasted and chopped; cookie crumbs; or tofu cream

Makes 5 to 9 servings, or 4 cups

Calories: 109

Protein: 5g

Saturated Fat: 0

Fiber: 0g

Carbohydrates: 19g

Fat: 2g

Cholesterol: 0

Sodium: 109mg

Calories from Carbohydrate: 68%

Calories from Fat: 15%

Calories from Protein: 17%

1. In a 3-quart saucepan, whisk together soy milk, sweetener, agar, and salt. Bring to a boil over medium heat, watching carefully to prevent foaming over. Turn heat down and simmer uncovered until agar completely dissolves, about 5 minutes. Whisk occasionally.

2. Turn off heat and whisk in vanilla. Pour into a standard 8-inch square baking dish or individual custard cups. Dust the surface with nutmeg. Cover with waxed paper or plastic wrap to prevent skin from forming on top and the surface from darkening; avoid parchment, which sags and sticks. Refrigerate to set, 1 to 1½ hours.

Variations

Almond Custard: Substitute homemade almond milk (see page 242) for soy milk. Add ¼ teaspoon almond extract with vanilla. Omit nutmeg.

Parfait of Fresh Fruit with Almond Cream: In French, "parfait" means "perfect or flawless." Whipped almond custard satisfies the desire for layers of billowy whipped cream. (See the photo.)

Make custard with 6 tablespoons agar flakes. Refrigerate. When firm, blend until smooth (this takes awhile), adding a couple of tablespoons of almond or cashew butter, if desired.

In 6 wine goblets, press sliced colorful fresh fruit against sides of glass. Fruits that work well are sliced strawberries, halved raspberries, blackberries, and grapes, and mandarin orange segments (blanched in apple juice or canned). Fill center with layers of whipped custard and fruit. Refrigerate until serving. Garnish with mint sprigs.

Pastry Cream for Tarts: For the lightest color, prepare a quarter the volume of Almond Custard or, if you don't feel like making almond milk, prepare a quarter the volume of the Vanilla Custard. Figure 1 cup almond milk or soy milk, 3 tablespoons Fruitsource syrup (preferred sweetener) or 2 tablespoons pure maple syrup, 1 tablespoon plus 1 teaspoon agar flakes, a few grains of salt, and ⅛ teaspoon vanilla.

Tapioca Pudding

Makes 5 servings, or 4 to 5 cups

Calories: 357
Protein: 10g
Saturated Fat: 1g
Fiber: 0.4g
Carbohydrate: 69g
Fat: 5g
Cholesterol: 0
Sodium: 323mg
Calories from Carbohydrate: 77%
Calories from Fat: 12%
Calories from Protein: 12%

This tapioca recipe is free of the usual custard ingredients: eggs, milk, and white sugar.

1 cup small tapioca pearls

5 cups homemade almond milk (see page 242), plain oat milk (not sweet), or soy milk

½ cup brown rice syrup

1 to 2 tablespoons pure maple syrup, or to taste

½ teaspoon sea salt

¼ teaspoon nutmeg

1 teaspoon vanilla

1 cup Tofu Cream (optional), see page 133

Nutmeg for garnish (optional)

Barley malt syrup for garnish (optional)

1. Place tapioca, milk, sweeteners, and salt in a 3- or 4-quart saucepan. Bring to a full boil, whisking occasionally. Turn heat down and simmer uncovered until almost all the pearls turn transparent, 15 to 20 minutes. Continue to whisk mixture occasionally to prevent sticking to the bottom of the pot.

2. Remove pot from heat and stir in spice and vanilla. Pudding thickens further as it cools. Serve warm or chilled. Spoon a dollop of Tofu Cream atop each serving of tapioca and sprinkle nutmeg over all. Or heat barley malt syrup and spoon a portion over the center for a caramel-like taste.

Variations

To make even quicker tapioca, the "instant" version (Minute Tapioca by General Foods) contains precooked, granulated tapioca. Boil the tapioca for just 5 minutes.

Large pearl tapioca requires a presoaking period of from several hours to overnight and takes much longer to cook, about 1 hour.

Coco Tapioca: Truly an ambrosial dessert! Coconut milk gives this pudding an extra creamy richness and an intriguing taste. Include light coconut milk or dilute regular coconut milk with water, 3 parts coconut milk to 1 part water. Garnish with coconut chips or shreds, half of them very lightly toasted, or with freshly grated coconut and a couple of slices of banana.

Amazake Tapioca Pudding: Amazake rice nectar makes a pudding that looks good (it darkens just a bit) and gels perfectly. Dilute its thick texture by substituting 1 cup water for amazake. Start with no sweetener and add to taste.

Pumpkin Flan

Makes 5 to 8 servings

Calories: 220

Protein: 4g

Saturated Fat: 0

Fiber: 2g

Carbohydrates: 49g

Fat: 1.8g

Cholesterol: 0

Sodium: 170mg

Calories from
Carbohydrate: 86%

Calories from Fat: 7%

Calories from Protein: 6%

My good friend, pickling and organic gardening teacher, and former cooking student Linda Redfield, designed this very popular custard. So perfect in its season, it's fancy enough to be served in any fine restaurant. Linda says both small pie pumpkins and sweet winter squashes work well in this recipe.

The recipe uses prune purée, one of today's hottest healthy substitutes for fat (butter or oil) in baked goods. Prunes contain a high level of pectin, a plant-based gel that acts like butter or shortening by trapping leavening gasses and air, which allows it to cream well with other ingredients. To reduce the fat in recipes, substitute prune purée in equal amounts to butter or oil. Prune purée keeps refrigerated for weeks.

It's best to make your own prune purée because the commercial version, Solo brand lekvar, contains highly refined sweeteners in the list of ingredients—corn syrup, water, sugar, pectin, and citric acid.

Prune Purée (makes ¾ cup)

1 cup pitted prunes, 5½ ounces

2 teaspoons vanilla

½ to ¾ cup water

Flan (makes 4 cups)

2 cups pumpkin purée (from 2½ pounds winter squash or pumpkin—see page 134)

¼ cup prune purée

¼ cup pure maple syrup

¼ cup brown rice malt syrup

2 teaspoons peeled and freshly grated ginger

½ teaspoon cinnamon

¼ teaspoon nutmeg

Pinch of cloves

½ teaspoon sea salt

2 cups soy milk

4 teaspoons agar flakes

Topping (makes ¾ cup)

6 tablespoons pure maple syrup

6 tablespoons brown rice syrup

1½ teaspoons cinnamon

¾ teaspoon nutmeg

1. To prepare prune purée, whip ingredients in a food processor or blender until smooth. This is most easily done in half batches in a mini-prep processor or the small container of a blender.

Prunes must be moist, not hard and dry, or they will not blend easily. If prunes are dry, rehydrate by soaking or poaching in water to cover, then purée with measured amount of the soaking water.

2. To make flan, blend ingredients, except soy milk and agar, until smooth.

3. Bring soy milk and agar flakes to a boil in a 2-quart saucepan, and watch for foaming over upon boiling. Simmer until agar dissolves, about 5 minutes. Blend into pumpkin mixture. Pour into 6- or 8-ounce French white porcelain ramekins (also known as custard or flan cups) or muffin tin cups or other lightly oiled molds. Allow to set, about 2 hours.

4. Warm the topping ingredients in a small saucepan. Run a thin knife blade around the edges of the flan, unmold, and drizzle with topping to serve.

Pumpkin Mousse with Pecan Brittle

Makes 4 servings

Calories: 525

Protein: 14g

Saturated Fat: 1g

Fiber: 4g

Carbohydrates: 93g

Fat: 15g

Cholesterol: 0

Sodium: 373mg

Calories from

Carbohydrate: 67%

Calories from Fat: 23%

Calories from Protein: 10%

Thanks to Harriet McNear, founder of Harriet's Kitchen, the whole foods cooking school in Winter Park, Florida, for this luscious pudding with its exquisitely crisp brittle topping.

Pumpkin Mousse (makes about 4 cups)

2½ cups soy milk

⅔ cup pure maple syrup

3 tablespoons agar flakes

3 tablespoons arrowroot powder

2 teaspoons cinnamon

1 teaspoon powdered ginger

½ teaspoon nutmeg

½ teaspoon cloves

½ teaspoon sea salt

1 cup pumpkin purée (see page 134)

Pecan Brittle (makes 2 cups)

1 cup sorghum syrup

½ teaspoon light vegetable oil (walnut or canola)

Pinch of sea salt

½ cup pecans, toasted and chopped

1. Place 2 cups of the soy milk with the syrup and agar flakes in a 3- or 4-quart saucepan. Bring to a boil over medium-low heat, stirring occasionally. Turn heat down and simmer until agar is dissolved, about 5 minutes, continuing to stir every once in awhile.

2. Mix remaining ½ cup soy milk with thickener (arrowroot or kuzu), seasonings, and pumpkin purée. Whisk into soy milk.

3. When simmering resumes, transfer to a heatproof serving bowl to chill.

4. To prepare brittle, place all ingredients except nuts in a 2-quart saucepan. Bring to a boil over medium-high heat, then cook until a candy thermometer registers the hard crack stage at 300°F in about 10 minutes.

5. Stir in nuts and pour mixture onto a lightly oiled baking sheet with sides or on a marble slab. Soak pot in hot water. Allow mixture to cool in refrigerator, then break into small pieces.

6. Serve mousse garnished with chunks of brittle.

Variation

Brown rice syrup may be substituted for sorghum syrup, but it takes longer to reach the hard crack stage. Watch for foaming over upon boiling and turn heat to low thereafter. Refrigerate or texture is more like taffy than brittle.

Nut Milks, Pastes, & Creams

Nuts and seeds lend a satisfying richness and depth of flavor to otherwise low-fat desserts. Their texture adds interesting appeal and lightness (when the nuts are finely ground), a crunchy quality (when the nuts are coarsely chopped), or a luscious smoothness (when ground completely for nut butters such as almond, hazelnut or filbert, peanut, cashew, or sesame butter).

Nuts and seeds are high in fiber, vitamins, minerals, and protein. Nut butters derive around 75 percent of their calories from fat, most of which is unsaturated, and contain no cholesterol or hydrogenated oils. Peanut butter is abundant in protein, iron, calcium, and fiber, while butter and margarine have practically none of these. Also delicious are tahini and sesame butter, made from unroasted or roasted hulled seeds and roasted unhulled seeds respectively. They are lower in saturated fat than peanut butter and are a rich source of B vitamins, vitamin E, phosphorus, and calcium.

Note that commercial peanut butter is made from peanuts from which the skin and nutritious germ have been removed. Often dextrose (sugar), corn syrup solids (fillers), emulsifiers, and hydrogenated vegetable oil are added so that instead of a normal saturated fat content of 10 percent, some peanut butter contains as much as 55 percent saturated fat.

On the other hand, peanut butter found in natural foods stores is made from whole peanuts that are roasted and ground. Salt is the only other ingredient and even that is absent in unsalted varieties.

Choose unsweetened coconut available in natural foods stores. Supermarket varieties may contain sugar, water, propylene glycol for a preservative, salt, and sodium metabisulfite to retain whiteness.

OVEN TOASTING TIMES FOR NUTS AND SEEDS

To bring up the flavor, activate the natural oils in nuts and seeds by toasting them before use. A relatively low temperature of 300°F preserves the heat-sensitive oils. Place nuts or seeds in a single layer on a dry baking sheet. The following chart serves as a time guideline for baking. Otherwise, you may smell their fragrance after the nuts or seeds have overbaked. Keep refrigerated after baking.

Coconut, shredded—4 minutes

Pine nuts—8 minutes

Poppy seeds—8 minutes

Sliced or slivered almonds—8 minutes

Pecans—10 minutes

Pumpkin seeds—15 minutes

Sesame seeds—15 minutes

Macadamia nuts—15 minutes

Sunflower seeds—20 minutes

Walnuts—20 minutes

Almonds—20 minutes

Cashews—20 minutes

Peanuts—20 minutes

Hazelnuts—20 minutes

Almond Milk, Almond Cream, and Toasted Almond Sprinkles

Makes 2½ to 3 cups milk, 2½ to 3⅓ cups cream, and 1 cup sprinkles

This cream is good poured over cake at any temperature—hot to room temperature to chilled.

Almond Milk

Calories: 1038

Protein: 28g

Saturated Fat: 7g

Fiber: 17g

Carbohydrates: 81g

Fat: 74g

Cholesterol: 0

Sodium: 109mg

Calories from Carbohydrate: 29%

Calories from Fat: 60%

Calories from Protein: 10

Almond Cream

Calories: 1123

Protein: 28g

Saturated Fat: 7g

Fiber: 18g

Carbohydrates: 102g

Fat: 74g

Cholesterol: 0

Sodium: 109mg

Calories from Carbohydrate: 34%

Calories from Fat: 56%

Calories from Protein: 10%

1 cup almonds, plain or blanched to remove skins

3 cups water

3 to 4 tablespoons arrowroot powder or kuzu root starch—less with maple syrup, more with brown rice malt syrup

¼ cup pure maple syrup or ½ cup brown rice malt syrup, or half of each

Pinch of sea salt

½ teaspoon almond extract

½ teaspoon vanilla extract

1. For slightly whiter almond milk and to eliminate an almost undetectable bitter taste from the skins, blanch the almonds. Before blending, pour 2 cups boiling water over the nuts and let them sit for a couple of minutes. Drain. Remove the almond skins by squeezing each almond between your index finger and thumb. This process takes about 15 minutes, so you may choose to enlist the help of a friend. The color and taste differences aren't dramatic and so I usually omit this step. (The process doesn't work with hazelnuts.)

2. To prepare almond milk, place almonds in a food processor and grind until nuts are finely pulverized, about 1 minute. Gradually drizzle in water and continue to purée. Pour liquid through two thicknesses of cheesecloth laid in a strainer. Twist cloth and squeeze through as much milk as possible. Almond milk lasts for a week refrigerated.

3. Reserve the pulp for use in pressed pie crusts, cookies, crisp or crumble toppings. For a richer flavor, make toasted almond sprinkles. Spread wet ground almonds on a baking sheet and bake at 250°F until golden, stirring a couple of times during cooking, 35 to 40 minutes.

4. To prepare almond cream, place thickener (arrowroot powder) in a small bowl and pour enough almond milk over thickener to barely cover. Transfer remaining almond milk to a 2-quart pot with sweeteners and salt. Bring to a boil. Whisk thickener mixture to dissolve it and add to pot. Gently whisk mixture until it gently bubbles in the center and thickens somewhat, in a matter of seconds. Turn off heat and stir in extracts. Cover surface with waxed paper or plastic wrap to prevent skin from forming. Make cream on day of serving for texture to hold.

NOTES

Almond milk made with 1 part almonds to 2 parts water is a bit richer in flavor, but the expense in terms of yield and cost doesn't seem to be justified for this purpose. Yield is 1 ¾ cups. A better alternative to cheesecloth is a nylon mesh paint strainer bag available at paint stores. Cut it in half. It lasts a long time, is easily rinsed clean, and does a better job.

Nut Pastes and Creams

Makes 1 ½ to 2 cups paste or 1 ½ to 3 cups cream

Nut creams are very popular in Europe. Of all the nuts, blanched almonds yield the nicest cream, one that is white in color with a mild but intriguing flavor, especially when enhanced with almond extract. Some gourmet markets stock time-saving whole blanched almonds.

Cashews are mild in flavor and tan in color when raw (not toasted). They are naturally sweeter and more suitable for use in making a nut cream filling or topping than either pine nuts or hazelnuts. Pine nuts are bland when raw and very oily when ground. Hazelnuts don't skin with blanching like almonds do. They must be oven-toasted until the skins are brittle enough to be rubbed off with a towel. (Not all of the nuts relinquish their skins.) The resulting cream is definitely light brown in color, but it tastes great.

Rich and smooth, nut creams make great alternatives to regular whipped cream and even tofu cream. Depending on the amount of liquid added, the consistency can be varied to serve as a dessert cream or sauce, a spreadable icing, or a paste that can be piped through a pastry bag. Color changes from white to cream and tan according to how much sweetener is added and to the liquid chosen, e.g. juice makes color tanner than does water.

You'll see that this recipe for the nut paste and cream for the Almond Torte recipe on page 194 is not as sweet or as strongly flavored as in the following Marzipan recipe.

2 cups nuts (almonds, plain or blanched, and/or cashews)

⅓ to ⅔ cup brown rice syrup or ¼ to ½ cup pure maple syrup, start with less

I to 2 teaspoons vanilla or almond extract

¼ to I½ cups water, almond milk, rice milk, amazake, apple juice, or soy milk.

1. To blanch almonds, bring 2 cups water to a boil in a small pot and add almonds. Turn off heat and let sit for a minute or two. Drain and slip off their skins by pinching nuts between your thumb and forefinger, one at a time.

2. In a food processor, blend nuts until they become a fine meal (this may take about 2 minutes in a food processor). Gradually blend in sweetener and extract until texture is suitable for a paste. Otherwise, very gradually drizzle in liquid, blending until texture resembles heavy cream.

3. Mixture thickens as it sits at room temperature or in the refrigerator and may require adding more liquid before serving. Nut creams freeze well.

Variations

Almond Cream: Feature blanched (or whole) almonds and include ¼ teaspoon almond extract with 1 teaspoon vanilla extract.

Ginger-Almond Cream: To above variation, add 1½ to 2 tablespoons juice squeezed from 3-inch piece of peeled and grated ginger.

Cashew Cream: Feature cashews for the smoothest texture of any nut cream.

Orange-Cashew Cream: Include juice from an orange as part of the liquid.

Cashew-Almond Cream: Include 1 cup each cashews and almonds and add ¼ teaspoon almond extract with vanilla extract.

Sweetener-Free Nut Cream: Omit sweetener, adding vanilla and apple juice to texture desired.

Nut Paste or Cream

Calories: 2041

Protein: 57g

Saturated Fat: 14g

Fiber: 35g

Carbohydrates: 144g

Fat: 151g

Cholesterol: 0

Sodium: 52mg

Calories from Carbohydrate: 27%

Calories from Fat: 63%

Calories from Protein: 11%

Marzipan

**Makes 1½ cups, or
about 12 ounces**

Here is a homemade marzipan, the sweetened almond purée or paste, without the powdered or granular white sugar, egg white, and liquid glucose found in some commercial versions.

2 cups water

1½ cups almonds, ½ pound

½ cup granular FruitSource (brown rice syrup and grape juice concentrate)

¼ cup FruitSource syrup

1 tablespoon almond extract

Calories: 1889

Protein: 45g

Saturated Fat: 11g

Fiber: 26g

Carbohydrates: 200g

Fat: 111g

Cholesterol: 0

Sodium: 119mg

Calories from
Carbohydrate: 40%

Calories from Fat: 51%

Calories from Protein: 9%

1. To blanch almonds, bring water to a boil in a 2-quart saucepan. Add the almonds and turn off heat. Let almonds sit for a minute or two. Drain and squeeze each almond to slip off the skin.

2. Grind blanched almonds with dry sweetener in a food processor until very fine, about 1 minute. Add wet sweetener with almond extract and process until texture is the consistency of a paste that forms itself into a ball in the processor, about 30 seconds more.

MAIL ORDER COMPANIES

Natural Lifestyle Supplies (retail and wholesale), 16 Lookout Drive, Asheville, NC 28804-3330, 800-752-2775. Informative catalog. Source for organic brown rice malt syrup (Sweet Cloud brand).

The Grain and Salt Society, 273 Fairway Dr., Asheville, NC 28805, 800-867-7258. Celtic Sea Salt and brown rice malt syrup under the Chi Cuisine label.

Mountain Ark (also Macrobiotic Company of America), 799 Old Leicester Hwy., Asheville, NC 28806, 800-643-8909. Source for organic brown rice malt syrup (Sweet Cloud brand).

Kushi Institute Store, P.O. Box 7, Becket, MA 01223-0007, 800-645-8744. Quality macrobiotic products including organic brown rice malt syrup (Sweet Cloud brand).

Wellspring Natural Foods, 23 Wild Wood Lane, Amherst, MA 01002, 413-323-7809. Source for organic brown rice malt syrup (Sweet Cloud brand).

Granum Inc., 2901 NE Blakeley St., Seattle, WA 98105, 206-525-0051. Importers of the highest (macrobiotic) quality Japanese natural foods from the Mitoku Co. Bulk agar flakes and kuzu root starch, good sea salt.

Gold Mine Natural Food Co., 3419 Hancock St., San Diego, CA 92110, 800-862-2347. Informative catalog. Source for many items, including high quality sea salt, and organic peeled and dried chestnuts and chestnut flour.

Shepherd's Garden Seeds, 30 Irene St., Torrington, CT 06790-6658, 860-482-3638. Inspiring catalog with recipes. Edible flower seed collection.

FOOD, HEALTH, AND ENVIRONMENT RELATED ORGANIZATIONS

Physicians Committee for Responsible Medicine (PCRM), P.O. Box 6322, Washington, DC 20015, 202-686-2210. Organization representing more than four thousand doctors who believe diet and lifestyle are one's first line of defense from and treatment for disease. *Good Medicine* magazine helps serve as a liaison between the medical and public sectors.

EarthSave International, 620B Distillery Commons, Louisville, KY 40206, 800-362-3648. Information-packed member's newsletter on how our food choices affect personal health and the environment.

Oldways Preservation and Exchange Trust, 266 Beacon St., Boston, MA 02116, 617-421-5000. Nonprofit education group that promotes healthy eating based on "the old ways," the traditional healthy cuisines of world cultures. Publications and international conferences on a variety of topics, including the new dietary pyramids—Mediterranean, Asian, Latin American, and Vegetarian.

Chef's Collaborative is a network of American chefs who collectively advance sustainable food choices, close relationships with local farmers, and an emphasis on organic ingredients. Educational programs for consumers, especially children.

Kushi Institute, P.O. Box 7, Becket, MA 01223-0007. Macrobiotic education center founded by Michio and Aveline Kushi.

George Ohsawa Macrobiotic Foundation, 1999 Myers St., Oroville, CA 95966, 916-533-7702. Publisher of macrobiotic books.

The Natural Gourmet Cookery School, 48 West 21st St., 2nd floor, New York, NY 10010, 212-645-5170. Licensed by the New York State Department of Education, this school offers a 600-hour career program in natural foods cooking.

The associated *Natural Gourmet Institute for Food and Health* offers classes for the general public taught by Annemarie Colbin, the school's founder, and many other teachers. Ms. Colbin's books include *The Natural Gourmet, Food and Healing,* and *Food and Our Bones.*

Harriet's Kitchen Whole Foods Cooking School, 1136 Oaks Blvd., Winter Park, FL 32789, 407-644-2167.

Whole foods cooking classes with Rebecca Wood, author of *The Splendid Grain* and *The Whole Foods Encyclopedia.* Contact www.rwood.com.

The Culinary Arts Institute—A Whole Foods Cooking School, 7981 Old Redwood Highway, Suite P, Cotati, CA 94931, 707-794-8781.

Food for Thought Culinary Kitchen, 1181 Yulupa Ave., Santa Rosa, CA 95405, 707-575-5363. Natural foods cooking school.

The Natural Epicurean Academy of Culinary Arts, 902 Norwalk Lane, Austin, TX 78703-4314, 512-476-2276. Natural whole foods and macrobiotic cooking school.

The Soyfoods Center, P.O. Box 234, Lafayette, CA 94549, 510-283-2991. World's largest database on soyfoods by William Shurtleff, author of *The Book of Miso, The Book of Tofu, The Book of Tempeh,* and *The Book of Kuzu.*

The KUSA Seed Research Foundation and Seed Society, P.O. Box 761, Ojai, CA 93024. Both of these nonprofit organizations provide consumer information and serve as a seed resource specializing in the bio-diversity values of ancient grains for modern human nutrition. Founder, Lorenz Schaller, is an expert on edible seed crops.

Center for Science in the Public Interest (CSPI), 1875 Connecticut Ave. NW, Suite 300, Washington, DC 20009-5728, 202-332-9110. *Nutrition Action Healthletter.*

American Institute for Biosocial Research, P.O. Box 1174, Tacoma, WA 98401, 253-922-0448. Books by Alexander Schauss, Ph.D.: *Nutrition and Behavior* and *Diet, Crime and Delinquency.*

Recovery Systems—A New Approach to Alcohol, Drugs and Food Problems, 14 Lomita Dr., Suite D, Mill Valley, CA 94941, 415-383-3611.

MANUFACTURERS AND DISTRIBUTORS

Eden Foods, Inc., 701 Tecumseh Rd., Clinton, MI 49236, 800-248-0320. Organic soy milk, soy-rice milk blend, and grain malt syrups—barley and wheat. Agar flakes and kuzu root starch imported from Muso Co., one of two premier natural foods companies in Japan (the other being Mitoku Co.).

Great Eastern Sun, 92 McIntosh Rd., Asheville, North Carolina 28806, 800-334-5809. Importers of Sweet Cloud organic brown rice malt syrup produced by Meeurens Co. in Belgium, the leading traditional malting company in Europe.

Advanced Ingredients, 331 Capitola Ave., Suite F, Capitola, CA 95010, 888-238-4647. FruitSource sweeteners.

Lundberg Family Farms, P.O. Box 369, Richvale, CA 95974, 530-882-4551. Enzyme-converted brown rice syrup, some organic.

Arrowhead Mills, Inc., Box 2059, Hereford, TX 79045, 806-364-0730. High quality baking ingredients.

Imagine Foods, Inc., 350 Cambridge Ave., Suite 350, Palo Alto, CA 94306. Organic Rice Dream rice milks and nondairy frozen desserts.

Westbrae Natural Foods, The Hain Food Group Western Regional Offices, 255 West Carob St., Compton, CA 90220, 310-886-8200. Organic soy beverages and enzyme-converted brown rice syrup.

Vitasoy USA Inc., P.O. Box 2012, S. San Francisco, CA 94083, 800-VITASOY. Organic soy beverages.

Turtle Mountain Inc., P.O. Box 70, Junction City, OR 97448. Sweet Nothings fat-free nondairy frozen desserts.

Grainaissance Inc., 1580 62nd St., Emeryville, CA 94608, 510-547-7256. Amazake rice nectar beverages.

Spectrum Naturals, 133 Copeland St., Petaluma, CA 94952, 707-778-8900. Quality oils and excellent educational materials.

Knudsen and Sons, Inc., P.O. Box 369, Chico, CA 95928, 530-899-5000. Fancy fruit spreads, some organic, sweetened with fruit juice concentrate.

Timber Crest Farms, 4791 Dry Creek Rd., Healdsburg, CA 95448, 707-433-8251. Sun-dried fruits, often organic, free of sulfites and preservatives.

Cascadian Farm, 719 Metcalf St., Sedro-Wolley, WA 98284, 800-624-4123. Organic frozen fruit and fruit concentrates.

Natural Food Technologies, Inc., 14241 E. Firestone Blvd., Suite 205, La Mirada, CA 90638, 562-802-0102. WonderSlim cocoa powder, low-fat and 97 percent caffeine-free.

California Natural Products, P.O. Box 1219, Lathrop, CA 95330, 209-858-2525. Developer of rice products, including enzyme-treated brown rice syrups.

Sunspire, 2114 Adams Ave., San Leandro, CA 94577, 510-569-9731. Grain-sweetened chocolate and carob chips.

Wholesome Foods, P.O. Box 2860, Daytona Beach, FL 32120, 904-258-4708. Organic sweeteners from sugar cane.

Cook Flavoring Co., P.O. Box 890, Tacoma, WA 98401, 800-735-0545. Natural extracts.

Frontier Cooperative Herbs, 3021 78th St., P.O. Box 299, Norway, IA 52318, 800-669-3275. Extracts including organic vanilla extract, non-irradiated spices.

Norsouth Products, Box 12412, Prescott, AZ 86304, 520-776-8364. SiSalt from Baja California.

Multi-Pure Drinking Water Systems, Meredith McCarty, P.O. Box 2605, Mill Valley, CA 94942. Solid carbon block and reverse osmosis filtration produces the best pure water for cooking and drinking. National Safety Foundation (NSF) certification guarantees the claims made by the manufacturer.

Purity Foods, Inc., 2871 W. Jolly Rd., Okemos, MI 48864, 800-99SPELT. Organic whole spelt flour under the Vita-Spelt label and good information.

Kamut Association of North America (KANA), 295 Distribution St., San Marcos, CA 92069, 760-752-5234.

Montana Flour and Grains, H.C. 77, P.O. Box 808, Big Sandy, Montana 59520, 406-378-3105. Grower/supplier of organic kamut and information.

Quinoa Corporation, P.O. Box 1039, Torrance, CA 90505, 310-530-8666. Quinoa flour from grain grown in the Colorado Rockies.

Health Best, 295 Distribution St., San Marcos, CA 92025, 760-752-5230. Nationwide suppliers of natural and organic products, including date sugar.

Papa Cristo's Products, C & K Importing, Inc., Los Angeles, CA 90006, 213-737-2970. Whole wheat phyllo dough.

Russ Bianchi, Managing Director, Adept Solutions, Inc., 331 Capitola Ave., Suite L, Capitola, CA 95010, 888-477-6644. Expertise in ingredient information, formula help, and recipe conversion with emphasis on knowledge of sweeteners and fat replacers.

Rumford Baking Powder Company, 900 Wabash Ave., Terra Haute, IN 47801, 812-232-9446. Aluminum-free baking powder.

Bibliography

RESOURCE BOOKS

The Whole Foods Encyclopedia (new and revised), by Rebecca Wood. New York: Penguin, 1999.

Shopper's Guide to Natural Foods, from the editors of *East West Journal.* Garden City Park, NY: Avery Publishing Group, 1987.

The Oxford Book of Food Plants, text by S. G. Harrison and G.B. Masefield and Michael Willis, illustrations by B.E. Nicholson. New York: Oxford University Press, Inc., 1985.

Fruit Trees and Shrubs, a special edition of *Plants and Gardens,* Vol. 27, No. 3. Brooklyn: Brooklyn Botanic Garden. August 1971.

Culinary Treasures of Japan, by John and Jan Bellame. Garden City Park, NY: Avery Publishing Group, 1992.

Sugar Blues, by William Dufty. New York: Warner, 1975.

Food and Healing, by Annemarie Colbin. New York: Ballantine Books, 1986.

Diet for a New America—How Your Food Choices Affect Your Health, Happiness and the Future of Life on Earth, by John Robbins, H.J. Kramer, Tiburon, CA. 1998

Holistic Health Through Macrobiotics, by Michio Kushi. New York: Japan Publications, 1993.

Let Food Be Thy Medicine—750 Scientific Studies and Medical Reports Showing the Physical, Mental, Social and Environmental Benefits of Whole Grains, Vegetables and Other Natural Foods, edited by Alex Jack. Becket, MA: One Peaceful World Press, 1999. A compact, impeccably documented resource for health and healing with food.

Healing with Whole Foods, by Paul Pitchford. Berkeley: North Atlantic Books, 1993.

Dr. Spock's Baby and Child Care, by Benjamin Spock. New York: Pocket Books, 1998. A plant-based diet is the prescription for American health in this updated version of the classic.

Eat Right, Live Longer, by Neal Barnard. New York: Crown, 1995.

McDougall's Medicine—A Challenging Second Opinion, by John McDougall. Clinton, NJ: New Win Publishing, Inc., 1986.

Dr. Attwood's Low-Fat Prescription for Kids, A Pediatrician's Program for Preventive Nutrition, by Charles Attwood. New York: Viking, 1995.

Don't Drink Your Milk!, by Frank Oski. Brushton, NY: Teach Services, Rt. 1, Box 182, 1996.

The Book of Kuzu—A Culinary and Healing Guide, by William Shurtleff and Akiko Aoyagi. Garden City Park, NY: Avery Publishing Group, 1985.

Nutrition and Behavior, by Alexander Schauss, Ph.D., 1985. This booklet/monograph is available from American Institute for Biosocial Research, P.O. Box 1174, Tacoma, WA 98401, 253-922-0448.

Diet, Crime and Delinquency, by Alexander Schauss, Ph.D. Berkeley: Parker House, 1980. Out of print, this book is being updated by the organization in the previous listing.

Deadly Feasts: Tracking the Secrets of a Terrifying New Plague, by Richard Rhodes. New York: Simon & Schuster, 1997.

Food, by Waverley Root. New York: Simon & Schuster, 1980.

Acid and Alkaline, by Herman Aihara. Oroville, CA: George Ohsawa Macrobiotic Foundation, 1986.

Aspartame (NutraSweet): Is It Safe? by H.J. Roberts. Philadelphia: Charles Press, 1990.

Nutrition Almanac, by Gayla J. and John D. Kirschmann. New York: McGraw-Hill, 1996.

Pleasant Valley, How a Way of Life was Restored by Going Back to Organic Farming, by Louis Bromfield. Mattituck, NY: Amereon Ltd., 1943.

The Nutritive Value of American Foods, USDA Handbook No. 456. Washington, DC, 1975.

The Complete Book of Food Counts, by Corrine T. Netzer. New York: Dell Publishing, 1994.

COOKBOOKS

Fresh from a Vegetarian Kitchen, by Meredith McCarty. New York: St. Martin's Press, 1989.

American Macrobiotic Cuisine, by Meredith McCarty. Garden City Park, NY: Avery Publishing Group, 1986.

The Natural Foods Cookbook—Vegetarian Dairy-Free Cuisine, by Mary Estella. New York: Japan Publications, 1988.

Whole Grain Baking, by Dina Scesny Greene. Freedom, CA: The Crossing Press, 1984.

Baking for Health, by Linda Edwards. Garden City Park, NY: Avery Publishing Group, 1988.

Naturally Sweet Desserts, by Marcea Weber. Garden City Park, NY: Avery Publishing Group, 1990.

Lorna Sass's Complete Vegetarian Kitchen, by Lorna Sass. New York: Hearst Books, 1992.

The Peaceful Palate, by Jennifer Raymond. Calistoga, CA: Heart and Soul, 1996.

The Natural Gourmet, by Annemarie Colbin. New York: Ballantine Books, 1989.

Cooking with Japanese Foods—A Guide to the Traditional Natural Foods of Japan, by Jan and John Bellame. Brookline, MA: East West Natural Health Books, 1986.

Cooking with Sea Vegetables, by Peter and Montse Bradford. London: Thorsons Publishing Group, 1986.

The Sea Vegetable Book—Foraging and Cooking Seaweed, by Judith Cooper Madlener. New York: Clarkson N. Potter, 1977.

The Sea Vegetable Gelatin Cookbook and Field Guide, by Judith Cooper Madlener. Santa Barbara, CA: Woodbridge Press Publishing Co., 1981.

A Tuscan in the Kitchen, by Pino Luongo. New York: Clarkson N. Potter, Inc., 1988.

Bistro Cooking, by Patricia Wells. New York: Workman Publishing Co., Inc., 1989.

Le Cordon Bleu at Home, New York: Hearst Books, 1991.

Thomas Jefferson's Cook Book, by Marie Gorbel Kimball. Charlottesville: University Press of Virginia, 1976.

NEWSLETTERS

EarthSave International, 620B Distillery Commons, Louisville, KY 40206. Very informative seasonal newsletter on living, and especially eating, ecologically. See "What About Chicken?" (Spring 1997) and "What About Dairy?" (Summer 1997) by Steve Lustgarten and Debra Holton.

Dr. John McDougall's To Your Health, Agora Health Publising, 819 North Charles St., Baltimore, MD 21201, 800-851-7100.

The Wellness Letter—The Newsletter of Nutrition, Fitness and Stress Management, from the University of California at Berkeley, P.O. Box 420148, Palm Coast, FL 32142, 904-445-6414.

Self Healing, 42 Pleasant St., Watertown, MA 02172, Dr. Andrew Weil's newsletter.

One Peaceful World, Box 10, 308 Leland Rd., Becket, MA 01223, 413-623-2322. Newsletter of One Peaceful World Society, a macrobiotic organization.

Nutrition Action Healthletter, Center for Science in the Public Interest, Suite 300, 1875 Connecticut Ave. NW, Washington, DC 20009-5728.

Food Allergy News, The Food Allergy Network, Inc., 10400 Eaton Place, Suite 107, Fairfax, VA 22030-2208.

The Wonder Food—Spelt, by Dr. Wighard Strehlow, Purity Foods, Inc., 2871 W. Jolly Rd., Okemos, MI 48864, 800-99SPELT.

The Baking Sheet, King Arthur Flour, Box 1010, Norwich, VT 05055, 802-649-3361. Baking newsletter.

MAGAZINES

Good Medicine, the magazine of Physicians Committee for Responsible Medicine, 5100 Wisconsin Ave. NW, Suite 404, Washington, DC 20016

Spectrum—The Wholistic News Magazine, 3519 Hamstead Ct., Durham, NC 27707-5736, 919-493-2181, www.SpectrumLink.com. Bimonthly summary of pertinent health news information from reliable sources.

Vegetarian Times, 4 High Ridge Park, Stamford, CT 06905, 203-322-2900.

Natural Health, The Guide to Well-being (formerly *EAST WEST* and *East West Journal*), 17 Station St., P.O. Box 1200, Brookline, MA 02147, 617-232-1000.

MacroChef, 243 Dickinson St., Philadelphia, PA 19147, 215-551-1430.

Macrobiotics Today, George Ohsawa Macrobiotic Foundation, 1994 Myers St., Oroville, CA 95966, 530-533-7702.

Taunton's Fine Cooking, 63 South Main St., P.O. Box 5506, Newtown, CT 06470, 203-426-8171.

Index